Supervision and Agency Management for Counselors

Elizabeth R. O'Brien, PhD, LPC, is a University of Chattanooga Foundation associate professor at the University of Tennessee at Chattanooga. She currently serves as the coordinator of the counselor education program and maintains a private practice in the Chattanooga area. Dr. O'Brien received her PhD from the University of Central Florida in Orlando, Florida, in 2007. She holds an educational specialist degree in marriage and family counseling from the University of South Carolina in Columbia, South Carolina. Dr. O'Brien is a licensed professional counselor in Tennessee and is certified as a professional school counselor in West Virginia.

Dr. O'Brien's research interests include integrating wellness training in counselor training and supervision, mindfulness training with women transitioning out of incarceration, and integrating yoga-based spiritual practices into counseling with adults and adolescents. Prior to her academic appointment, Elizabeth was a school-based counselor working with elementary, middle school, high school, and alternative-school children and their families in Lexington, South Carolina.

Michael A. Hauser, PhD, LPC, NCC, is currently working for the federal government in central Texas as a clinical coordinator and marriage and family therapist. His primary work is with veterans suffering from posttraumatic stress disorder (PTSD). As the clinical coordinator, he ensures quality clinical services and provides training to various community agencies in order to educate and advocate for veterans with PTSD. Prior to this position, he was a lecturer at the University of Tennessee at Chattanooga (UTC) in the leadership doctoral program and the counseling master's program. Dr. Hauser is retired from a career in the U.S. Army after serving in training and leadership positions for 23 years. After 6 years in the corporate world in Michigan he moved to Georgia and began his counseling education. He has worked in an inpatient hospital environment and a partial hospitalization program supporting seniors and the physically impaired. Prior to his current position he worked in a private practice in northeastern Georgia, serving adolescents and adults suffering from a variety of mental health issues, as well as conducting marriage and family counseling. He has published various works, and served as an editor for *Counseling Outcome Research and Evaluation*.

Dr. Hauser's research interests include PTSD and its effects on the individual, couples, and families, as well as therapeutic outcome efficacy. His dissertation was entitled "The Role of Optimism and Working Alliance and Its Utility in Predicting Therapeutic Outcomes in Counseling Relationships."

Supervision and Agency Management for Counselors

A Practical Approach

Elizabeth R. O'Brien PhD, LPC

Michael A. Hauser, PhD, LPC, NCC

Editors

SPRINGER PUBLISHING COMPANY
NEW YORK

Springer Publishing Company, LLC
11 West 42nd Street
New York, NY 10036
www.springerpub.com

Acquisitions Editor: Nancy S. Hale
Production Editor: Pamela Lankas
Composition: S4Carlisle

ISBN: 978-0-8261-2798-3
e-book ISBN: 978-0-8261-2799-0

15 16 17 18 19 / 5 4 3 2 1

Library of Congress Cataloging-in-Publication Data

Supervision and agency management for counselors : a practical approach / [edited by] Elizabeth R. O'Brien, Michael A. Hauser.
p. ; cm.
Includes bibliographical references and index.
ISBN 978-0-8261-2798-3 — ISBN 978-0-8261-2799-0 (e-ISBN)
I. O'Brien, Elizabeth R., editor. II. Hauser, Michael A. (Michael Alan), 1956- , editor.
[DNLM: 1. Counseling—organization & administration. 2. Leadership. 3. Staff Development. WM 55]
RC467.95
616.890068—dc23

2015028252

Printed in the United States of America by Gasch Printing.

Contents

Contributors

Lisa Aasheim, PhD, NCC, ACS, Associate Professor, Coordinator of the School Counseling Master's Program, Director of the Community Counseling Clinic at Portland State University, Portland State University, Portland, Oregon

Dana Lee Baker, PhD, Associate Professor for School of Politics, Philosophy and Public Affairs, Associate Director of the College of Arts & Sciences, Washington State University, Vancouver, Washington

Elizabeth K. Crawford, EdD, Assistant Professor, University of Tennessee at Chattanooga, Chattanooga, Tennessee

Richard Deaner, PhD, LPC, Associate Professor of Counselor Education, Georgia Regents University, Augusta, Georgia

Rebecca M. Goldberg, PhD, LPC, NCC, GC-C, Assistant Professor for the Department of Counseling and Educational Psychology, Mississippi State University, Starkville, Mississippi

Michael A. Hauser, PhD, LPC, NCC, Harker Heights, Texas

Amiko W. McPherson, University of Tennessee at Chattanooga, Chattanooga, Tennessee

Elizabeth R. O'Brien, PhD, LPC, UC Foundation Associate Professor, Counselor Education Program Coordinator, University of Tennessee at Chattanooga, Chattanooga, Tennessee

David W. Rausch, PhD, Associate Provost for Academic Affairs, University of Tennessee at Chattanooga, Chattanooga, Tennessee

Deanna L. Sharpe, PhD, CFP®, Associate Professor for the Personal Financial Planning Department, University of Missouri, Columbia, Missouri

Lorrie B. Slater, LPC-MHSP, Chattanooga, Tennessee

Allison Louise Smith, LCSW, Chicago, Illinois

Sherry Todd, PhD, LPC, ATR-BC, CTS, Master of Arts Counseling Program Director, Assistant Professor, Regent University, Virginia Beach, Virginia

Preface

Becoming a counselor is a lifelong journey, with many learning opportunities along the way. Although many helping professionals will say that their first passion is helping facilitate others' growth, there are opportunities to facilitate that growth that move beyond engaging in counseling and the therapeutic process. If you are in a place along your journey where you have been counseling for a number of years, you feel confident that you have found your strengths, and have made a point to continue to strengthen your weaker areas, you may find that you are wondering where your next challenges may lie.

This book is designed to provide a road map for the next steps along your journey: supervising newer helping professionals, engaging in leadership positions within an agency, or perhaps considering opening your own professional practice. As with any new endeavor, having an idea of the challenges that may await you is one of the best ways to prepare yourself for future success. At this point, much like at the beginning of your counseling career, you may not know what you do not know—this book aims to start you thinking about how you may want to proceed. The next steps of your journey as a professional counselor can be as exciting and invigorating as those first few counseling sessions as a new professional, but now they can be tempered with your experiences, making them richer and something to be shared with your professional community. Let the journey begin!

ORGANIZATION OF THE BOOK

This book contains 10 chapters and is divided into two sections: supervision and agency management. Chapters 1 to 4 are dedicated to issues related specifically to the supervisory process, such as roles and responsibilities, ethics, and various due-process procedures. Within these chapters, you will find resources that you can adapt to your own practice as a supervisor and additional resources that can help you explore more deeply your journey toward becoming a supervisor.

Chapters 5 to 10 focus on the aspects of agency management (including issues that pertain to private practice) that may be less familiar to counselors, simply because counseling preparation programs typically don't explore these issues in depth. You will find chapters focusing on budgeting, information management, leadership, and marketing. The budgeting chapter not only gives the reader information about how to financially plan, but provides the information in a very accessible manner. You can also explore how marketing in your community is not only a vital component of your success, but a great way to network with other community agencies and businesses that you may not be as exposed to when you are concentrating on your role as a professional helper.

With all of the information provided herein, you will follow our protagonist, Amy, as she charts a course that is similar to that of many clinicians in transition—making mistakes and learning how she can become a better supervisor to move toward a leadership position within her agency.

Acknowledgments

To become professional counselors and counselor educators there have been many people Elizabeth and Mike have met along the way who have helped them to become who they are and who will always be integral to their continued development.

Elizabeth would like to thank Mark Young, Joshua Gold, Margaret Burgraff, Beth DuRant, and Beth Hook. All of these individuals have likely shared both the joy and frustration of working with Elizabeth in her development as a beginning counselor and later as a counselor educator. She is particularly grateful to the "Beths," who supervised her throughout some of her most challenging moments as a young professional and were unwavering in their support of her development. Elizabeth would also like to thank her friends Mimi Meriwether, Sarah Protheroe, Crissy Roddy, Amy Gruber, Beth Crawford, and Beka Bohannon.

Elizabeth would like to thank her coeditor, Mike Hauser, without whom this project would not have happened. Mike was always there for a reality check when needed. Thank you to Nancy S. Hale, Editorial Director at Springer Publishing, for supporting this project and giving the answers Elizabeth and Mike needed when they needed them! Finally, Elizabeth would like to thank her family—her parents, Hans and Carolyn O'Brien; her husband, Kyle Oden; and her pooch, Woodrow—without their high standards and unfailing support Elizabeth would not be where she is today.

Mike would like to thank God, who answered his prayers and provided for his needs. Mike thanks his wife, Brenda, his greatest supporter, who is always there when needed and always provides space and time when needed. Her loving kindness can never be repaid. He would also like to thank the many contributors who signed on to this project. They graciously supported this work with their resources and expertise. Thanks are due to Springer Publishing Company for encouragement and much-needed input. And, of course, Mike is appreciative of his friend and coeditor, Elizabeth. She generated the overall concept of this book and wove the various threads into a meaningful and wonderful fabric. With a mind that never stops, generating ideas wasn't much of a problem for Elizabeth; however, constraining her thoughts was demanding.

Elizabeth and Mike would both like to thank Amiko Warren McPherson for her diligent work in assisting with this project.

O • N • E

Orientation to Agency Management and Supervision

Elizabeth R. O'Brien

Amy is a clinical mental health counselor working in a small start-up community mental health agency. The agency is located in a midsized urban area and serves individuals who are dependent on the state for physical and mental health assistance; the agency is funded by local, state, and federal programs as well as community grants. Before this job, Amy worked for 4 years at a psychiatric hospital, during which time she earned her professional counseling license. Prior to earning her master's degree, Amy worked as a case manager at a mental health clinic in a different state for 5 years.

During the interview process, Amy's supervisor informed her that she could look forward to assuming some leadership responsibilities in the agency if she was able to demonstrate the requisite competencies for such an appointment. So far, her supervisor has been vague in describing what those competencies might be. Amy is working to ensure her clinical skills are beneficial to the community, but, at the same time, she is trying to acquire the leadership experiences she thinks will help forward her career. She is attending night classes and seeks mentorship and supervision from sources well versed in the challenges she will face.

As the agency becomes established within the community and the hurried pace of a start-up begins to die down, Amy's boss begins inviting her to attend management meetings with other staff. As she listens to the discussions, Amy realizes that she will find it challenging to balance the roles and responsibilities of providing clinical supervision to personnel, of helping to manage the agency's nonclinical employees, and learning the business responsibilities of running the agency. After one of these meetings, Amy's boss discusses her first step in leadership: She will begin clinical supervision of three of the new master's-level therapists whom the agency hired.

INTRODUCTION

Most beginning counselors graduate from preparation programs with the ability to amalgamate specialized learning to create a framework for counseling practice. For beginning practitioners, the challenge then becomes one of honing and refining their skills so that they become both competent and confident in their clinical ability (Stoltenberg, 1981). As they advance, beginning practitioners will likely have opportunities to experience a wide variety of counseling settings and treatment modalities. Some clinicians may become adept at using brief evidenced-based practices (EBPs) with multidisciplinary treatment teams for efficient and holistic client care, some may choose to engage in a solo or private practice, and others still will oscillate between various settings throughout their careers. Under supervision from senior counselors and other helping professionals, these counselors will obtain licensure and other professional credentials that will mark their passage from beginner to experienced professional.

Amy's story is similar to that of many clinical mental health counselors after they have moved out of their initial phase of development, have graduated, and have gained initial experience in moving toward licensure and beyond. Their peers see these counselors as able to train newer clinicians and as having obtained institutional knowledge (at the agency, community, and state levels) that helps them to create appropriate treatment plans for their clients. When these professionals consistently demonstrate a high level of clinical skill and professional knowledge, their agencies often identify them as emergent leaders. Conversely, some professionals may find that they are comfortable with their knowledge base and are ready to embark on a journey toward establishing their own mental health agency or private practice. The challenge becomes finding a guide to delineate the next steps toward success in either of these endeavors.

To that end, the purpose of this text is twofold: (1) to educate emerging agency leaders on best practices in clinical supervision and (2) to educate established clinicians on basic business practices that are integral in either managing an agency or establishing a private practice. Subsequently, the text is presented in two sections that will address both of these goals. Within this chapter, we discuss broad changes that have taken place in clinical mental health agencies and then lay the groundwork for understanding the supervision process and responsibilities. Subsequent chapters in the first section of the book further elaborate on best practices in clinical supervision. Please note that although this text provides an overview of supervision and business practices, it is not a comprehensive guide. Therefore, suggestions for further research and readings are included at the end of each chapter.

CLINICAL MENTAL HEALTH AGENCIES IN THE 21ST CENTURY

In the United States, it is estimated that approximately 9.6 million individuals (adults and children) were diagnosed with a serious mental illness (SMI) during the 2012 calendar year (National Institute of Mental Health [NIMH], 2012). Of the adults in this estimate, approximately 58% received mental health services in the form of inpatient hospitalization, outpatient treatment, and/or prescription medication. Of the 9.6 million aged 18 and under, approximately 50% engaged in the aforementioned services. These numbers indicate that although there is a great need for mental health services, there are still large numbers of adults and children who do not receive the services that they need in order to manage the symptoms of an SMI. Those who do obtain services typically access care through hospital emergency rooms, psychiatric facilities, and community clinical mental health agencies. Our discussion will focus on the latter.

Clinical mental health agencies aim to provide care and services to individuals and the community and seek to enhance individual development and functioning. Often, these agencies offer specific types of mental health service delivery, such as substance abuse treatment, medication management services, psychiatric evaluations, psychological treatment, psychoeducational programs, and case management services, to target interventions for specific populations as needed. The overarching mission of helping individuals to obtain and maintain optimal mental health functioning is a newer concept, as, historically, mental illness has been treated as something shameful and untreatable (Rosenberg, Rosenberg, Huygen, & Klein, 2013). Although the incidence of stigma is somewhat less prevalent than it once was, mental illness and mental health conditions have been stigmatized both publically and personally. Public stigma of individuals can include the prejudice that those with mental illness are dangerous, violent, and unpredictable. Discriminatory practices can result from this type of prejudice, such as friends and family disengaging from relationships with these individuals or difficulty in obtaining housing and/or employment. Personal stigma can result in individuals' feeling shame and experiencing lower levels of self-esteem. Additional consequences can include individuals' adopting self-sabotaging behaviors that fulfill the expectations of public perception (Coorigan & Lee, 2013). However, as mental health and mental illness issues have received greater acknowledgement in the recent past, there has been a societal shift toward treatment and prevention of mental health-related issues.

The 21st century has brought changes in the way clinical mental health agencies function. The adoption of the 10 Essential Public Health Services in 2014 as an addendum to the Affordable Care Act (ACA) extended mental health care benefits to many by requiring that mental and substance use disorder services be included in health plans offered to individuals and group markets. These must be included in health insurance plans and be comparable to other types of medical coverage, such as general medicine and surgical care (Berionio, Po, Skopec, & Glied, 2013). The acknowledgment of mental health care as an essential service is a welcomed feature of the ACA; however, maintaining public acceptance of the necessity of mental health care will depend on outcome data showing that treatments and programs are efficacious—hence the emphasis on evidence-based practices (Berionio, Po, Skopec, & Glied, 2013). Further discussion regarding the financial ramifications of the ACA is found in Chapter 7; now let us briefly explore ideas related to outcome data.

Investigators engage in therapeutic outcome research to determine whether a particular treatment modality is useful for a given disorder. Although this definition is more germane to medical research, the field of psychology engages in similar research when validating EBPs. EBPs tend to be interventions that are researched in relation to specific client populations, such as trauma-focused cognitive behavioral therapy (TF-CBY) for individuals diagnosed with posttraumatic stress disorder (PTSD). This and other EBPs are sometimes considered "manualized" treatments, meaning specific techniques and approaches of the therapy are taught to clinicians with the intention that they will use this knowledge to treat or counsel clients and their families (Ledley et al., 2009). The strengths of these EBPs are such that they have been shown to be successful for a large number of client issues, such as (a) illness management and recovery, (b) medication management, and (c) family education/involvement (Sands & Gellis, 2001). In addition, they tend to be cost-effective and offer recommendations for specific assessments that one can use in data collection and analysis for agency-level efficacy studies. Agency-level studies generate data that can provide important evidence when these entities are looking for new funding or are attempting to maintain their funding.

Please note that although EBPs are useful for treating clients with particular clusters of symptoms and/or diagnoses, the efficacy of counseling is also deeply affected by common factors inherent in all counseling. These common factors, first articulated by Rosenzweig (1936), are part of the inherent set of circumstances and/or characteristics that exist within therapeutic treatment modalities that lend themselves to the overarching success of counseling. The reality is that all therapeutic interactions contain aspects of these common factors, and that even though specific theories or treatment modalities are ascribed to have more or less of a particular factor, these transtheoretical aspects permeate counseling (Hauser & Hayes, 2010). Although the common factors have been presented in many different permutations, the most succinct come from Bordin (1979) who streamlined them to the following components: (a) an agreement on goals, (b) having tasks or a series of tasks to complete, and (c) the development of bonds and/or the therapeutic relations (p. 253). Although EBPs have benefits, they are not without shortcomings. Individuals who experience mental illness can present with a variety of symptoms and have issues within their lives that can make treatment challenging. Because EBPs are generalizable by design, some argue that they are not designed for "outliers," or those who may present with more severe symptomology. One other problem with EBPs is that it is virtually impossible to research the efficacy of all treatment modalities against all forms of mental illness, particularly with the recognition that clients rarely present with a singular mental illness. Most clients tend to have co-occurring disorders, which severely complicates the principles involved in efficacy research. In addition, one must consider the aforementioned common factors, and the degree to which they are present or absent within treatment, as this can have a deep impact on the overall success of treatment, yet be unmeasurable by an EBPs assessment. Although counselors can augment their practices and treatment modalities to tailor interventions for clients, this may threaten the validity of a particular EBP. Finally, those responsible for evaluating the usefulness of an EBP within a particular agency should be aware of research design and basic statistics so they can determine whether an approach has been well validated and is appropriate for the population that the agency serves.

COMMUNITY STAKEHOLDERS

Community partners or "stakeholders" are those individuals, groups, or organizations that have a "stake" in how the organization runs and the services it provides to the community. In particular, certain community partners can have specific expectations regarding services the agency provides and the manner in which the agency provides these services. By adapting the Centers for Disease Control and Prevention's (CDC's) model of stakeholders (Figure 1.1), one can categorize these groups in the following ways:

1. Program operators, such as managers, staff, and funding agencies
2. Constituents, those served by the program, such as clients, advocacy groups, and elected officials
3. Decision makers, those who have a vested interest in the success of a program, such as the general public, funding agencies, and partners (CDC, 2015)

Public health issues are very complex and include a range of stakeholders, all of whom have an important role to play. It must also be said that although all partners have a vested interest in how agencies are run and how they serve their community constituents, these partners' interests do not always align with the mission of the agency. In examining the previous list, one can see that a power hierarchy may exist among stakeholders, with some having more formalized and institutional power and influence than others. More institutionally powerful stakeholders, such as local and state government agencies, are imperative for funding and licensure. However, one should acknowledge that although clients and community groups may have less formalized power, they

FIGURE 1.1 • Program evaluation.

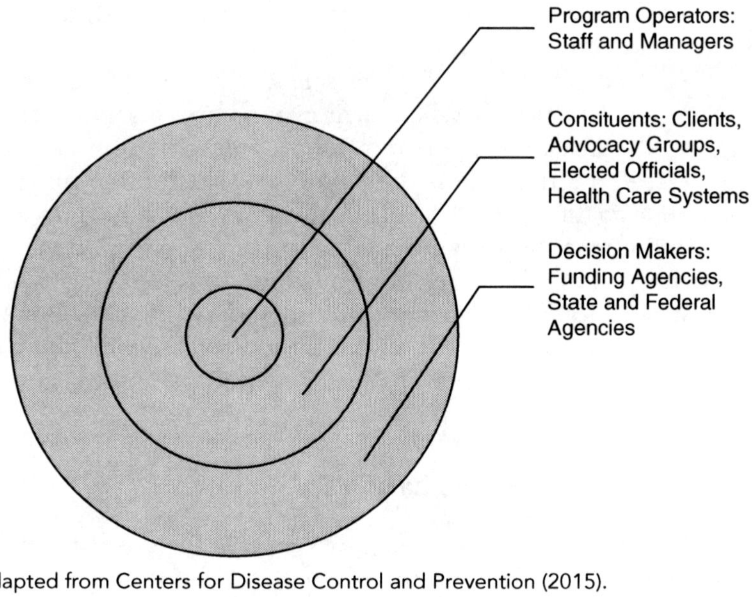

Source: Adapted from Centers for Disease Control and Prevention (2015).

are the rationale for the existence of these agencies and should be respected members of the stakeholder community. In other words, they need to be heard.

Ideally, stakeholders should use a utilitarian approach when defining the purpose of a mental health agency: to do the greatest good for the greatest number of people within the community. However, issues typically arise when the priorities of one group do not align with the priorities of a second group. For example, imagine a local advocacy group is looking at mental health services provided in a city and sees that the only agency is located in an area that is inaccessible to individuals living in a high-poverty area with limited transportation options. The advocacy group decides to conduct a cost-effectiveness analysis on establishing a small mental health clinic in the impoverished area. A cost-effectiveness analysis compares the relative costs of a service compared to the effectiveness of the benefits that the service will provide. Although this may sound similar to a cost–benefit analysis, *effectiveness* is a term that is used when evaluating the usefulness of health services because health is a difficult quotient to quantify. In this case, the cost-effectiveness analysis would examine the cost of opening and operating a small clinic in a high-need area compared to the overall health benefits to individuals and the community. Suppose the advocacy group found that the health benefits of opening the clinic (e.g., lower rates of hospitalization and police interventions in domestic disputes) would indeed offset the overall cost of the clinic—it would seem this would be a no-brainer, right?

But then we must consider this example from the perspective of the government—the state mental health office—and its budgeting issues. Funding for the upcoming fiscal year has been cut, and there is less money allocated in the budget to fund mental health agencies. Because of this cut, the local mental health agency will have to downsize its staff to two thirds of the previous workforce. This downsizing will diminish the services that the clinic can provide to the whole community. Now the idea of trying to take the resources that remain and create a small clinic would be extremely difficult, and, in the eyes of the state mental health office, could further diminish the health benefits to the overall community.

So, how can stakeholders reconcile this idea of doing the greatest good for the greatest number when each group can present a rationale for how its ideas are beneficial to the community? This type of misalignment can cause a great deal of strife among stakeholders, which often plays out in public forums, such as the media. Too often, these types of struggles disempower those stuck in the middle, who are unable to voice their opinions. Ultimately, these decisions are often based on funding, and, in our example, although the state office wishes to help all community members, the decision at this point is to fund only one clinic and put off discussions of a second clinic until more funding can be secured.

Stakeholders and Program Evaluation

One of the most important roles that stakeholders play in the life of a mental health agency is helping in the evaluation process. Agencies as a whole must engage in continuous evaluation so they can gather evidence regarding their impact on the community they serve, which is somewhat similar to the discussion of EBPs in the previous section. Program evaluation is an intensive process that helps agencies determine the efficacy and efficiency of their current practices and can yield important information regarding areas for improvement. Chapter 5 features a more in-depth discussion of program evaluation; what follows here is a concise description of how stakeholders can be a part of this process.

As mentioned previously, one can sort stakeholders into specific categories that make them easier to identify. After identifying these categories, contact stakeholders to ascertain whether they are interested in providing input to the agency regarding its benefits to the community. Often, interested parties will convene in focus groups, open community meetings, and have meetings with officials. These forums allow stakeholders to discuss the components of mental health intervention and/or agency outcomes that matter to them. Identifying outcomes, or what stakeholders want the mental health agency to "do," is integral when creating an evaluation plan. Questions that are important for stakeholders to answer can include:

- Whom do you represent and what is your interest in this agency?
- What would you like this agency to accomplish?
- How would you measure progress toward accomplishing these goals?
- How much progress would you expect this agency to have made at this time?
- What do you see as a critical evaluation question at this time?

After answering these questions, it is important to find common themes that are included in stakeholders' answers. This is important for two reasons: (1) it will help evaluators understand the salient issues that are shared between groups and (2) it will help unite stakeholders in a shared vision for the agency.

After identifying these themes, presented as desired agency outcomes, stakeholders should begin examining ways that the agency can collect data to evaluate the degree to which the outcomes are being met. Representatives from different stakeholder groups can meet on a regular basis in the form of an advisory board to discuss the relevance of the outcomes, data that are being collected to determine whether outcomes are being met, and augmentation to practices that may be needed in the face of evaluation results.

Dissemination of evaluation results and reports to stakeholders and others on a regular basis is a part of agency transparency within the community and beyond. As previously stated, the ACA and other funding entities are deeply interested in the impact that agencies have on their clients and the cost–benefit scenarios of agencies in terms of their results. Evaluation reports allow for stakeholders, funding entities, and agency critics to make data-informed decisions regarding the overall efficacy of an agency with its treatment populations.

DEMOGRAPHICS

Demographic changes in the United States have also made it imperative that clinical mental health agencies are able to provide culturally appropriate interventions to an increasingly multicultural society. U.S. Census data from 2000 to 2010 show an increase in the number of Hispanic or Latino individuals, as well as those identifying as two or more races (U.S. Census Bureau, 2012). Census updates from years subsequent to 2010 show that this trend is continuing. Data on poverty show that the number of adult individuals sharing a household (beyond the primary adult) increased for all age levels, and that the rate of children living in poverty was 21.6% in 2010—at that time, the highest rate ever recorded.

Racial minorities and individuals living in poverty often do not have adequate access to mental health resources and/or have access to mental health providers who are inadequately equipped to help with the specific needs of these populations (Sands & Gellis, 2001). The additional mental stress that can be present for minorities and those living in poverty can often compound and exacerbate symptoms. Counselors must be aware of these issues so that they are able to engage in therapeutic interventions that are respectful of the potential challenges that these populations face.

The consequences of interventions that are culturally inappropriate can include client attrition, prolonged symptomology, and client estrangement from therapeutic interventions. Professional organizations, such as the American Counseling Association, the official professional organization for counselors, have attempted to respond to this disparity by delineating multicultural competencies within ethical codes. In counselor preparation programs, such as those accredited by the Council for the Accreditation of Counseling and Related Educational Programs (CACREP), programmatic requirements delineate multicultural competencies that students are required to learn (CACREP, 2009).

However, individually, counselors must make the commitment to engage in continuous education (see Chapter 2) and immersion experiences so that they are able to acknowledge the differences that exist within communities that are culturally and ethnically diverse and to provide culturally responsive care to their clients. Supervisors of clinical counselors must also stay abreast of multicultural issues that can affect the counselor–client relationship and the supervisor–supervisee relationship. In its *Best Practices in Clinical Supervision*, the Association for Counselor Education and Supervision (ACES) states, "The supervisor recognizes that all supervision is multicultural supervision and infuses multicultural considerations into his/her approach to supervision" (Borders et al., 2011, p. 8). These stances reflect the need for mental health services to be available to fulfill a wide range of diversity needs in society and that continuous training must be in place to help counselors meet these needs.

HISTORICAL FACTORS

Whereas multiculturally responsive counseling typically encompasses issues related to racial identity, socioeconomic status, and gender issues, there are other diversity and historical factors that influence service delivery. Examples include the following:

1. The acceptance of same-sex relationships and national legalization of same-sex marriages in the Supreme Court decision on the case of *Obergefell v. Hodges* on June 26, 2015

2. The advent of terms, such as "technology addiction," and treatment modalities for individuals who engage in compulsive Internet and technology usage
3. Increased mental health services and support for veterans and their families experiencing trauma from deployment and family reintegration issues

These specialized issues, and recognition of how they contribute to mental health, are becoming more prevalent in society and deeply affect the overall development of individuals throughout the life span. For example, recent research has shown that children and nondeployed parents tend to have higher levels of psychological, behavioral, and academic/work distress during military deployment, and families experience these same symptoms during reintegration of the deployed spouse (Chandra et al., 2010; Siegel & Davis, 2013).

MULTIDISCIPLINARY TEAMS

To this point, the discussion of mental health agencies has focused on forces that exist largely outside of the agency. However, this final section focuses on an important component of agencies that resides within: multidisciplinary teams (MDTs). MDTs are a vital part of comprehensive treatment and are defined as "individuals from various disciplines who are involved in a project but work independently" (Ciofi, Wilkes, Cummings, Warne, & Harrison, 2010, p. 62) Agency teams often comprise counselors, nurses, social workers, case managers, psychiatrists, and general physicians. Research shows that MDTs are advantageous when working with clients who present with complex issues, such as co-occurring disorders or SMIs (Belanger & Rodriguez, 2008). Team members tend to possess different talents, knowledge, and experiences, all of which can help the group to create interventions tailored to the specific needs of individual clients. The outcomes of these interventions can increase clients' access to quality care, reduce individual and familial stress, reduce hospitalization rates, and improve overall client outcomes (Ciofi et al., 2010).

When they are working well, MDTs can be extremely beneficial to clients and help to create a collegial working environment. However, issues can arise within teams that can hinder productivity. Team structure and functioning can be derailed if members feel threatened or unsure of their roles within the group. For example, if a power hierarchy exists within the group (such as physicians as the head members of the treatment team), it could make other members wary of sharing their opinions if they are contradictory to those of the more powerful members. Defining the roles and responsibilities of each team member could help in mitigating some of these issues. It is also recommended that communication training and/or team building should be included in the ongoing education of MDTs. This becomes particularly important when professionals from diverse disciplines are engaged in treatment planning and have differing points of view.

OVERVIEW OF SUPERVISION

Supervision is an important process that protects clients and helps all clinicians maintain ethical behavior and engage in best practices. With that being said, it was once described to me in terms of the Dr. Seuss book *Did I Ever Tell You How Lucky You Are?*: "his job is to watch. Is to keep both his eyes on the lazy town bee, a bee that is watched will work harder you see" (1973, p. 26). Later in the story, it is determined that the watcher needs his own watcher, who then needs his own watcher, until finally a long string of watchers is engaged to watch what the original bee is doing. Supervision is similar in its layers of people who are "watching"; new counselors are supervised by individuals who themselves are accountable to their own organizational and/or clinical supervisors, consultation partners, and regulatory agencies such as state licensure boards.

Gaining the responsibility of supervision can come in two ways: formally and informally. Formal supervision responsibility is obtained by gaining a specialized license through one's state credentialing board or being promoted within an agency to supervise other clinicians. More informal mechanisms include allowing interns/new clinicians to observe one's practice when conducting psycho educational groups, group counseling, or individual therapy. Other modes of informal supervision include answering questions regarding institutional processes, treatment planning and aftercare services, and community resources. Consider Amy's journey toward becoming a clinical supervisor:

> *Amy's first responsibility as an emerging leader is to begin supervising three newly hired master's-level clinicians. With guidance from her agency supervisor and her clinical supervisor, she contacts the state licensure board to find out what requirements she must meet in order to supervise new clinicians toward their own licensure. Amy lives in a state that requires that supervisors have 2 years of clinical experience beyond their initial licensure and complete three continuing education credits (CEs) per licensure renewal on supervision practices.*
>
> *Amy completes the supervisor application and the board approves her as a licensed professional counselor supervisor (LPC-supervisor). This responsibility means that she can supervise newer clinicians on their cases, is well versed in local and state laws that affect practices, and can recommend clinicians for licensure when they have completed the clinical requirements.*
>
> *Although Amy has completed her three CEs in supervision, she now knows that balancing the roles and responsibilities of being a clinical supervisor will be challenging. She considers her supervisees, who until this point have been casual friends of hers at work. She decides that in her first supervision session, she wants to begin with a conversation about the role she now plays as their clinical supervisor and their perceptions of what this means for their working relationships in the agency and in supervision.*

In the next pages, we will explore the process of supervision, the roles and responsibilities of supervisors, and the various entities and agencies that influence supervision practices.

DEFINING *SUPERVISION* IN A CLINICAL SETTING

Merriam-Webster (n.d.) defines *supervision* as "the action or process of watching and directing what someone does or how something is done." The responsibilities of mental health supervision can be grouped into two distinct categories: organizational supervision and clinical supervision. Organizational supervision in agencies typically pertains to "directing," particularly as it relates to having clinical and other employees follow established agency policies and procedures. The organization creates these policies and procedures based on standards of care established by agency accrediting bodies, and state and federal laws drive them. Examples can include documentation of client interventions, time frames for linking clients to services outside of the agency, or assessment procedures used in determining interventions that will best suit clients' needs and yield outcome data for the agency regarding efficacy.

Clinical supervision is a more specialized process and involves "watching"—for example, ensuring that clinical employees are engaging in theoretically and ethically sound treatment practices that they are fully qualified to use. Ultimately, a clinical supervisor's first responsibility is to ensure the safety and welfare of the client, and this is done by engaging new clinicians in the supervision process. Bernard and Goodyear's (2009) definition of *clinical supervision* states that it "is an intervention provided by a more senior member of a profession to a more junior member or members of that profession" (p. 7). The authors also articulate that the relationship is hierarchical in nature, that supervision is an ongoing process, and that the supervisory process is imperative as a *gatekeeping* measure to ensure clients' welfare. The gatekeeping role is particularly important in training and maintaining clinical professionals who are competent and ethical practitioners who abide by their state laws, licensure codes, and professional ethics codes.

Gatekeeping is, in this author's opinion, one of the greatest responsibilities that a supervisor has in the supervision process. Essentially, the supervisor ensures that an individual is competent to ensure clients' welfare, is able to engage in appropriate clinical interventions, is ethical, and is able to practice within the standards set forth by the state and other credentialing agencies. However, this role is not simply a confirmatory process; the gatekeeper also maintains the burden of preventing incompetent clinicians from entering into the field or continuing practice for reasons of unethical behavior and/or impairment. Although this may seem to be a didactic process, it in fact rests on a continuum, with supervisors also helping supervisees to ameliorate inappropriate practices so that they can be successful clinicians. Supervisors who provide ongoing evaluation (as discussed in the next section) are transparent in the gatekeeping process so that supervisees are able to make a successful transition from apprentice to independent clinician.

The irony is that most professionals who engage in supervision and the gatekeeper role are experienced clinicians who have had either limited or no formalized training in supervision processes. Typically, professional credentialing groups and accrediting bodies set eligibility and qualifications criteria necessary to engage in supervision, but the entities that have the most impact on supervisors are standards set by individual state regulatory boards. These standards vary from state to state; for example, several states require that supervisors be approved by their state licensure board (e.g., Arkansas), whereas other states delineate that supervision with any licensed mental health professional is approved (e.g., District of Columbia). However, a few states clearly articulate that supervisors must have obtained training in supervision before they are approved to supervise (e.g., Oklahoma; American Counseling Association, 2010). Because Amy is from a state with guidelines similar to those of Oklahoma, she completed some education in supervision before she was board approved to supervise; however, even this requirement gives a limited scope to the responsibilities of clinical supervision.

Professional credentialing groups, such as the National Board for Certified Counselors (NBCC), also engage in credentialing both professional counselors and supervisors. Specifically, the American Association for Marriage and Family Therapy (AAMFT) offers credentials for individuals who can demonstrate a level of competence that is more advanced compared to that of their professional peers. The AAMFT also has a specific set of criteria for credentialing clinical supervisors. Finally, accrediting bodies, such as the CACREP, have specific standards that educational programs must follow in order to prepare all counselors and counselor educators.

The number of CACREP education standards regarding teaching supervision to master's-level clinicians is relatively small, only two, when compared with the requirements for those completing doctoral work in counselor education and supervision—a discrete section that includes six outcomes that articulate the knowledge, skills, and practices doctoral candidates must learn (CACREP, 2009). Understandably, individuals preparing to train counselors in an educational setting must have extensive knowledge of clinical supervision practices. However, given that master's-level clinicians supervise most beginning counselors in the field, it stands to reason that some attention should be given to these processes within counselor preparation programs.

SUPERVISION PROCESS AND ROLES

Supervision is a didactic process, meaning that supervisors and supervisees should engage in a dynamic learning environment that focuses on constructing knowledge and skills. This description may imply that supervision follows a specific set of steps or pedagogy; rather, it can be an ambiguous process that requires a great deal of flexibility on the part of the supervisor in order to meet the needs of supervisees and their clients.

Supervision has many parallels to teaching, counseling/psychotherapy, and consultation (see Figure 1.2); each of these will be discussed further. However, it is important to be mindful that although supervision is a combination of the aforementioned, it is a separate construct with specific ethical guidelines and processes.

As stated previously, supervision does have some parallels to teaching. A more advanced practitioner is actively engaged in teaching and modeling behaviors that the less experienced counselor is expected to learn and/or

FIGURE 1.2 • Supervision Venn diagram.

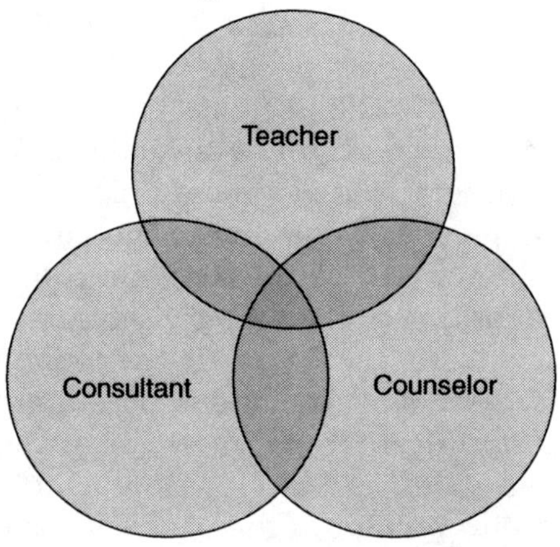

emulate in his or her own style. As professional gatekeepers, supervisors are responsible for the evaluation of supervisees' performance and giving appropriate feedback regarding their performance. Because the relationship is hierarchical, supervisors have both power and responsibilities. In mental health agencies, clinical supervisors are typically responsible for completing or contributing to employee performance reports, reporting supervision hours completed toward licensure requirements, and making recommendations to licensure boards regarding the ethical practice of supervisees.

Ideally, supervision happens in a dynamic learning environment, but there is not a specific teaching formula that supervisors follow in order to inculcate their supervisees with knowledge. The term *dynamic* is used because there are so many working parts to a given supervision session, and there can be many opportunities for learning experiences beyond discussing cases. Although this may sound similar to a counseling session, sometimes the ambiguity of supervisees' needs can be frustrating for those who are beginning supervisors. It is at this point that the supervisory relationship becomes especially important—just as counselors ascribe to the idea that the therapeutic relationship is the impetus for change, so too is the supervisory relationship the impetus for counselor growth. Through supervisee self-report, therapy recordings, and case records, supervisors can learn the specific needs of the supervisee and tailor their interventions in order to promote optimal professional growth.

In addition to teaching, supervision also has some parallels to the counseling process. In Chapter 4, you will see that supervision theories have some similarities with counseling theories—particularly important is that supervision theories are very interested in a supervisee's worldview. Worldview is determined by an individual's attitudes, values, and opinions, which in turn can affect how the individual thinks and behaves, and influence decision making (Sue & Sue, 2013). Within supervision, worldview is a crucial aspect of how the supervisee conceptualizes the client and can be the root of problematic thoughts, feelings, and behaviors that hinder the success of the therapeutic relationship. Supervisors must be able to use their counseling skills in order to probe supervisees regarding how these issues are influencing their interactions with clients. At the point of insight, supervisors then move supervisees toward reflective practice that focuses on minimizing the negative impact of the client–counselor working relationship. Supervisors must be vigilant when working with supervisees in this type of modality for many reasons. Supervision is a hierarchical relationship in terms of power, and the evaluative aspect that exists therein should not be influenced unduly by the intimacy that is inherent in a counseling relationship. In effect, supervisors should know that supervisees are not impaired and are professionally competent, but more knowledge could impair supervisors' ability to evaluate supervisees in a fair manner. If a supervisor suspects a supervisee is experiencing a significant impairment, he or she should refer the supervisee for personal counseling and work with the individual to determine whether he or she is able to remain in the counselor role. Although these conversations can be intimidating, they are an inherent part of ensuring client welfare, as well as helping supervisees with issues that can lead to attrition in the profession.

Finally, the supervisor fulfills the role of consultant when working with supervisees. The consultant role is well conceptualized by Hart and Nance's (2003) two-by-two model, which delineates a supervision style that is lower in support and directionality than its teacher/counselor counterparts. When consulting, the supervisor and supervisee engage in more egalitarian and peer-like conversation that can range from discussing client cases to how to use therapeutic interventions with client populations with which the supervisee is less familiar.

It is recommended that certain competencies be met before consultation is used as a supervision modality. First, supervisors must ascertain that supervisees are capable of performing their duties and are not in need of the "hand-holding" that supervisees may need when they are newer in the field or new at a particular agency. Note that supervision roles shift throughout relationships, and new experiences can require more direction; however, when supervisees are becoming more autonomous in their practice, consultation can fulfill the important role of helping supervisees reframe their experiences from that of novice to colleague.

ROLES AND RESPONSIBILITIES

As mentioned previously, supervisors have very specific functions in terms of training both pregraduate and prelicensure counselors in an agency setting. In this section, we explore the supervisor's role as an evaluator and recorder. It should be noted that there is some discussion of how supervisors' roles can vary depending on whether they are engaged in organizational supervision, clinical supervision, or both types at the same time. This is an important distinction to make because not all clinical supervisors have influence over supervisees' work environments, but they are still considered responsible for client welfare, whereas organizational supervisors are likely to be responsible for client welfare regardless of their involvement in their supervisees' clinical supervision and development.

A supervisor is responsible for assessing and evaluating the performance of a supervisee, regardless of whether the position is that of clinical or organizational supervisor. Part of this evaluation entails informed consent of the supervisee; this means supervisors must inform supervisees in their purview of the policies and procedures that they must adhere to as well as due-process procedures for appealing supervisory actions. Although this is discussed more fully in Chapter 3, it bears mentioning here that all of those who engage in supervision should take the time to reflect on their expectations for both their supervisees and themselves within the supervisory relationship. One could assume that supervision is simply two people in a room discussing cases and that is all, but, in fact, supervision is much more successful when there are clearly delineated expectations, procedures, and evaluations in place.

Examples of record keeping include supervision notes, supervisory evaluations of new clinicians' performance, and evaluations, as well as agency-generated evaluations such as annual reviews. Anyone who has worked in an agency or business setting has likely experienced the process of an annual review. For those who may not have, an annual review usually occurs once per year and entails a supervisor assigning performance ratings for particular tasks that the supervisor expects employees to complete as a course of their duties. A great example of record keeping is keeping client records or charts up to date. Because medical records and documentation are tied to how agencies are reimbursed for services, peer audits are often performed monthly or bimonthly to ensure that employees are documenting services in a timely and approved format. Audits are typically performed by having clinicians randomly select their clinical peers' client records and review them with a checklist; the clinicians then submit the checklist to a supervisor. Checklists often include items such as treatment plans, physician orders, completed intake assessments, and similar items. This type of intervention is designed to ensure that employees are reminded to keep records up to date as well as compliant with agency and governmental requirements for documentation.

Peer audits also help supervisors to determine how well employees are performing on this particular task. Most of the time employees are documenting in a timely manner; however, if there is a clinician who is not, supervisors must work with the clinician to ensure that this does not happen, given that the results of nondocumentation can result in loss of revenue, paybacks to insurance companies, and fines levied on the agency. Typically, noncompliant employees are given a warning; however, if they persist in noncompliance they may risk being written up. In egregious cases, employers can fire employees for failure to document appropriately.

Supervisors are responsible for reviewing several aspects of employee performance, such as in the record-keeping example, as well as other aspects of professionalism such as ethical practice, comportment, and adherence to company policies. They are also responsible for communicating to supervisees when they have violated professionalism or policies and the due process for appealing decisions regarding poor performance reviews, professional censures, and termination of employment. The adage that "with power comes responsibility" is very true, and potential supervisors must consider whether they can fulfill this important role and whether they are able to handle taking on the difficult tasks of supervision, such as employee termination, along with the more enjoyable tasks, such as signing final paperwork before a supervisee submits an application for licensure.

Additionally, reflective supervisors consider and acknowledge the impact that their role can have in working relationships and their personal lives. Supervisors must be able to cope with the isolation that can sometimes accompany the supervisory role. Questions that anyone interested in taking on supervisory responsibilities should ask himself or herself include:

1. Do I want to take responsibility for the actions of others?
2. Do I want to be the individual who will be "on-call" when others are ill or unable to perform their duties?
3. Do I want to be responsible for negotiating the needs of the agency with the workload of my workforce, particularly in difficult times?
4. Do I want to be part of a vision team that devotes time to the development of the agency rather than engaging in helping?
5. Am I comfortable with participating in the social and networking events that will become part of my job description?
6. Am I (and my family) comfortable with losing some aspects of privacy due to work impacts?
7. Am I ready to be the person who will have to reprimand and/or terminate another clinician?

Although this is not an exhaustive list, it is a good start for those who are evaluating their readiness to supervise. Another aspect that supervisors and potential supervisors should consider is how they model professionalism and comportment to their peers and supervisees, as discussed next.

Commitment to Continuous Professional Engagement and Training

Perhaps one of the most important ways that a supervisor can model professionalism is by continuously engaging in professional service and training. Examples of professional service/engagement include membership and/or leadership in one's local, state, or national-level counseling organizations; presenting at a local, state, or national conference; and serving as a board member for a nonprofit organization. Professional training is just as it sounds: attending conferences and/or education sessions to procure knowledge in areas that one is interested in (such as supervision training, play therapy training, etc.), as well as training that reinforces best practices in the field (e.g., continuing education in ethics and multicultural competencies).

Another responsibility of professional engagement is staying up to date on one's state licensure laws and regulation board requirements. Licensure laws vary from state to state, and supervisors should be knowledgeable of the rules that govern licensed professional counselors (LPCs) and LPC interns in their area. Supervisors who live near state borders should also be aware of the licensure laws of those states as well. Additionally, supervisors should be aware of the written laws that govern their practice—that is, the legislation that is part of the legal code, such as the age of consent. Again, those living near state borders should be aware of laws pertaining to their clients in the states in which they reside. Typically, one can download licensure laws for reference as well as call licensure boards to resolve questions that may arise in the course of professional practice and/or supervision.

It can be easy to regard these types of endeavors with a bit of a sigh; most people are busy, and these activities can seem like one more item to be checked off of one's never-ending "to do" list. However, there are inherent benefits to these activities that professionals often forget, such as being presented with the opportunity to engage with peers who understand your professional joys and difficulties, learning new techniques that can be adapted to your clients and/or supervisees that will invigorate your practice, and being reminded of those best practices that you may have "drifted away" from because you are busy minding other responsibilities. It is also easy to forget that newer clinicians, peer clinicians, and your supervisors are watching you to see how you conduct yourself and how you represent the profession. This is not to assign an additional burden, but rather is meant as a gentle reminder of the responsibilities that are inherent in the role of supervisor. For this author, the opportunity to be a teacher and supervisor has been a great gift; if most supervisors are being honest, they will say that they learn more from those they supervise than by any other means. It is the gift of the role: Supervisors encounter so many different worldviews and ways to counsel that they are given the opportunity to see helping with fresh eyes.

SUMMARY

Individuals who wish to move into positions with greater responsibilities within an agency must consider both the current trends within agency management and efficacy as well as what it means to become a supervisor. Balancing the requirements of both managing an agency and ensuring the ethical conduct and continued development of counselors and staff can be a large task that may seem overwhelming. However, interested individuals can take steps to learn more about these aspects of supervision so that the task seems less intimidating.

In the 21st century, there has been an increase in the acceptance of mental health issues and an acknowledgment that individuals diagnosed with mental health disorders should be given access to treatment and care. The Affordable Care Act, and its inclusion of mental health care as part of provided services, is evidence that the government recognizes that individuals should have access to treatment. However, with this type of endorsement comes the requirement to provide data-driven evidence that treatments are successful for a wide variety of clients. Although some mental health issues no longer generate stigma, multicultural and historical factors continue to affect individuals' abilities to access care and receive appropriate services. Additional issues that can influence agency services and delivery include relationships with community stakeholders and within multidisciplinary teams.

Supervision within an agency can be conceptualized as organizational or clinical supervision. Organizational supervision is the act of directing others, such as being a manager. Clinical supervision includes aspects of teaching, counseling, and consultation, such as working with peer clinicians to supervise their clinical practice and development. However, supervisors of either type must be prepared to document and evaluate those they are supervising, and this inherent power comes with responsibility. One of the most important of these responsibilities is continuously modeling appropriate ethical behavior and comportment through continuing education, knowledge of one's agency and area, and service to the profession.

REFLECTION QUESTIONS

1. Who are your stakeholders?
2. How do you see mental health and mental health agencies evolving in the next 10 years?
3. How do you think your historical era has changed the mental health services that are currently delivered and should be delivered in the future?
4. What are your thoughts regarding the current push for the use of evidence-based practices in mental health settings?
5. Consider the roles of both an agency supervisor and clinical supervisor; which role appeals to you more? What steps do you think you would need to take to prepare for your desired role?

SUGGESTED RESOURCES

Danish, S. J., & Antonides, B. J. (2013). The challenges of reintegration for service members and their families. *American Journal of Orthopsychiatry, 83*(4), 550–558.

Essig, T. (2012). The addiction concept and technology: Diagnosis, metaphor, or something else? A psychodynamic point of view. *Journal of Clinical Psychology, 69*(11), 1175–1184.

Norcross, J. C. (Ed.) (2002). *Psychotherapy relationships that work: Therapist contributions and responsiveness to patients*. New York, NY: Oxford University Press.

Oshri, A., Lucier-Greer, M., O'Neal, C. W., Arnold, A. L., Mancini, J. A., & Ford, J. L. (2015). Adverse childhood experiences, family functioning, and resilience in military families: A pattern-based approach. *Family Relations, 64*, 44–63.

Riggle, E. D. B., Rostosky, S., & Horne, S. G. (2010). Psychological distress, well-being, and legal recognition in same-sex couple relationships. *Journal of Family Psychology, 24*(1), 82–86.

REFERENCES

American Counseling Association. (2010). *Licensure requirements for professional counselors*. Retrieved from http://www.counseling.org/docs/licensure/72903_excerpt_for_web.pdf ?sfvrsn=2

Belanger, E., & Rodriguez, C. (2008). More than the sum of its parts: A qualitative research synthesis on multi-disciplinary primary care teams. *Journal of Interprofessional Care, 22*(6), 587–597. doi:10.1080/13561820802380035

Berionio, K., Po, R., Skopec, L., & Glied, S. (2013, February 20). *Affordable Care Act expands mental health and substance use disorder benefits and federal parity protections for 62 million Americans*. Retrieved from http://aspe.hhs.gov/health/reports/2013/mental/rb_mental.cfm

Bernard, J. M., & Goodyear, R. K. (2009). *Fundamentals of clinical supervision* (4th ed.). Boston, MA: Allyn & Bacon.

Borders, L. D., DeKruyf, L., Fernando, D. M., Glosoff, H. L., Hays, D. G., Page, B., & Welfare, L. E. (2011, January 18). *Best practices in clinical supervision*. Retrieved from https://

view.officeapps.live.com/op/view.aspx?src=http%3A%2F%2Fwww.saces.org%2FResources%2FDocuments%2Faces_best_practices.doc

Bordin, E. S. (1979). The generalizability of psychoanalytic concept of the working alliance. *Psychotherapy: Theory, Research and Practice, 16*, 252–260.

Centers for Disease Control and Prevention. (2015). *Introduction to program evaluation for public health programs.* Retrieved from http://www.cdc.gov/getsmart/program-planner/Step1.pdf

Chandra, A., Lara-Cinisomo, S., Jaycox, L. H., Tanielian, T., Burns, R. M., Ruder, T., & Han, B. (2010). Children on the homefront: The experience of children from military families. *Pediatrics, 125*(1), 16–25.

Ciofi, J., Wilkes, L., Cummings, J., Warne, B., & Harrison, K. (2010). Multidisciplinary teams caring for clients with chronic conditions: Experiences of community nurses and allied health professionals. *Contemporary Nurse, 36*(1–2), 61–70.

Coorigan, P., & Lee, E-J. (2013). Recovery and stigma in people with psychiatric disabilities. In J. Rosenberg & S. Rosenberg (Eds.), *Community mental health: Challenges for the 21st century* (pp. 3–21). New York, NY: Routledge.

Council for the Accreditation of Counseling and Related Educational Programs. (2009). *Program standards.* Retrieved from http://www.cacrep.org/wp-content/uploads/2013/12/2009-Standards.pdf

Hart, G. M., & Nance, D. (2003). Styles of counselor supervision as perceived by supervisors and supervisees. *Counselor Education and Supervision, 43*, 146–158.

Hauser, M., & Hayes, D. G. (2010). The slaying of a beautiful hypothesis: The efficacy of counseling and therapeutic process. *Journal of Humanistic Counseling, Education and Development, 49*, 32–44.

Ledley, D. R., Heimberg, R. G., Hope, D. A., Hayes, S. A., Zaider, T. I., Van Dyke, M., . . . Fresco, D. M. (2009). Efficacy of a manualized and workbook-driven individual treatment for social anxiety disorder. *Behavior Therapy, 40*, 414–424.

National Institute of Mental Health. (2012). *Serious mental illness (SMI) among U.S. adults.* Retrieved from http://www.nimh.nih.gov/health/statistics/prevalence/serious-mental-illness-smi-among-us-adults.shtml

Obergefell v. Hodges, 576 U.S. ____ (2015).

Patient Protection and Affordable Care Act of 2010, Pub. L. 111-148, 124 Stat. 119, codified as amended at 42 U.S.C. § 18001.

Rosenberg, J., Rosenberg, S. J., Huygen, C., & Klein, E. (2013). Marginal no more: Serious mental illness, sexual orientation, and gender preference. In J. Rosenberg & S. Rosenberg (Eds.), *Community mental health: Challenges for the 21st century* (pp. 22–32). New York, NY: Routledge.

Rosenzweig, S. (1936). Some implicit common factors in diverse methods of psychotherapy. *American Journal of Orthopsychiatry, 6*, 412–415.

Sands, R., & Gellis, Z. D. (2001). *Clinical social work in behavioral mental health: An evidenced based approach.* Boston, MA: Allyn & Bacon.

Seuss, D. (1973). *Did I ever tell you how lucky you are?* New York, NY: Random House.

Siegel, B. S., & Davis, B. E. (2013). Health and mental health needs of children in US military families. *Pediatrics.* doi:10.1542/peds.2013-0940

Sue, D. W., & Sue, D. (2013). *Counseling the culturally diverse: Theory and practice* (6th ed.). Hoboken, NJ: John Wiley & Sons.

Stoltenberg, C. (1981). Approaching supervision from a developmental perspective: The counselor complexity model. *Journal of Counseling Psychology, 28*(1), 59–65. doi:10.1037/0022-0167.28.1.59

Supervision. (n.d.). In *Merriam-Webster's online dictionary.* Retrieved from http://www.merriam-webster.com/dictionary/supervision

U. S. Census Bureau. (2012). *Components of population change by race and Hispanic origin.* Retrieved from http://www.census.gov/compendia/statab/cats/population/estimates_and_projections_by_age_sex_raceethnicity.html

T • W • O

Individual and Group Supervision

Rebecca M. Goldberg

Leticia (Supervisee):	(*Sighs heavily*) I feel lost. I don't know what to do with my client.
Amy (Supervisor):	Well, you came to the right place (*laughing*)!
Leticia:	(*Chuckles*) Good, I hope so.
Amy:	Alright, so talk to me about feeling "lost."
Leticia:	I am just stuck; I don't feel like I'm really going anywhere with my client. She just keeps telling the same stories over and over again, and I don't feel like there is any resolve to them. It's like we're going in circles or something.
Amy:	I watched your video recording of the last counseling session you had with her, and I sensed that you felt lost.
Leticia:	(*Cringing*) Oh great, so it's not just my imagination. (Shakes her head) I don't know what I'm doing with this client.
Amy:	That's exactly why we have supervision. It takes two to see one.
Leticia:	(*Pauses*) I'm going to give you my best counselor response now: "Tell me more about that."
Amy:	(*Smiling*) That was a great directive!
Leticia:	(*Blushing*) I've learned from the best.
Amy:	Okay, so what I mean by "it takes two to see one" is that your client is so close to her own problems that she cannot work through them on her own, and that is the reason why she comes to see you for counseling—it's helpful to have an outside perspective in order to better understand one's issues. The two of you together can see her problems more clearly than she can on her own,

and then the two of you can also craft solutions to problems that she might not have come up with on her own.

Leticia: That makes sense.

Amy: And then that same phenomenon can be paralleled in supervision—sometimes the counselor has a hard time seeing the client's issues clearly, and then the supervisor becomes that outside perspective. So now, you and I make up the party of two in order to see the one set of problems associated with the counseling relationship; in this case, having tangential sessions and feeling "lost" or like you aren't going anywhere with the client.

Leticia: Hmm, "it takes two to see one." I like that.

Amy: Well, thank you. I'm glad it makes sense to you.

Leticia: It really does! I also feel like I can use that message with my clients to help normalize things or validate them for going to counseling in the first place.

Amy: Absolutely! So let's take a step back from your counseling relationship with this client, and try to look at the session from an outside perspective. That way, we can pinpoint ways for you to not allow the session to become tangential, so you won't feel "lost" or like you're losing control of the session.

Leticia: I would love that!

Amy: Let's start by watching some of the video recording from your last session, and I want you to pause the DVD when you feel like things are becoming tangential and you are losing control of the session. Then, we're going to talk about ways for you to take back control of the session so you don't feel "lost."

Leticia: (*Exhales deeply*) That would make me feel much better (*smiles*).

INTRODUCTION

Clinical supervision is a necessary part of the licensure process for counselors. The process of clinical supervision, although actually involuntary, is one that requires commitment and participation from all involved parties in order to establish beneficial working relationships and to make the best use of the time spent together. Supervision should be considered an opportunity for learning; however, the legal mandate of clinical supervision can be overwhelming and intimidating for some counseling trainees working toward licensure.

The history of counseling supervision is rooted in early 20th-century Europe in the days of Sigmund Freud and Max Eitington. Dating back to 1902, Freud used to hold meetings each Wednesday night at his house in Austria, where invited professionals could discuss psychological cases and issues. First called the Wednesday Psychological Society, and later renamed the Vienna Psychoanalytic Society, these weekly meetings provide, perhaps, the first evidence of unofficial therapeutic supervision (for a review, see Urlic & Brunori, 2007; White & Winstanley, 2014; Worthington, 2010). Freud's subsequent teachings also reflected this burgeoning understanding that less experienced analysts should learn from those individuals with more experience in order to produce more effective practitioners. Almost 20 years later in 1920, Eitington, a German psychoanalyst, was one of the founding members of the Berlin Psychoanalytic Polyclinic, later renamed the Göring Institute. It was there, between 1925 and 1930, where Eitington officially proposed the idea of supervision for psychoanalysts still in training. In the 1930s, Vilma Kovacs and Helena Deutsch contributed to the standards for clinical supervision, specifying what makes supervisors qualified to mentor inexperienced therapists. In 1958, Rudolf Ekstein and Robert Wallerstein wrote their seminal text *The Teaching and Learning of Psychotherapy*, introducing the specific purposes of clinical supervision for therapists in training. Practitioners started paying attention to this new training technique (i.e., supervision), and the next few decades were replete with scientist practitioners investigating and lauding the benefits of clinical supervision.

To create effective supervisory relationships, trainees must find supervisors to be available and approachable. Trainees under supervision must balance autonomy with dependence, engage in self-reflection, and adhere to supervisor directives when client welfare is of concern. The relationships between supervisors and supervisees must be built on transparency and trust because the supervisors have vicarious legal responsibility for the actions of the supervisees, who, in essence, are working under the supervisors' licenses until they earn their own counseling licenses. Likewise, the supervisees must be willing to trust their supervisors, as they are responsible for guiding them through prelicensure requirements. As counseling licensure is bound to the state level, counseling supervisees must check with their state licensure boards regarding specific rules, requirements, and guidelines for clinical supervision. Many states (e.g., Alabama, Florida, Georgia, Louisiana, and Mississippi) require that clinicians receive specialized training in supervision before credentialing them as qualified or approved clinical supervisors for prelicensure counselors. Approved clinical supervisor (ACS) is an example of one such certification offered through the Center for Credentialing and Education (CCE).

Why is licensure (and the supervision required for it) governed by the states in which counselors work? Why is licensure not national, like many counseling certifications? Differences between scopes of practice necessitate statewide licensure processes. Concern for local public policy drives state licensure, as each state defines its minimum standards of care, attempting to ensure that counselors do not practice outside of their areas of competence. State licensure boards also get to determine what qualifies an individual to be an approved supervisor. For example, state licensure boards often require that supervisors have degrees in the same fields as their supervisees (e.g., a licensed clinical social worker cannot supervise a counseling graduate working toward being a licensed professional counselor). Statewide licensure ensures that practitioners are trained in the areas crucial to the particular regions in which they work. Rural mental health providers will have clients who present with problems that can differ greatly from those of clients who live in urban areas. Depending on the demographics of a state, as well as the resources therein (or lack thereof), there are likely to be vast differences among the presenting problems of clients. Therefore, counselors need to be trained according to their state licensure boards' requirements for local mental health needs.

CHARACTERISTICS OF EFFECTIVE SUPERVISORS

There are many important characteristics associated with effective clinical supervisors, the first of which is that effective supervisors must also be proficient clinicians. Competent supervisors must have sufficient clinical experience from which to draw examples and understanding of the supervisees' processes. The adage, "those who cannot do, teach" is not applicable here; the effective supervisor is both an ethical clinician and proficient teacher. When teaching supervisees, effective supervisors are confident in their knowledge; at the same time, they are open to questions and discussion. Effective supervisors are committed to the professional development of supervisees and engage them in critical discussions regarding issues such as ethics and law (e.g., dual relationships, confidentiality with minor clients), current counseling research (e.g., evidence-based practices, multiculturally appropriate interventions), clinical case conceptualizations (e.g., problem-solving skills, conflict management), and practical concerns about the helping professions (e.g., paperwork, third-party payments and insurance, job prospects). Supervisors must invest emotionally in their relationships with supervisees, show empathy and respect for both their trainees and trainees' clients, as well as work to establish trust and cooperation with supervisees. Supervisors must be able to adapt their roles when necessary (e.g., consultant, educator/trainer in specialized knowledge, counselor; see Chapter 1 for review). Additionally, supervisors should provide support and understanding for supervisees, which may come in the practical forms of modeling and coaching or the emotional forms of reassurance and encouragement. For example, supervisors may need to model for supervisees how to take criticism without becoming defensive or discouraged. Another example is when supervisors model self-reflection and encourage the same from supervisees. Similar to clients' experiences in counseling, supervisees should learn about themselves as a result of the supervisory relationship and process. Effective supervisors survey and guide the trainees' therapeutic experiences with clients, and are willing to offer meaningful suggestions for improvement, when appropriate, to trainees regarding varying therapeutic situations with clients. Effective supervisors provide regular, consistent, constructive feedback and evaluations to supervisees in a nonthreatening manner, and, finally, they restrict the relationships to supervision only and do not create (or attempt to avoid) dual relationships with supervisees. Ethical supervisors understand and follow ethical guidelines, and model them appropriately for supervisees (for a review, see Barnett, Erickson Cornish, Goodyear, & Lichtenberg, 2007; Bernard, 1994; Pearson, 2004).

CHARACTERISTICS OF EFFECTIVE SUPERVISION

An integral component of effective clinical supervision is a positive working relationship between the supervisor and supervisee. The success of the relationship is dependent on both supervisor and supervisee being active participants in the supervision process. Transparency is important for the supervisor–supervisee relationship, meaning that both parties have a clear understanding of their roles and expectations for the supervision experience, with no hidden agendas. The supervisor should orient the supervisee to the supervision experience, essentially demystifying the process; when the supervisee better understands what to expect, he or she is more likely to be actively involved. The supervisor–supervisee relationship must be built with rapport and permit all parties involved to freely speak their minds. When there is a modicum of closeness between supervisors and supervisees, they are more likely to feel comfortable addressing difficult topics that surround clinical relationships (e.g., ethical transgressions, feelings of attraction for a client). Regardless of supervision theory or type of supervision (e.g., individual or group), characteristics of effective supervision experiences should remain fairly constant. Effective supervision sessions include focused and established action plans, which should be collaboratively created and agreed on at the beginning of each supervision session. Action plans guide supervision sessions and attend to the changing goals and needs of supervisors and supervisees; they are akin to clinical treatment plans, informing the supervisors and supervisees of the requirements of that day's meeting. They also provide opportunity for both parties to verbalize and understand the expectations for that day's supervision session. An action plan should cover daily goals as well as any specific tasks that need to be accomplished during that particular supervision meeting (e.g., procure signature for paperwork). Action plans can be verbal, written, or both. There needs to be enough flexibility built into the plan to cope with new issues that arise during the session; supervisors should always leave enough time to check back in with their supervisees to process any immediate concerns or problems. There should also be enough time built into the plan to account for any spontaneous questions or discussion that may arise. Most important, at the outset of each scheduled supervision session, supervisors must first address any emergent needs before proceeding with that day's action plan. For example, if supervisees are experiencing crisis situations related to clients (e.g., client safety is of concern because of suicide risk), those issues take precedence and need to be addressed and resolved before concentrating on the rest of the daily agenda. Issues such as ethical dilemmas and transgressions, client welfare, and other immediate concerns take top priority in any supervision session (for a review, see Barnettet al., 2007; Bernard, 1994; Pearson, 2004). Exhibit 2.1 provides a sample supervision agenda and record.

TOOLS OF SUPERVISION

Supervisor Rights

Defining Your Expectations for Self and Supervisees

Supervisors must make explicitly clear their expectations for supervisees at the outset of any new supervision relationship. Certain expectations are outlined in the professional disclosure statement (e.g., preparation for sessions,

EXHIBIT 2.1 • Supervision Agenda and Record

____

Supervisee: ____

1. Immediate concerns (e.g., emergencies, ethical transgressions): __________
____
____
____

2. Review/sign paperwork (e.g., site agreement form, supervision log, case notes): ____
____
____
____

3. Update case conceptualization and review (e.g., counseling theory, clinical judgment, diagnosis): ____
____
____
____

4. Review recording(s) (as applicable): ____
____
____
____

5. Interventions and client progress: ____
____
____
____

6. Discussion and treatment recommendations: ____
____
____
____

7. Evaluation and feedback: ____
____
____
____

(*continued*)

EXHIBIT 2.1 • Supervision Agenda and Record (*continued*)

8. Plan for next session: ______________________________________
____
____
____

9. Other concerns/comments: ______________________________________
____
____
____

______________________________ ____________

Supervisor Signature Date

showing client recordings), which is explained in more detail in the next section. Other expectations, such as supervisee attitude and participation, should be discussed with the supervisee. There are numerous qualities that supervisors consider to be highly desirable in supervisees, and these expectations should be communicated early in the supervision experience in order to make the most efficient use of the time spent together (for a review, see Rodenhauser, Rudisill, & Painter, 1989; Vespia, Heckman-Stone, & Delworth, 2002). It is preferable that supervisees express openness to and curious interest in the process of supervision, as well as desire, motivation, and initiative to be active participants therein. Supervisors must also express open-mindedness and enthusiasm, and be dependable partners within the supervision relationship. Both supervisees and supervisors must always remember that the supervisory relationship is bidirectional and interpersonal; neither participant should be a passive member of the process.

If supervisees exhibit problematic behaviors, supervisors are mandatory reporters and must immediately and appropriately respond in a manner consistent with their state licensure boards' code of ethics. Supervisees can experience a continuum of problems, ranging from benign to harmful. Supervisors should be aware, for example, when supervisees do not seem to be transitioning well to their clinical sites. This may include counseling students in new practicum and internship sites who are insecure or timid, or new graduates at the prelicensure stage who are stressed about transitioning from being students to young professionals. Supervisors must be able to recognize and assess this problem and respond accordingly, addressing supervisees' needs for successful transition and acclimation to their clinical sites. This may be particularly helpful with new graduates who are struggling with the differences between being in the classroom as compared with full-time application through working. Another issue that may concern supervisors is when supervisees do not seem open to critique or feedback. Direct feedback and evaluation are important parts of the supervision process, and if supervisees are not willing to accept and adapt appropriately in relation to supervisors' feedback, this can become a major concern for supervisors. Supervisees must remember that while they are prelicensure, they are working under the umbrellas of their supervisors' licenses; they must be willing to take direction and respond accordingly to feedback. This becomes extremely important when supervisees' behaviors negatively affect client welfare, which is the ultimate concern of all counselors. For example, if supervisors suspect supervisees' impairment (e.g., chemical dependency, mental illness) or major boundary violations (e.g., sexual relationships with clients), the level of urgency is high for immediate intervention and remediation. Other concerns that supervisors need to acknowledge and address with supervisees include poor counseling skills, lack of empathy for clients, limited theoretical knowledge and application, inappropriate use of counseling interventions, ineffective interpersonal skills, and personal or professional characteristics that limit counseling effectiveness.

Supervision Contract Negotiations

It is recommended that supervisors provide supervisees with written informed consent forms for supervision called "professional disclosure statements" (for examples, see Borders & Brown, 2005; McCarthy et al., 1995). These documents typically include (a) the supervisor's contact information; (b) the supervisor's professional and educational background and experience, including relevant credentials and areas of expertise; (c) information about the nature of supervision, including supervision model(s), modalities of case review (e.g., audio or video recording, live supervision), and how evaluation will be used; (d) a statement of confidentiality and its limitations; (e) the number and frequency of contracted supervision sessions; (f) the location and time of meetings; (g) plans for necessary rescheduling of sessions; (h) required fees and fee schedule, as well as methods of payment accepted; (i) the supervisee's responsibilities in supervision (e.g., how to prepare for sessions, maintaining records); (j) the supervisor's responsibilities (e.g., record keeping, case note review); (k) contact information for the state licensure board in case of concerns with or complaints regarding the supervisor; and (l) emergency procedures in-between supervision sessions. This supervision consent form is usually several pages long because, similar to a client informed consent form, it must be as inclusive as possible in order to cover the plethora of issues integral to the supervision experience. The supervision contract should be a process of mutual understanding and may include some limited negotiations. Although the hierarchy between supervisors and supervisees is understood, supervisees should still feel empowered to get their needs met, and the professional disclosure statement should address these needs as equitably as possible.

Professional disclosure statements also present information regarding supervision session preparation requirements for supervisees, such as what will be expected of supervisees on a weekly basis and what materials they will need to prepare for the sessions. The contract should also help supervisees understand how supervisors review counseling sessions, including requirements related to recording (e.g., audio, video) and parameters for how counseling sessions will be chosen for review in the supervision session. The professional disclosure statement used in supervision, similar to the informed consent necessary for counseling, should also explain to supervisees what kind(s) of supervision theories and interventions will be used during the supervision experience in order to demystify the process for supervisees and engage them in role induction.

In addition to professional disclosure statements, supervisors should also maintain other types of documentation, such as notes and logs related to supervision sessions and supervisees, as well as any types of evaluative tools they may use to determine supervisees' progress. Supervision is meaningless if there is not a minimum standard to which the evaluative tools are tied, such as pass/fail criteria or a Likert-type scale denoting levels of progress. In order to produce both formative and summative evaluation, supervisors will need to assess and appropriately document their supervisees' use of counseling skills and application of theory, understanding and practice of ethical competencies, multicultural awareness and diversity appreciation, and level of personal and professional growth and development, as well as personal and professional limitations or concerns. Criteria for evaluation will likely be provided by supervisees' educational institutions if they are graduate students; regardless, supervisors should still practice their own methods of assessment and evaluation, documenting accordingly. For examples of the documentation just discussed, see Exhibits 2.2, 2.3, and 2.4.

EXHIBIT 2.2 • Supervisee Profile and Contact Information

____

Date: __________

Supervisee:______________________ Position: ____________

Home address: ______________________________________

Street City, State Zip

Site address: ______________________________________

Street City, State Zip

Preferred phone: ____________ Site phone: ________________

E-mail address: ______________________________________

Completed degrees: __________________________________

Professional credentials (if applicable):________________________

Current academic program (if applicable): ______________________

Proof of current malpractice insurance on file: Yes ☐ No ☐

(continued)

EXHIBIT 2.2 • Supervisee Profile and Contact Information (*continued*)

Current level of clinical experience (please circle one):

Master's practicum student	Doctoral internship student
Master's internship student	Postdoctoral graduate
Postmaster's graduate	Other (please explain):
Doctoral practicum student	

Please list hopes/goals for the supervision experience (e.g., clinical skills, ethics, case management):

____

____

____

____

Please list fears/concerns for the supervision experience: ________________

____

____

____

Please list your strengths and weaknesses as a clinician: ________________

____

____

____

Has this supervisee ever received a complaint of malpractice or ethical transgression?

Yes ☐ No ☐ If yes, please explain: ____________________

____

____

____

Going Beyond "Talk" Supervision

Supervision is more than just talking. It is important for supervisors to remember that not all supervisees are audio learners (i.e., those who learn from talking and listening). Many supervisees are kinesthetic and visual learners, and they will benefit most from experiential exercises for supervision whereby they are able to learn by doing, seeing, and experiencing. Experiential exercises allow

EXHIBIT 2.3 • Supervision Outcome Scale

Please answer the following set of questions about you and your **current (or most recent) individual supervisor.** Again, remember if you have MORE THAN ONE individual supervisor in your current (or most recent) clinical training setting, please choose one and use the **same one** throughout the survey.
Please describe the degree to which supervision with your **current (or most recent) individual supervisor** has contributed to the IMPROVEMENT of the following:

Not helpful at all	Helpful, but very little	Somewhat helpful	Very helpful	Extremely helpful
1	2	3	4	5

1. Client symptoms (decrease in symptoms)	1	2	3	4	5
2. Your relationship with clients	1	2	3	4	5
3. Your counseling skills	1	2	3	4	5
4. Your case conceptualization ability	1	2	3	4	5
5. Your multicultural counseling skills (e.g., skills that are culturally appropriate in working with diverse clients)	1	2	3	4	5
6. Your multicultural beliefs/attitudes/awareness (e.g., awareness of your own worldviews)	1	2	3	4	5
7. Your multicultural knowledge (e.g., knowledge of worldviews of culturally different clients)	1	2	3	4	5

Note. The Clinical Competence Subscale includes items 1, 2, 3, and 4; the Multicultural Competence Outcome Subscale includes items 5, 6, and 7.
Source: Tsong and Goodyear (2014). Reprinted with permission.

supervisees the opportunity to engage in the experience of making observations about self and/or others, receiving and offering feedback, and generally working through the process of supervision instead of just talking about it. Creative approaches can be incorporated into both individual and group supervision, such as using creative arts drawing activities, sculpting with clay, or sand-tray activities; using and staying with metaphors; and integrating different media, such as books (i.e., bibliosupervision), music, and video. These processes can be even more dynamic with group supervision because there are multiple parties with whom to interact and learn from as well as to create shared knowledge through reflection, observation, discussion of case analysis and client conceptualization, and appropriate use of counseling skills and application of ethics.

EXHIBIT 2.4 • Sample Professional Disclosure Statement

Contact Information

Rebecca M. Goldberg, PhD, LPC, NCC, GC-C
Department of Counseling and Educational Psychology
Mississippi State University
Box 9727, Allen Hall 509F
Mississippi State, MS 39762
(o) 662.325.7925 / (c) 662-325-8262
rebecca.goldberg@ssrc.msstate.edu

Objectives

The purpose of this professional disclosure statement is to acquaint you with your supervisor and the supervision services being offered. This form will provide structure to and explanation of the supervision process, including the rights and responsibilities of supervisor and supervisee, parameters of the supervision relationship, administrative details, assessment and evaluation methods, potential outcomes, as well as the risks and benefits of entering a supervision relationship. Overall, this professional disclosure statement is designed to ensure that there is common understanding of the supervision process and relationship, as well as the expectations therein.

Supervisor's Professional Background

My highest degree earned is a doctor of philosophy in counselor education from the University of Florida, I am a licensed professional counselor in the State of Mississippi, a national certified counselor through the National Board for Certified Counselors, a certified grief counselor through the American Institute for Health Care Professionals (American Academy of Grief Counseling), and a qualified supervisor in accordance with the Mississippi State Board of Examiners for Licensed Professional Counselors. I currently hold memberships with the American Counseling Association, the Mississippi Counseling Association, and the Association for Counselor Education and Supervision. My clinical specialties are in grief counseling for loss and bereavement, couples counseling and family therapy, and counseling at-risk youth and adjudicated offenders ages 12 to 18. I have been a counselor for 9 years and provided supervision for licensure for the past 4 years in individual and group formats. My counseling theoretical orientation is an integration of existentialism, feminist theory, and solution-focused brief therapy, and as a supervisor, I generally use the interpersonal process recall (IPR) model, which is described in more detail in the next section.

(*continued*)

EXHIBIT 2.4 • Sample Professional Disclosure Statement (*continued*)

Supervision Methods

In short, using IPR entails reviewing preselected portions of recordings of counseling sessions (i.e., video, audio), and stopping the recordings at appropriate points in order to facilitate communication, raise inquiries, and deepen awareness of your self- and other-perceptions. Examples of probes might include, "What were you feeling when that happened?" "What were you thinking when that happened?" and "What would you do differently if given the chance?" You will be responsible for reviewing the recordings of your counseling sessions and selecting portions thereof to process in our supervision sessions. We can discuss any questions that you have during our introductory supervision meeting.

Supervisor Responsibilities

As your supervisor, I will thoughtfully and intentionally prepare for and attend all supervision sessions. I plan to provide you with feedback during each supervision session, as well as any formal evaluations needed for your educational program or clinical site (see Evaluation section for more information). I will review the client case notes you have prepared and any other pertinent clinical materials for gatekeeping purposes. I will complete a record of each supervision session (see Documentation section for more information), and will maintain licensure and credentials to be a qualified supervisor for the duration of our supervision relationship.

Supervisee Responsibilities

You understand that, for supervision to be most effective, you will need to be actively engaged and participate in your own personal and professional growth and development. Additionally, you understand that the work you complete outside of supervision sessions (e.g., homework or assignments, viewing recordings of counseling sessions and completing self-critiques) will greatly impact your progress in supervision. Simply put, you must thoughtfully and intentionally prepare for and attend the supervision sessions if you want them to be impactful for you. If you are unable to keep an appointment, please notify me within 24 hours to cancel or reschedule. You will need to keep me informed regarding all client issues and concerns, as well as counseling progress. You are required to maintain professional liability insurance at all times (minimum $1,000,000 single incident/$3,000,000 aggregate). If you are submitting these hours of clinical supervision for your professional licensure, you are responsible for keeping track of the number of supervision hours completed (and still needed).

(*continued*)

EXHIBIT 2.4 • Sample Professional Disclosure Statement (*continued*)

Confidentiality Policies and Documentation

Just as your clients have the right to privacy, supervisees also have privacy rights. I will be keeping a written record of the supervision sessions, which you may view at any time. This consists of written notes from your clinical cases and some summary of our interactions. These remain with me and will be confidential. Disclosures that occur in triadic or group supervision cannot be guaranteed as confidential; however, I will take every measure to encourage confidentiality and act appropriately if confidentiality is not upheld. Breaking our confidentiality occurs only in the eventuality of:

- Actual threat of harm to self or others, or knowledge thereof
- Reasonable suspicion of abuse/neglect to elders, minor children, or individuals who are considered cognitively impaired or otherwise incapacitated
- Ordered by a court of law or national security agency
- Defense against legal action or formal complaint made before a court of law or regulatory board

Your request for release of records must be submitted in writing and filed with me before any of your records are released.

Financial Policies

My fee for your supervision is $120 per individual supervision and $60 per group supervision hour, due at the beginning of each supervision session. Cash or personal checks will be accepted and I will provide you with a receipt for all fees paid at the end of each month. A nonrefundable fee of $35.00 will be charged for bounced checks.

Evaluation

I believe in formative evaluation (i.e., continuously giving you feedback about how you are doing), but I will also provide you with summative evaluation (i.e., final cumulative feedback). Please always feel free to ask me for more specific feedback if you would like it during our supervisory process. If you need evaluation paperwork completed for your educational program or clinical site, please provide me with the necessary paperwork two (2) weeks prior to the deadline.

Duration and Termination of the Supervision Contract

Our sessions will continue until you have completed your hours for licensure. Sessions will occur on a regular weekly basis and be scheduled at the

(*continued*)

EXHIBIT 2.4 • Sample Professional Disclosure Statement (*continued*)

convenience of both parties. Makeup supervision sessions will occur as soon after the scheduled session as possible.

Ethical Concerns

I will be following the ethical guidelines adopted by the Mississippi State Board of Examiners for Licensed Professional Counselors. These ethical guidelines were developed by the Association for Counselor Education and Supervision in 1993 and will be provided for your consideration. Please feel free to voice any complaints or issues of disagreement in our supervision sessions. However, if you feel dissatisfied with services and we are not able to resolve your concerns, you may report your complaints to:

Mississippi State Board of Examiners for Licensed Professional Counselors
239 North Lamar Street, Suite 402
Jackson, MS 39201
(o) 601.359.1010 / (f) 601.359.1030

Emergencies

If you need to contact me in-between sessions, you may call or e-mail me (see contact information on page 1). If I am unavailable, please leave a message and I will get back to you as soon as possible. If you are in an emergency situation, call proper authorities or 911.

Statement of Agreement

I have read and understand the information contained in this professional disclosure statement, and I agree to abide by the guidelines therein.

Rebecca M. Goldberg, PhD, LPC, NCC, GC-C

______________________________ __________
Supervisor Signature Date

______________________________ __________
Supervisee Signature Date

Supervisee Rights

Determining Your Needs

The best way for supervisees to determine their needs in clinical supervision is to engage in reflection and self-assessment. Supervisees make for more active participants in the supervision process when they have clarified their own expectations for the experience. See the Supervisee Profile and Contact Information form (Exhibit 2.2), which can be used at the beginning of a supervision relationship and checked throughout its duration to ensure that goals and objectives are being met. Wellness and counselor impairment are essential topics to consider, as counselor wellness directly affects quality of services (Lawson, 2007). This is critical for all supervisees, regardless of their progress within educational programs (e.g., practicum level, internship level, doctoral student) or whether they are prelicensure; everyone should practice self-reflection in order to be effective supervisees within clinical supervision (Swank, 2014) and engage in wellness practices. This is also true regardless of whether the supervisees engage in individual or group supervision. Some questions that counselors should consider answering prior to engaging in clinical supervision include the following:

- What is/are my main theoretical orientation(s)?
- What are my strengths and weaknesses?
- What are my goals for professional growth?
- What are my goals surrounding counseling skill development?
- Do I have particular hopes or intentions for supervision?
- Are there any client populations, specialized interests, or interventions/theoretical methods that I want to learn about or discuss in supervision?

While engaging in clinical supervision, supervisees must be willing to express their needs to supervisors, especially if they are not being met and client care is negatively affected as a result. This requires the supervisees' willingness to ask for specific feedback, for example, as well as the supervisors' openness to hearing those requests and giving the necessary feedback. Supervisees are not as likely to ask for help when they are scared or intimidated by their supervisors, or if they fear negative judgment or evaluation as a result of asking for help. It is important for supervisors to self-reflect on their experiences and the possible perceptions that supervisees may have of them. Supervisors should consider asking themselves, "Have I been approachable?" "Could I possibly have come across as intimidating to the supervisees?" and "Are there any issues that I need to broach with my supervisees, knowing that they are too scared/nervous/fearful to approach me with those topics?" Supervisors have to remember that counseling students and prelicensure graduates are often anxious about the unknown process of becoming counselors, and there are times when supervisors must be willing to acknowledge and address the stress that accompanies this process.

Supervision Contract Negotiations

Supervisees need to be prepared to ask questions regarding the supervision contract if certain information is not explicitly addressed in the professional disclosure statement. Additionally, the supervisees must provide the supervisors with any relevant information that will affect the supervision process, such as university requirements in the case of supervisees who are still counseling students (e.g., counseling program requirements for recording counseling sessions, direct and indirect client contact hours needed, paperwork such as a site agreement, and formative and summative evaluation procedures). Supervisees are responsible for submitting all required paperwork to their supervisors, allowing adequate time for document preparation (e.g., 1 or 2 weeks prior to the deadline). Feedback and evaluation should be guaranteed to the supervisees; this can include formative and/or summative evaluation in the form of oral or written responses, or a combination of the two. Additionally, if supervisors employ assessments for evaluation purposes, supervisees have the right to see any instrument that will be used.

Supervisee Evaluation

Evaluation is a crucial part of both individual and group supervision, and is a right of the supervisees. Supervisee evaluation should address clinical strengths and weaknesses, professional development, the quality of performance, and specific feedback regarding areas in which the supervisee is improving, as well as areas that still have room for improvement. Evaluation might assess areas such as multicultural competence, verbal and nonverbal counseling skills, client case conceptualizations, implementation of interventions, use of counseling theory, professionalism, collaboration with community services, and case staffing. Evaluation should not feel critical, judgmental, mocking, or contemptuous in nature; instead, evaluation should provide opportunities for teachable moments to occur and lessons to be learned. Evaluation should not just be done by the supervisor. The supervisee must also engage in self-reflection and self-evaluation in order to gauge professional progress for him- or herself. Constructive self-evaluation can occur by allowing the supervisee to fill out the same evaluation form as the supervisor, then comparing the two perspectives and sharing feedback and impressions of supervisee progress.

It is more effective for evaluation to occur throughout supervision, rather than just as a capstone to the experience. Consistent progress reports are preferred over only using summative feedback. Evaluations must also be shared with supervisees in order for them to be helpful. It is wholly ineffective to fill out an evaluation form for a counseling student, for example, and send that form to the faculty supervisor without first sharing its content with the supervisee (however, this practice happens frequently). Supervisors are also counselors and empathetic beings who generally prefer to avoid directly hurting someone's feelings; therefore, many forego giving what might be potentially construed as negative feedback in order to avoid an uncomfortable confrontation. Instead, supervisors should present negative feedback as teachable moments that provide opportunity for learning and professional growth. For sample evaluations, please see the Supervisee Performance Assessment Instrument (SPAI; Fall & Sutton, 2004), the Minnesota Supervisory Inventory (MSI; Robiner, 1998), the Counselor Activity Self-Efficacy Scales (CASES; Lent, Hill, & Hoffman, 2003), and the Supervision Outcome Scale (SOS; Tsong & Goodyear, 2014), which is shown in Exhibit 2.3. The SOS has items that measure multicultural competence, and it is brief, both of which are great benefits for supervision evaluation. Further information regarding evaluation can be found in Chapter 5.

DETERMINING SUPERVISION MODALITY

The supervision modality is multidimensional because it involves both the theoretical orientations (e.g., integrated developmental model, interpersonal process recall) used by the supervisors and the type of supervision experience (i.e., individual or group). In this chapter, we will address individual and group supervision experiences; supervision theories are addressed in detail in Chapter 4.

INDIVIDUAL SUPERVISION

Dynamics and Interpersonal Interactions

Individual supervision is the simplest form of clinical supervision; it entails one supervisor interacting with one supervisee, focusing on both supervisee and client concerns. A variation to this model is triadic supervision, in which one supervisor works with two supervisees simultaneously; the Council for Accreditation of Counseling and Related Educational Programs (CACREP; 2009) and the licensure boards from many states (e.g., Illinois, Iowa, Tennessee, Wisconsin, and Wyoming) permit triadic supervision as a substitute for individual supervision when necessary and appropriate (for a review, see Goldberg, Dixon, & Wolf, 2012; Stinchfield, Hill, & Kleist, 2007). In individual supervision, the dynamics and interpersonal interactions between the supervisor and supervisee are of crucial importance because there are no other members of the supervision relationship on whom to rely. Both supervisors and supervisees must feel comfortable enough to be honest with each other, offering feedback when appropriate, providing evaluation when necessary, and listening intently when the other is speaking. The relationship between individual supervisors and their supervisees may, at times, resemble that of counseling relationships with regard to the expression of empathy for one another and maintenance of autonomy, fidelity, justice, nonmaleficence, and beneficence (Kitchener, 1984) within the supervision relationship. Some of the topics discussed, such as personal meaning-making, biases and stereotypes, and individual growth and development, may also place supervisees in the position to feel like clients. Individual supervisors must make sure to appropriately refer supervisees to personal counseling if needed; the supervision relationship is *not* a replacement for individual counseling.

Supervision Goals

First and foremost, clinical supervision must always be performed with the goal of maintaining client welfare above all else. Additionally, supervision goals must be created uniquely for and tailored to each supervisee; much like counseling itself, there is no one-size-fits-all approach to clinical supervision because each supervisor–supervisee relationship will look different and each supervisee's needs will vary. It is important for individual supervisors and supervisees to cocreate supervision goals depending on the needs of the clients, the needs of the supervisees, the requirements of the educational programs or clinical sites, and licensure requirements, as well as any additional points of concern that must be taken into account. Goals may entail refinement of counseling skills, implementation of interventions or treatment modalities, enhancement of theoretical understanding and application, professional behavior development, critical analysis of ethical transgressions, and self-reflection and personal awareness. Just like in counseling, goals are fluid, not concrete, and must be adapted when necessary. The overarching goal of clinical supervision is producing competent counselors, but the ways of accomplishing that are flexible.

Individual Supervision Interventions

Just as counselors have options when working with clients, supervisors working with supervisees have various interventions, methods, and even theories from which to choose. Supervision models are covered in detail in Chapter 4; however, this section addresses individual supervision interventions. Supervisors should select interventions based on supervisee needs, learning style, personality type (e.g., introverted or extraverted), and developmental level. Supervisees who focus on negative cognitions, such as anxieties about the counseling experience, may respond well to cognitive interventions that identify and replace these self-defeating thoughts with alternatives to the maladaptive cognitions. For example, supervisees who tell themselves, "I am never going to finish all of these contact hours for licensure" can be redirected toward positive self-talk and cognitive restructuring, such as, "There are a lot of hours to earn, but I will get them little by little." The Gestalt supervisor would approach the nascent supervisee differently, perhaps asking the supervisee to employ the paradoxical theory of change, whereby the counselor-in-training does not try to negate his or her anxiety about the counseling experience. Rather, the supervisee is taught that change can only happen when individuals accept themselves wholly and without stipulations. Only then can the supervisee work through the anxiety. The solution-focused supervisor might use the miracle question (de Shazer, 1988) to focus a supervisee on goals for the supervision experience (e.g., "If a miracle happened tonight while you were sleeping, and you were able to fast forward through the next 16 weeks of clinical practice and supervision, how would you know this miracle happened? What would be different about you?"). The solution-focused supervisor is also likely to use scaling questions in order to help the supervisee self-assess therapeutic success. For example, after watching a recording of a client session, the individual supervisor might ask the question, "On a scale of 1 to 10, with 10 being perfect and 1 being terrible, how would you rate your performance in that segment we viewed?" The answer to this question allows for discussion about perception and improvement.

Benefits and Disadvantages

As with each type of counseling and supervision modality, individual supervision has both advantages as well as shortcomings. The most obvious benefit of individual supervision is the one-on-one focus that supervisees receive from their individual supervisors. The opportunity to concentrate on one supervisee at a time can allow individual supervisors to assist without distractions from other supervisees. Supervisors might find that they have more time to offer feedback and evaluations to individual supervisees, as compared with group supervisees. A benefit of individual supervision is that vicarious learning is possible, whereby the supervisee watches the supervisor counseling a client. The supervisee has the opportunity to observe effective counseling performed by a more senior member of the profession. The aim of this experience is to build and promote counselor self-efficacy. Additionally, the individual supervisor–supervisee relationship is one that can become quite intimate with the amount of time spent together and the vulnerable nature of the counselor-in-training. Because the only two members of the individual supervision relationship are the supervisor and supervisee, there can be a lot of perceived pressure for bonding to occur. If the individual supervisor and supervisee do not bond with one another, there are no other members within the relationship to mitigate or deflect that lack of connection. Also, in individual supervision there is not the added benefit of multiple other perspectives, as is the case in group supervision.

Group Supervision

Group Dynamics

An integral factor of effective group supervision is having a cohesive group of supervisees who are willing to work collaboratively together to craft a dynamic, interpersonal supervision experience in which all participating parties benefit from the interaction. Characteristics of an effective group include trust for another and the supervision process, honest critique and feedback, openness to others' opinions, peer support, and willingness to empathize and bond with other group members. These become more difficult to accomplish when there are too many supervisees in the group, stunting each person's ability to contribute, play an active role, and bond with the other group members. The CACREP (2009) limits group supervision to no more than 12 supervisees for practicum and internship, ensuring that there is an ideal number for group interaction. The greatest benefit of group supervision, perhaps, is that multiple perspectives are offered by the supervisees. Each member of the group is likely to be exposed to differing counseling theories, interventions and methodologies, interpretations of ethical dilemmas, use of counseling skills, and client populations and issues, increasing their learning experiences and perhaps their professional repertoires. Peer-group learning also provides opportunities for practicing interventions and exercises that would be difficult in individual supervision (e.g., group counseling and family therapy exercises that require multiple people, such as family sculpting or role-plays). Using the supervision group to practice an intervention before doing it with an actual counseling group or client family is a great benefit of the peer-group learning experience provided by group supervision.

Group Supervision Interventions

There are many interventions that can be used for both individual and group supervision experiences with simple adaptations made for one person as compared with a group of people. Certain cognitive behavioral interventions, such as stress inoculation and relaxation techniques, can easily be adapted for use with a group. For example, the supervisor working with a group of inexperienced practicum students may frequently deal with issues surrounding stress and anxiety in the counselor role. Cognitive behavioral breathing exercises and progressive muscle relaxation can be taught to the whole group for personal and professional benefit. There are other interventions, though, that are created specifically for group supervision and require multiple parties to execute; the feminist intervention of tag-team supervision is one such technique (Edwards & Chen, 1999). In this technique, group supervision members play the roles of client(s) and counselor, taking turns in the counselor role. Observation of the tag-teams allows the actual counselor to consider different perspectives for future work with the actual client(s). Multiple individuals are also needed in order to engage in a family sculpting exercise, making group supervision the ideal setting in which to practice this family systems approach. Family sculpting, a technique created by Virginia Satir (Satir, Banmen, Gerber, & Gomori, 2006), involves physically arranging individuals to represent current relationships within a client family. The supervisee who wants to try family sculpting with a client family may want to first role-play the situation using group supervision members.

Benefits and Disadvantages

In group supervision, the benefits can also act as deficits, depending on the nature of the group and the level of cohesion among its members. Group cohesion is a particular benefit of group supervision, providing support for supervisees who are not bonding with the group supervisor. At the same time, if the members of the group do not bond with one another, this can make for uneventful group supervision sessions. Group supervision also provides supervisees with numerous perspectives to consider when engaging in case conceptualization. Again, this can be both a contribution and a disadvantage, depending on the members of the group supervision. Some individuals greatly appreciate having a variety of perspectives to consider, whereas others might feel confused because of the plethora of options provided. Feedback is both an advantage and a disadvantage in group supervision. Groups provide the benefit of more opportunity than individual supervision does for giving and receiving different kinds of feedback, the most helpful of which are concrete, specific, descriptive, tentative, and objective. Feedback benefits group supervision when it is presented as an invitation to share information and ideas. This becomes a disadvantage, however, when the feedback is vague, judgmental, directive, or authoritative, or when the amount or type of feedback overwhelms the supervisee. Feedback does not benefit group supervision when it is presented as advice giving. Feedback must also be reciprocated; the group member who offers suggestions to others must be willing to take others' suggestions as well.

MULTICULTURAL SUPERVISION

Maintaining a multicultural framework when addressing counseling supervision is crucial in the 21st century. Not only are clients from an increasing variety of backgrounds, but supervisors and supervisees are progressively becoming more diverse as well. Numerous researchers have reported estimates for the demographic composition of the United States over the next 30 to 40 years (Sue & Sue, 2012; Zunker, 2012). They predict that between the years 2030 and

2050, the U.S. population will be comprised of at least 50% ethnic multicultural groups (i.e., Latino Americans, Asian Americans, Native Americans, etc.). Multicultural counseling supervision must address multicultural awareness and competence, diversity understanding, and continuing personal growth in diversity areas, which will be covered in this section.

Assessing Multicultural Awareness

The American Counseling Association's *Code of Ethics* (2014) requires that counselors work to understand the diverse backgrounds of their client populations. However, multicultural awareness starts within oneself; it is understood that in order to be multiculturally competent, an individual must begin with self-knowledge and understanding of one's own cultural beliefs and practices, as well as presumptions, stereotypes, and biases. This is the first of three dimensions of multicultural counseling competence (Sue, Arredondo, & McDavis, 1992); counselors who are culturally skilled seek out awareness of their own beliefs, attitudes, and assumptions of human behavior and cultural conditioning. Not being aware of one's biases, for example, makes it more likely for that person to judge another based on those biases, and accidentally (or intentionally) impart those biases onto someone else. In the case of counseling supervision, multicultural awareness is treated with the same weight and deference as it receives in counseling. The supervisor must encourage the supervisee(s) to confront and challenge beliefs and assumptions about diverse groups. It is important to note that multicultural awareness refers to much more than just the color of skin; we are referring to all of the cultural factors that clients encompass, including ethnicity, religion or spiritual beliefs, gender, level of ability or disability, sexual identity, nationality, age, health status, developmental level, socioeconomic status or class, and so on. To learn more about investigating your own stereotypes and biases, consider reading Friere's (2000) *Pedagogy of the Oppressed* and Sue's (2003) *Overcoming Our Racism: The Journey to Liberation,* and using the Implicit Association Test (Greenwald, McGhee, & Schwartz, 1998); the Succession, Identity, and Consumption (SIC) Scale of Prescriptive Ageism (North & Fiske, 2013); and the Ambivalent Sexism Inventory (ASI; Glick & Fiske, 1996).

The second dimension of multicultural competence is knowledge of different cultural worldviews, and respect and appreciation for them (Sue et al., 1992). Counselors do not have to approve of different lifestyles, they just have to accept them as valid truths for their clients. Part of multicultural awareness is understanding the impact that a culture has on its members. Both supervisors and supervisees must be mindful of the role a culture plays in the lives of its members, creating rules by which to live and traditions to follow, often transgenerationally. Just as in counseling, cultural differences exist in supervision, too. The supervisor and supervisee(s) are likely to come from varying backgrounds, ethnicities, cultures, nationalities, and so forth. It is important to openly discuss issues, such as cultural socialization and gender identity, in supervision. When appropriate in supervision, it may be necessary to review pertinent cultural identity development models in order to continue to promote awareness and understanding of the multitude of clients with whom counselors will have contact. For review, see racial or ethnic identity measures, such as the Jewish Identity Development model (Kress & Elias, 2000), the White Racial Identity Attitude Scale (WRIAS; Helms & Carter, 1990), the Multigroup Ethnic Identity Measure (MEIM; Phinney, 1990), and the Cross Racial Identity Scale (CRIS; Cross & Vandiver, 2001). Additionally, it may be prudent to specifically review multicultural supervision models in order to better facilitate competency development and further promote understanding and acceptance of differences among clients and counselors, as well as supervisors and supervisees (for a review, see Carney & Kahn, 1984; Robinson, Bradley, & Hendricks, 2000; and Chapter 4).

Modeling Diversity Understanding in the Supervisory Role

It will not make for effective supervision if the individual or group supervisor has an attitude of "do as I say, not as I do" regarding diversity and multicultural awareness. Individual and group supervisors must first be multiculturally competent themselves if they ever expect to have a positive impact on their supervisees regarding embracing diversity. The third (and final) dimension of multicultural counseling competence is commitment to expanding counselors' skills and interventions to work with a variety of diverse cultural clients (Sue et al., 1992). This includes progression in relevant and specific modalities and strategies for working with clients with various cultural values and life experiences. Supervisors must model for their supervisees the same behaviors and attitudes that they ask of them. Additionally, supervisors must have open attitudes and welcome discussion and questions regarding issues of diversity. If supervisees do not feel comfortable asking their supervisors questions about multicultural issues and concerns, it will ultimately hurt the clients because their care may suffer due to lack of knowledge and understanding on the counselors' behalf.

When addressing cultural diversity, the issue of power must ultimately arise. Similar to differences in power levels between counselors and clients, supervisors and supervisees experience power distance within their relationships. Not discussing obvious power differentials is akin to approving of them; in order to create the most effective supervision experience, both supervisors and supervisees must be willing to broach difficult topics, such as oppression and bigotry, in order to better understand them. The supervisors should, again, take into account the supervisees' learning styles when determining the best approaches for modeling diversity understanding. Audio learners may benefit from bidirectional discussions, whereas visual learners may appreciate psychoeducational PowerPoint presentations and kinesthetic learners may like role-plays.

Continuing Personal Growth in Diversity Areas

Becoming multiculturally competent is not like running a race; you will not cross a finish line and say, "I am done learning about culture. I know everything I need." Rather, multicultural competence is a lifelong pursuit, continually evolving and adapting as society and cultures change. Self-reflection does not end when supervision does. Questioning one's own biases, stereotypes, and preconceived notions should not cease just because supervision has terminated. As counselors, you owe it to your clients and your profession to always search for meaning as it relates to diversity. You should never stop caring about the plethora of learning opportunities and teachable moments that cultural differences present.

SUMMARY

Regardless of whether supervision is in individual or group format, the experience has the potential to deeply affect the lives of the participating members should they commit to the process and allow themselves to be changed as a result. The learning that is cocreated through supervision can not only benefit clients, but also the professionals involved, as long as they are willing to truly be active participants and open up themselves to a process that is challenging and fulfilling. Both supervisor and supervisee have the opportunity to invest in the supervision experience and relationship and reap great rewards as a result.

The purpose of individual and group supervision is to benefit the client by focusing on the supervisee's application of counseling skills, counseling theory, ethics, and professional behavior. Effective supervision relies on having a positive working relationship between supervisor and supervisee(s), as well as using action plans for supervision sessions to ensure that the time together is spent usefully and efficaciously. A useful tool for supervision is the professional disclosure statement, similar to informed consent, in which the contract of the supervision experience is documented. Expectations for both supervisor and supervisee(s) should be discussed and agreed on at the outset of the supervision experience. Determining the learning styles of the supervisees is useful because supervision experiences can be crafted and tailored to fit the unique needs of the supervisees in order to promote optimal learning outcomes. Both individual and group supervision require participating members to be actively involved and invested in the process in order to facilitate valuable experiences. Multicultural competence is an invariable journey to which there is no endpoint.

REFLECTION QUESTIONS

Reflection Questions for Supervisees

1. What are your perceptions of the benefits and deficits of individual supervision? Group supervision?
2. How do you see your role in the supervision experience? What kind of supervisee do you want to be?
3. What do you need from your supervisor? What do you need from fellow supervisees (if applicable)?
4. What are your expectations for supervision? Specific goals?
5. How are you becoming multiculturally competent?

Reflection Questions for Supervisors

1. What kind of supervision did you receive prelicensure? What was most helpful about that experience? What was least helpful?

2. What kind of supervisor is the most successful at promoting effective supervision? What personal traits and professional characteristics does this supervisor have? How is this person like you? How are you dissimilar from this person?
3. What do you want your relationships with your supervisees to be like? How will you build rapport?
4. How do you want to structure supervision sessions so they are efficacious and purposeful?
5. What are your expectations for supervision? Specific goals?
6. How are you helping supervisees to become multiculturally competent?

SUGGESTED RESOURCES

American Association for Marriage and Family Therapy. (2013). *User's guide to the AAMFT Code of Ethics*. Washington, DC: Author.

Bernard, J. M., & Goodyear, R. K. (2013). *Fundamentals of clinical supervision* (5th ed.). Boston, MA: Pearson Education.

Campbell, J. M. (2000). *Becoming an effective supervisor: A workbook for counselors and psychotherapists*. New York, NY: Routledge.

Campbell, J. M. (2005). *Essentials of clinical supervision*. Hoboken, NJ: John Wiley & Sons.

Corey, G., Corey, M. S., & Callanan, P. (2010). *Issues and ethics in the helping professions* (8th ed.). Pacific Grove, CA: Brooks/Cole.

Falendar, C. A., & Shafranske, E. P. (2004). *Clinical supervision: A competency-based approach*. Washington, DC: American Psychological Association.

Falendar, C. A., & Shafranske, E. P. (2008). *Casebook for clinical supervision: A competency-based approach*. Washington, DC: American Psychological Association.

Hawkins, P., & Shohet, R. (2012). *Supervision in the helping professions* (4th ed.). Philadelphia, PA: Open University Press.

Ladany, N., Friedlander, M. L., & Nelson, M. L. (2005). *Critical events in psychotherapy supervision: An interpersonal approach*. Washington, DC: American Psychological Association.

Pearson, Q. M. (2001). A case in clinical supervision: A framework for putting theory into practice. *Journal of Mental Health Counseling, 23*(2), 174–183.

Tyson, L. E., Culbreth, J. R., & Harrington, J. A. (Eds.). (2008). *Critical incidents in clinical supervision: Addictions, community, and school counseling* (2nd ed.). Alexandria, VA: American Counseling Association.

REFERENCES

American Counseling Association. (2014). *Code of ethics*. Alexandria, VA: Author.

Barnett, J. E., Erickson Cornish, J. A., Goodyear, R. K., & Lichtenberg, J. W. (2007). Commentaries on the ethical and effective practice of clinical supervision. *Professional Psychology: Research and Practice, 38*(3), 268–275. doi:10.1037/0735-7028.38.3.268

Bernard, J. M. (1994). Receiving and using supervision. In H. Hackney & S. Cormier (Eds.), *Counseling strategies and interventions* (pp. 169–189). Needham Heights, MA: Allyn & Bacon.

Borders, L. D., & Brown, L. L. (2005). *The new handbook of counseling supervision* (2nd ed.). Mahwah, NJ: Lawrence Erlbaum.

Carney, C. G., & Kahn, K. B. (1984). Building competencies for effective cross-cultural counseling: A developmental view. *Counseling Psychologist, 12*, 111–119.

Council for the Accreditation of Counseling and Related Educational Programs. (2009). *CACREP standards*. Alexandria, VA: Author.

Cross, W. E., Jr., & Vandiver, B. J. (2001). Nigrescence theory and measurement: Introducing the Cross Racial Identity Scale (CRIS). In J. G. Ponterotto, J. M. Casas, L. A. Suzuki, &

C. M. Alexander (Eds.), *Handbook of multicultural counseling* (2nd ed., pp. 371–393). Thousand Oaks, CA: Sage.

de Shazer, S. (1988). *Clues: Investigating solutions in brief therapy*. New York, NY: W. W. Norton.

Edwards, J. K., & Chen, M-W. (1999). Strength-based supervision: Frameworks, current practice, and future directions. *Family Journal: Counseling and Therapy for Couples and Families, 7*(4), 349–357. doi:10.1177/1066480799074005

Ekstein, R., & Wallerstein, R. (1958). *The teaching and learning of psychotherapy*. New York, NY: Basic Books.

Fall, M., & Sutton, J. M., Jr. (2004). *Clinical supervision: A handbook for practitioners*. Boston, MA: Pearson Education.

Friere, P. (2000). *Pedagogy of the oppressed* (30th anniversary ed.). New York, NY: Bloomsbury.

Glick, P., & Fiske, S. T. (1996). The Ambivalent Sexism Inventory: Differentiating hostile and benevolent sexism. *Journal of Personality and Social Psychology, 70*(3), 491–512.

Goldberg, R. M., Dixon, A. L., & Wolf, C. P. (2012). Facilitating effective triadic counseling supervision: An adapted model for an underutilized supervision approach. *Clinical Supervisor, 31*(1), 42–60. doi:10.1080/07325223.2012.670077

Greenwald, A. G., McGhee, D. E., & Schwartz, J. L. K. (1998). Measuring individual differences in implicit cognition: The Implicit Association Test. *Journal of Personality and Social Psychology, 74*(6), 1464–1480.

Helms, J. E., & Carter, R. T. (1990). Development of the White Racial Identity Inventory. In J. E. Helms (Ed.), *Black and white racial identity: Theory, research, and practice* (pp. 67–80). Santa Barbara, CA: Praeger.

Kitchener, K. S. (1984). Intuition, critical evaluation, and ethical principles: The foundation for ethical decisions in counseling psychology. *Counseling Psychologist, 12*(3), 43–55. doi:10.1177/0011000084123005

Kress, J. S., & Elias, M. J. (2000). Infusing community psychology and religion: Themes from an action-research project in Jewish identity development. *Journal of Community Psychology, 28*(2), 187–198.

Lawson, G. (2007). Counselor wellness and impairment: A national survey. *Journal of Humanistic Counseling, Education and Development, 46*(1), 20–34.

Lent, R. W., Hill, C. E., & Hoffman, M. A. (2003). Development and validation of the Counselor Activity Self-Efficacy scales. *Journal of Counseling Psychology, 50*(1), 97–108. doi:10.1037/0022-0167.50.1.97

McCarthy, P., Sugden, S., Koker, M., Lamendola, F., Maurer, S., & Renninger, S. (1995). A practical guide to informed consent in clinical supervision. *Counselor Education and Supervision, 35*(2), 130–138.

North, M. S., & Fiske, S. T. (2013). A prescriptive intergenerational-tension ageism scale: Succession, Identity, and Consumption (SIC). *Psychological Assessment, 25*(3), 706–713. doi:10.1037/a0032367

Pearson, Q. M. (2004). Getting the most out of clinical supervision: Strategies for mental health. *Journal of Mental Health Counseling, 26*(4), 361–373.

Phinney, J. S. (1992). The Multigroup Ethnic Identity Measure: A new scale for use with diverse groups. *Journal of Adolescent Research, 7*(2), 156–176. doi:10.1177/074355489272003

Robiner, W. N. (1998). *Quality assessment and improvement systems*™. Minneapolis, MN: University of Minnesota.

Robinson, B., Bradley, L. J., & Hendricks, C. B. (2000). Multicultural counseling supervision: A four-step model toward competency. *International Journal for the Advancement of Counseling, 22,* 131–141.

Rodenhauser, P., Rudisill, J. R., & Painter, A. F. (1989). Attributes conducive to learning in psychotherapy supervision. *American Journal of Psychotherapy, 43*(3), 368–377.

Satir, V., Banmen, J., Gerber, J., & Gomori, M. (2006). *The Satir model: Family therapy and beyond*. Palo Alto, CA: Science and Behavior Books.

Stinchfield, T. A., Hill, N. R., & Kleist, D. M. (2007). The reflective model of triadic supervision: Defining an emerging modality. *Counselor Education and Supervision, 46*(3), 172–183.

Sue, D. W. (2003). *Overcoming our racism: The journey to liberation*. San Francisco, CA: Jossey-Bass.

Sue, D. W., Arredondo, P., & McDavis, R. J. (1992). Multicultural counseling competencies and standards: A call to the profession. *Journal of Multicultural Counseling and Development, 20*(2), 64–88.

Sue, D. W., & Sue, D. (2012). *Counseling the culturally diverse: Theory and practice* (6th ed.). Hoboken, NJ: John Wiley & Sons.

Swank, J. M. (2014). Assessing counseling competencies: A comparison of supervisors' ratings and student supervisees' self-ratings. *Counseling Outcome Research and Evaluation, 5*(17), 17–27. doi:10.1177/2150137814529147

Tsong, Y., & Goodyear, R. K. (2014). Assessing supervision's clinical and multicultural impacts: The Supervision Outcome Scale's psychometric properties. *Training and Education in Professional Psychology, 8*(3), 189–195. doi:10.1037/tep0000049

Urlic, I., & Brunori, L. (Eds.). (2007). Editorial introduction [Special section: Supervision]. *Group Analysis, 40*(2), 163–166. doi:10.1177/0533316407077060

Vespia, K. M., Heckman-Stone, C., & Delworth, U. (2002). Describing and facilitating effective supervision behavior in counseling trainees. *Psychotherapy: Theory, Research, Practice, Training, 39*(1), 56–65. doi:10.1037//0033-3204.39.1.56

White, E., & Winstanley, J. (2014). Clinical supervision and the helping professions: An interpretation of history. *Clinical Supervisor, 33*(1), 3–25. doi:10.1080/07325223.2014.905226

Worthington, A. (2010). Supervision as oversight: A new era in the history of psychoanalytic practice and training? *Psychodynamic Practice, 16*(2), 131–150. doi:10.1080/14753631003688233

Zunker, V. G. (2012). *Career counseling: A holistic approach* (8th ed.). Independence, KY: Cengage Learning.

T • H • R • E • E

Ethical Issues in the Supervisory Relationship

Richard Deaner

After 3 months of working at the agency, Amy's supervisor left the agency in order to start her own private practice. As a result, Amy was asked by the director of the agency to coordinate the intensive in-home services program. In this capacity, she would be responsible for supervising three new therapists who were recently hired due to additional funding from a large grant. Additionally, she would still be expected to carry a caseload and provide counseling to the children and families. The director was confident that she was a good candidate for the new position and would be able to succeed in her new role.

Although Amy felt supported by her coworkers, she was somewhat concerned that she did not adequately possess the necessary skills to properly supervise other counselors. Additionally, the new grant included the use of interns from the university at which she is currently enrolled as a part-time student. Therefore, she would be responsible for the supervision of employees and interns. To make matters more complicated, one of the therapists she is supervising is a friend who graduated from the same counselor education program. The new position includes a slight pay increase but Amy is concerned with the already significant responsibilities inherent in the position. In her current position, she has already noticed that she has less free time than she had prior to taking the position. She has been unable to go to the gym due to long hours, and her friends have been complaining that she is always tired and unable to spend time with them. Nevertheless, Amy feels that the clients will benefit greatly from the increase in services and that she is the best candidate for the supervisory position because she has the most experience with the services, clients, and agency. The local university will not offer a class in supervision until the following academic year because it is a newly designed course in the program. Therefore, it does not appear that she will be able to enroll in classes related to supervision in order to enhance her professional development in this area. However, she is eager to find ways in which she can enhance her ability to provide counseling services as well as the services provided by others.

INTRODUCTION

The purpose of this chapter is to provide an overview of critical elements related to ethics and supervision. First, a concise overview of ethical issues related to counseling and supervision is outlined. Emphasis is placed on ethical supervisory issues described within the American Counseling Association (ACA) *Code of Ethics* (2014). Significant revisions within the ACA *Code of Ethics* (2014) include reference to supervision, and this chapter highlights these changes to facilitate understanding of ethical decision making in supervision. It is important to acknowledge that state licensing boards provide their own unique standards of practice for counselors and supervisors, and there are ethical codes regarding supervision for other mental health professionals, including psychologists (American Psychological Association, 2010) and social workers (National Association of Social Workers, 2008). However, the discussion of various state licensing boards and the ethical codes of conduct for multiple professions is beyond the scope of this chapter.

This chapter highlights ethics in supervision and includes discussion related to the roles and responsibilities of the supervisor and supervisee. First, an overview of the ACA *Code of Ethics* (2014) is provided. Notable additions to the *Code* are discussed. Next, related supervisory ethical responsibilities are outlined, including the following:

1. Competence
2. Feedback and evaluation
3. Informed consent and due process
4. Ethical decision making
5. Confidentiality
6. Multiple relationships
7. Liability

The supervisor and supervisee have distinct obligations within the supervisory relationship. Therefore, this chapter includes specific information related to both roles. The intent of these sections is to increase awareness, knowledge, and skills for individuals who plan to supervise counselors in a postmaster's capacity.

OVERVIEW OF THE ACA *CODE OF ETHICS*

Preamble

Recent revisions to the ACA *Code of Ethics* (2014) include several noticeable and significant additions. For instance, a notable addition to the Preamble includes a description of six ethical principles that form "the foundation for ethical behavior and decision making" (ACA, 2014, p. 3): *autonomy, nonmaleficence, beneficence, justice, fidelity,* and *veracity.* Because these principles inform ethical behavior and decision-making processes, let's begin with a brief description of each principle. After all, these principles apply to counseling and supervision.

First, the principle of *autonomy* involves fostering a sense of responsibility on the part of the client and the right to control the direction of her or his treatment. Next, the principle of *nonmaleficence* involves the avoidance of doing harm. The principle of *beneficence* involves striving to benefit the individual while promoting wellness. The principle of *justice* describes the importance of providing and fostering equitable services for individuals and society. The fifth principle, *fidelity*, emphasizes the importance of dependability, reliability, and trustworthiness on the part of the counselor. Last, the sixth principle of *veracity* underscores the notion of truthfulness when developing a working relationship with individuals. All of these principles provide a platform from which counseling professionals and supervisors can make ethical decisions in order to provide effective services in any setting. Indeed, the *Code* provides a resource and guide by which appropriate decisions, behaviors, and services can be delivered by all counselors, supervisors, and counselors-in-training.

Terminology

On close examination of the revised ACA *Code of Ethics* (2014), one can observe substantial edits regarding terminology and its application regarding supervision. The previous ACA *Code of Ethics* (2005) includes language that specifically applies to counselors-in-training, counselor educators, researchers, faculty, students, and supervisors in a variety of manners. These terms are used in multiple instances throughout the document. Conversely, the 2014 ACA *Code of Ethics* contains language that applies to counselors-in-training, counselor educators, researchers, faculty, students, and supervisors as well. However, the revised *Code* (2014) seems to significantly reduce the inclusion of the term *counselors-in-training*. In both versions of the *Code*, the term *counselors-in-training* is used interchangeably with the term *students* (Sections F.6.b, F.8.a, F.8.b). For some, it may have been unclear whether or not the material regarding supervision (professional disclosure, adherence to the standards, and impairment) was applicable to other "counselors-in-training" who were not merely students and who were in the process of training to be professional counselors as postgraduates.

Meanwhile, the revised *Code* (2014) only includes the term *counselors-in-training* in two instances. This difference is significant because the revised *Code* (2014) appears to clarify the role of a supervisee, especially within the main area where ethics and supervision are discussed (Section F). First, it includes the term *counselors-in-training* in one of the six "purposes" of the *Code*, which states, "The *Code* identifies ethical considerations relevant to professional counselors and counselors-in-training" (ACA, 2014, p. 3). Next, the term, *counselors-in-training* is used within the definition of *supervisee* in the Glossary of Terms (ACA, 2014, p. 21). In this instance, a supervisee is defined as "a professional counselor or counselor-in-training whose counseling work or clinical skill development is being overseen in a formal supervisory relationship by a qualified trained professional" (ACA, 2014, p. 21). Therefore, there seems to have been a concerted effort to clarify these roles, especially for supervisors and supervisees. Because both counselor education students and postgraduate counselors may be engaged in supervision, this chapter uses the term *supervisee* to include both *counselor-in-training* and *student* in order to simplify matters and facilitate better understanding.

Supervision

As noted, the ACA *Code of Ethics* (2014) includes language that applies specifically to the process of supervision (Section F). As such, there is language that delineates responsibilities for supervisors and supervisees. In sum, the *Code* includes guidance for supervisors in order to ensure appropriate and effective services to be rendered by the supervisee. Responsibilities include the importance of appropriate and effective supervision in order to enhance the professional development of the supervisee. Additionally, the *Code* clearly outlines the roles and responsibilities of supervisees as they navigate the process of supervision. Overall, the main components of this section involve issues related to values, professionalism, and readiness. An outline of integral components inherent within supervisory ethical responsibilities and a brief overview of legal principles are specifically covered in the next section. Additionally, recent revisions to the *Code* include notable guidelines related to the delivery of supervision via electronic formats. Therefore, it is necessary to briefly discuss how the *Code* considers elements associated with supervision in terms of technological advancements. All of the aforementioned ethical components are integral and unique to the process and structure of supervision. See Exhibit 3.1 for an example of a licensed professional counselor (LPC) supervision agreement contract.

SUPERVISORY ETHICAL RESPONSIBILITIES

There are several integral aspects related to ethical responsibilities inherent in the process of supervision. These unique ethical considerations are apparent for the supervisor and supervisee in the process of supervision. First, in order to deliver appropriate and effective services to clients, the supervisor and supervisee need to be competent practitioners. In fact, a major component related to supervisory responsibilities involves the notion of *competence*, which is a significant theme within the ACA *Code of Ethics* (2014). In supervision, there are three basic areas related to competence: (1) supervisory training; (2) awareness, knowledge, and skills; and (3) the notion of impairment. All of these areas are described in the following sections as they relate to supervisor and supervisee competence.

Because supervision is a process used to enhance the professional development of the supervisee, special considerations regarding *feedback and evaluation* are also important to address in this chapter. Prior to engaging in the evaluative process of supervision, the supervisor and supervisee should be aware of roles and responsibilities related to the process of supervision. Therefore, the notions of *informed consent* and *due process* are critical elements to consider when providing supervision. Last, in order to provide effective services to clients, the supervisors and supervisees must be able to navigate ethical decisions in a thorough and reflective manner. Consequently, a discussion concerning *ethical decision making* within the context of supervision is provided in the following sections.

Another critical element for this chapter to explore is the issue of *confidentiality* in supervision. *Confidentiality* in supervision presents unique aspects related to clients and supervisees. The process of supervision can evolve over

EXHIBIT 3.1 • Sample Licensed Professional Counselor Supervision Agreement Contract

I, ______________________________, as the supervisee, agree to the following requirements for licensed professional counselor (LPC) supervision:

- To attend supervision sessions on a regular and monthly basis at (specified location) for 3 hours of group/individual supervision
- To collaboratively set goals for supervision based on individual professional development, skill development, personal growth, and/or wellness as a professional counselor
- To participate with periodic evaluation of my goals and redefining of those goals
- To participate with periodic evaluation of my supervisor in order to facilitate professional development
- To participate with honest disclosure of client cases in order to adequately assess case conceptualization, ethical dilemmas, and/or emergency situations
- To provide monthly summaries of client development in order to adequately assess progress of client and professional development
- To be responsible for records of supervision, communication with licensure board, proof of liability insurance, as well as emergency contacts and to provide this information at the request of the supervisor
- To agree and abide by the most current professional and ethical standards of the American Counseling Association (ACA) and state licensing boards of (state) with careful attention to the culturally relevant issues; This tenet is especially critical due to unique ethical issues inherent within supervision—competence, confidentiality, informed consent and due process, feedback and evaluation, liability, ethical decision making, and technology (if supervision is provided via technology)
- To agree to pay (amount) for each scheduled hour of supervision per each monthly session and to abide by the cancellation policy developed during the first session of supervision

As your supervisor, you can expect me to navigate the roles of teacher, counselor, and consultant in my efforts to facilitate supervision. My role of teacher involves disseminating knowledge, skills, and scholarship related to effective counseling. At times, my role as teacher may involve the assignment of homework, such as scholarship review, in order to enhance your professional development. My role of counselor involves enhancing your awareness and insight regarding values, assumptions, beliefs, and expectations that may affect your clinical work. However, I do not provide counseling services to supervisees. Rather, supervision will include discussion of interpersonal and intrapersonal issues that may affect your ability to work with clients. My role as consultant involves working collaboratively with you in order to define goals, conceptualize cases, and discuss treatment options. You will be asked regularly to evaluate my services and to evaluate your awareness, knowledge, and skills in order to facilitate growth as a professional counselor. It is my hope that we indicate areas for growth while highlighting your strengths. However, the process of supervision may be challenging at times. You have the right to disagree with my evaluation of your progress and have the right to terminate my services at your discretion. However, if I determine that you are overly resistant to suggestions, feedback, or supervisory goals, I may recommend outside counseling services, revise our supervisory relationship, or terminate our supervisory relationship. The overall goals of supervision are to protect your clients and to assist you in your growth as a professional counselor. All of the aforementioned issues are essential for you to consider as we embark on this collaborative journey together.

Supervisee ______________________________ Date ____________________

Supervisor ______________________________ Date ____________________ time. The relationship between the supervisor and supervisee may change prior to, during, or after supervision has been initiated. As a result, the supervisor and supervisee may navigate multiple roles and responsibilities during supervision. Therefore, a brief discussion of *multiple relationships* is provided in the following sections. Finally, issues related to *liability* within supervision are explored. It is essential to consider *liability* as it relates to the supervisor and supervisee in order to fully examine this issue.

These aforementioned aspects related to (1) competence, (2) feedback and evaluation, (3) informed consent and due process, (4) ethical decision making, (5) confidentiality, (6) multiple relationships, and (7) liability are addressed in the next sections as they directly relate to the ACA *Code of Ethics* (2014). The individual ethical standards are provided as each aspect related to ethics and supervision is described. Emphasis is placed on the specific issues relevant for supervisors and supervisees who work in a postgraduate environment.

COMPETENCE

The ACA *Code of Ethics* (2014) includes reference to competence in specific areas. A major aspect of competence involves the ability to deliver appropriate and effective services to client(s). In order to fulfill this competency, it is necessary to address knowledge, skills, and personal readiness for the supervisor and supervisee. The constructs related to competence for supervisors and supervisees are distinct. Therefore, it is necessary to discuss issues related to competence separately for supervisors and supervisees. First, the following sections discuss issues related to supervisor competence, including (1) specialized training; (2) awareness, knowledge, and skills; and (3) impairment. Next, the chapter explores topics related to supervisee competence, including (1) awareness, knowledge, and skills, and (2) impairment.

Supervisor Competence

For supervisors, competence involves issues related to appropriate training, personal awareness, and impairment. The notion of competence can be an evolving concept of skills development, experience, and education used to enhance professional development. Competence also applies to the ability to maintain awareness and personal readiness in order to render effective services. Therefore, the supervisor and supervisee are required to maintain awareness in terms of personal wellness so that services are not negatively affected. As supervisors and supervisees navigate the provision of services to clients, they can use an ethical decision-making model to determine practical and competent delivery of services.

Training

The ACA *Code of Ethics* (2014) clearly defines issues related to competence for the supervisor. The *Code* specifically stresses the requirement for supervisors to be trained in the area of supervision (ACA, 2014, Section F.2.a). In fact, this standard states, "Prior to offering supervision services, counselors are trained in supervising methods and techniques. Counselors who offer supervision services regularly pursue continuing education activities, including both counseling and supervision topics and skills" (ACA, 2014, Section F.2.a). As such, it is imperative that supervisors seek training *prior* to becoming supervisors, according to this standard. Furthermore, the supervisor is required to seek education related to the provision of counseling *and* supervision services. With regard to Amy, she is clearly experiencing an ethical dilemma as she contemplates becoming a supervisor without having appropriate training related to supervision. As a result, she will need to reflect on the spirit of this standard because she isn't likely to experience professional development regarding supervision prior to her provision of supervision. She will have to consider her own needs, the needs of the clients, and the needs of the supervisees and decide on a course of action. Later in this chapter, we discuss a possible tool by which she can consider possible outcomes to this dilemma. An ethical decision-making model will allow Amy to reflect and consider various aspects of this dilemma in a systematic and concrete manner.

A new and noticeable addition to the *Code* (ACA, 2014) related to competence involves technology in supervision. As a result of technological advances, there are numerous ways in which supervisors can provide services to supervisees. The *Code* specifies, "When using technology in supervision, counselor supervisors are competent in the use of those technologies. Supervisors take the necessary precautions to protect the confidentiality of all information transmitted through any electronic means" (ACA, 2014, Section F.2.c). Therefore, supervisors should undergo training regarding technology in order to properly supervise counselors via technological means. Supervisors should be familiar with the structure, services, and delivery of the specific type of technology used for supervision. Additionally, supervisors should be aware of elements regarding informed consent and confidentiality if and when providing supervision via electronic formats.

In 2012, the National Board for Certified Counselors (NBCC; 2013) adopted the *Policy Regarding the Provision of Distance Professional Services* in order to expand on the unique elements related to the provision of professional services via technological means. Therefore, this policy can be used as a resource when considering all of the unique elements related to the provision of professional services via technological means. This policy includes unique standards related to informed consent, transfer of information, data storage, confidentiality, encryption, emergency precautions, qualifications, social media, and professional disclosure. The *Code* and the NBCC *Policy* emphasize that supervisors and supervisees should critically examine the benefits and limitations when supervision is provided via phones, Internet, Skype, e-mail, text, or any other web-based platform. For instance, limitations regarding confidentiality would be essential to consider when supervision is provided via web-based platforms. Discussing all of the elements within this policy is beyond the scope of this chapter. However, one can certainly benefit from reviewing this policy when providing professional services via technological means because it provides clear and specific options to consider.

Awareness, Knowledge, and Skills

Supervisors are required to be "aware of and address the role of multiculturalism/diversity in the supervisory relationship" (ACA, 2014, Section F.2.b). Therefore, supervisors should be reflective practitioners who are able to reflect on their own cultural biases, values, and beliefs and how these might affect the supervisory relationship. In the case of Amy, she will need to examine her own cultural biases, values, and beliefs and how these might affect her relationship with clients as well as the supervisees with whom she will work.

Sue, Arredondo, and McDavis (1992) urge counselors to use the Multicultural Counseling Competencies (MCCs) in order to become competent practitioners (www.counseling.org/Resources/Competencies/Multcultural_Competencies.pdf). These competencies involve three interrelated components that are required in term of becoming a culturally competent counselor: *awareness, knowledge*, and *skills*. First, the supervisor should be aware of her or his own values, beliefs, and assumptions. Pederson (1990) asserts that all individuals are cultural beings. Therefore, it is reasonable to assume that supervisors should examine their own cultural upbringing and the evolution of their values, beliefs, and assumptions within a unique cultural context in order to gain *awareness*. Next, the supervisor should seek professional development regarding the *knowledge* of various other cultures in order to effectively provide services. In this step, it is necessary to understand that there are different ways of perceiving the world, and these perspectives can be influenced by culture. If needed, the supervisor should research scholarship regarding particular cultures in order to gain understanding in this area. In this manner, the supervisor can seek to understand best practices as they relate to certain cultures.

Furthermore, professional development in terms of cultural sensitivity allows the practitioner to apply *awareness* and *knowledge* in order to use culturally sensitive *skills*. As such, the supervisor is able to attend to the needs of the culturally unique client in an effective manner by utilizing appropriate and effective *skills*. Supervisors (and supervisees) who are able to meaningfully reflect on these three culturally responsive elements will be able to work collaboratively with supervisees in order to meet the needs of clients. Because Amy works in an urban setting, she may be working with a diverse population of clients. Additionally, the supervisees with whom she will work may also represent diverse populations. Therefore, Amy should carefully consider these cultural elements when proceeding with supervision.

Impairment

Another feature of supervisory competency involves the personal readiness and wellness displayed by the supervisee. According to the ACA *Code of Ethics* (2014), "Students and supervisees monitor themselves for signs of impairment from their own physical, mental, or emotional problems and refrain from offering or providing services when such impairment is likely to harm a client or others" (p. 13). Although the *Code* uses the term *students* in this standard, it appears that it is referring to supervisees in general. As such, the supervisor is responsible for monitoring the wellness of the supervisee. Because the notion of wellness has been identified as a paradigm of the counseling profession

(Myers, 1991), how this notion is applied to supervisees and supervisors seems understandable.

Competence is a sensitive but important issue within supervision, especially when practitioners work in managed care organizations and mental health agencies (Acker, 2010, 2012). Acker (2010, 2012) suggests that mental health agencies often are required to provide increasingly efficient services. In this manner, practitioners are forced to provide increasingly complex and efficient services but with dwindling and limited resources. As a result, the mental health practitioner's perceptions can be negatively affected, which can lead to burnout, job dissatisfaction, and turnover. Lent and Schwartz (2012) investigated the relationship among personal variables, clinical work settings, and demographic variables in relation to burnout for professional counselors. In this study, professional counselors reported significantly more levels of burnout in mental health outpatient settings when compared with professional counselors working in private practice or inpatient services. Additionally, professional counselors working in mental health agencies reported significantly more emotional exhaustion.

For Amy, it seems critical to consider and abide by the recommendations offered through research related to burnout within her own work setting when providing supervisory services. Many supervisees may feel overwhelmed with the amount of work or may feel inadequate in terms of providing effective services due to the significant workload. As such, Amy will need to consider these perceptions when providing supervision in order to monitor any possible impairment issues displayed by the supervisee.

Although the supervisor must assess the personal readiness of the supervisee, it is also necessary for the supervisor to assess his or her own wellness or impairment. Amy will need to assess her own sense of wellness in order to model appropriate behavior and to enhance the parallel process of supervision. Perceived responses to the work environment are particularly salient for Amy, who works in an agency that may have higher levels of employee burnout. For Amy, it appears that the agency is indeed experiencing the need to provide additional services without having the requisite amount of resources. Amy may be unprepared to assume the role of supervisor. However, it seems that the needs of the agency have precluded any delay in her development as a supervisor. As a result, Amy is seemingly forced to provide additional services with fewer resources. It will be imperative for Amy to gauge her own level of readiness and assess possible burnout, exhaustion, and impairment throughout her work with clients and supervisees.

Supervisee Competence

The supervisor has a significant role within the supervisor/supervisee relationship. Indeed, the supervisor facilitates the professional development of the supervisee in order to enhance clinical skills. However, supervisees have significant obligations within the supervisory process. In order to become competent practitioners, supervisees will need to develop awareness, knowledge, and skills in order to effectively work with diverse populations. Also, the supervisee is responsible for monitoring his or her own wellness in order to avoid clinical impairment.

Last, supervisee competence includes aspects related to feedback, evaluation, due process, and informed consent in order to facilitate professional development.

Awareness, Knowledge, and Skills

One of the main goals of supervision is to assist the supervisee in becoming "prepared to serve a range of diverse clients" (ACA, 2014, p. 12). This seems to have been an important revision to the *Code* as evidenced by its wording. In fact, the terms *diverse* and *diversity* are used 31 times in the previous *Code* (2005), whereas the same terms are used 42 times in the current *Code* (2014). Meanwhile, reference to *values* occurs 12 times in the previous *Code* (2005), whereas reference to *values* occurs 20 times in the current *Code* (2014). One can assume that the recent court cases involving the personal values and beliefs of counselor education students may have had some impact on the inclusion and increase of discussion related to values. In three recent court cases (*Keeton v. Anderson-Wiley,* 2010; *Ward v. Wilbanks,* 2010; *Ward v. Polite,* 2012), the counselor-in-training's personal values conflicted with the values of clients and the nondiscrimination policy of the counseling profession. Although the results of each court case varied, the notion of values affecting the counseling relationship was emphasized in all. However, it is important to note that the values themselves should not be scrutinized and challenged. Rather, it is imperative that supervisors and supervisees examine how the values *may affect* the counseling (and supervisory) relationship. After all, according to the ACA *Code of Ethics* (2014), it is essential for counselors to be "aware of—and avoid imposing—their own values, attitudes, beliefs, and behaviors" (p. 5). Furthermore, the *Code* contains a new and notable addition that seems to expand on this awareness by offering a remedy to the situation if counselors are at risk of imposing values onto clients. The *Code* states, "Counselors respect the diversity of clients, trainees, research participants and seek training in areas in which they are at risk of imposing their values onto clients, especially when the counselor's values are inconsistent with the client's goals or are discriminatory in nature" (2014, Section A.4.b, p. 5). Therefore, it is crucial for the supervisor and supervisee to examine their values in order to increase awareness and to avoid imposing values on clients. In doing so, practitioners can be prepared to work with diverse populations in a competent and ethical manner while they seek culturally sensitive knowledge and skills in order to enhance services.

Impairment

Another critical component related to supervisee competence is the notion of impairment. As previously mentioned, supervisors are responsible for monitoring the impairment of supervisees. However, supervisees are also tasked with monitoring their own wellness and impairment. The ACA *Code of Ethics* (2014) states, "supervisees monitor themselves for signs of impairment from their own physical, mental, or emotional problems and refrain from offering or providing professional services when such impairment is likely to harm a client or others" (p. 13). Therefore, it is imperative for the supervisee to continuously monitor her or his wellness in a reflective manner in order to ensure appropriate and effective services. For example, the supervisee should consider any issues related to personal wellness, including physical symptoms, mental health, and emotional regulation. Acker (2010) studied social workers who worked in managed care settings and discovered that somatic complaints, such as headaches, illness, and other physical manifestations of stress, were associated with perceived competence, burnout, and exhaustion. Acker reported that as perceived competence increased for social workers, there was a decrease in frequency of the somatic complaints displayed by the social worker. Conversely, as burnout and exhaustion increased for the social worker, the frequency of somatic complaints displayed by the social worker increased. Although this study compared these issues for social workers, it seems realistic to apply these same notions when discussing counselors working in mental health agencies. Overall, this information provides a basis from which supervisees can monitor perceived competence, burnout, and exhaustion in order to assess possible impairment.

FEEDBACK AND EVALUATION

Bernard and Goodyear (2014) emphasize the role of the supervisor as an evaluator and gatekeeper in the counseling profession. In this sense, it is imperative for the supervisor to adequately assess and evaluate the competence of the supervisee (Exhibit 3.2, Professional Counseling Development Evaluation). Competencies may be based on skills, dispositions, and issues related to impairment. All of these issues affect supervisee performance. The ACA *Code of Ethics* (2014) states, "supervisors are aware of supervisee limitations that might impede performance" (p. 13). As such, supervisors are responsible for addressing any limitations of competency through ongoing evaluation. If the supervisees are unable to "demonstrate that they can provide competent professional services to a range of diverse clients" (p. 13), supervisors must consider and recommend remedial assistance depending on the needs of the supervisee. This remedial assistance may involve processing personal values, or it may involve requirements related to expanding awareness, knowledge, and skills.

Evaluation also involves appropriately identifying strengths as well as areas for growth. Furthermore, the ACA *Code of Ethics* (2014) clearly indicates that supervisors are responsible for ongoing evaluation "regarding their performance and schedule periodic formal evaluative sessions throughout the supervisory relationship" (p. 13). In this manner, evaluation and feedback should be an ongoing, constructive, and systematic process for the supervisee. The supervisee should be aware of the variables that will be considered for evaluation, and this leads our discussion to other important issue regarding competence: informed consent and due process.

INFORMED CONSENT AND DUE PROCESS

In order facilitate growth and competency for the supervisee, the supervisor should provide a clear basis from which the supervisee will be supervised and evaluated. Clearly, clients have a right to know what to expect in counseling. Clients should be aware of the process of counseling, and any risks or benefits

EXHIBIT 3.2 • Professional Counseling Development Evaluation

Counseling LPC Candidate: **Date:**

Rating Scale

4 = exemplary level—level of excellence/mastery
2 = in-progress level—approaching competence
3 = proficient level—level of competence
1 = unsatisfactory level—not competent at this time

Component	Not observed 0	Unsatisfactory 1	In Progress 2	Proficient 3	Exemplary 4
Supervision					
a. Displays positive attitude toward learning and supervision		Candidate rejects or actively disengages from opportunities for learning or ignores recommendations from supervisor; or interactions with supervisor may occasionally be confrontational; or candidate avoids self-disclosing personal concerns to supervisors that may impact performance as counselor.	Candidate occasionally takes advantage of learning opportunities or seeks opinions and advice from supervisors; or possesses minimal awareness or selectively self-discloses to supervisors personal concerns that may impact performance as counselor.	Candidate consistently acknowledges feedback from others, as evidenced by listening to, clarifying, evaluating, and implementing the feedback of others; shows willingness to self-disclose to supervisors personal concerns that may impact performance as counselor.	Candidate displays an unfailing zest for knowledge and readily seeks suggestions for improvement; shows unfailing willingness and ability to recognize when to self-disclose to supervisors personal concerns that may impact performance as counselor.
b. Develops positive relationship with supervisors		Candidate does little to develop or actively rejects a positive relationship with supervisors.	Candidate maintains a neutral relationship with instructors or supervisors, neither contributing to nor supporting a positive relationship with supervisors.	Candidate consistently maintains a positive relationship with supervisors.	Candidate displays exceptional affiliation and rapport with instructors and supervisors.

Multicultural Competence				
a. Demonstrates a commitment to developing multicultural competencies; acknowledges personal biases and works to reduce them	Candidate displays little to no commitment to developing multicultural competencies or lacks willingness to acknowledge and reduce personal biases.	Candidate is developing a commitment to developing multicultural competencies while intermittently acknowledging and reducing personal biases.	Candidate consistently demonstrates a commitment to developing multicultural competencies while reliably acknowledging and reducing personal biases.	Candidate displays exceptional commitment to developing multicultural competencies while actively acknowledging and reducing personal biases.
b. Demonstrates awareness, valuing, and knowledge of diverse worldviews	Candidate consistently demonstrates closed-mindedness or is unable or unwilling to value or attain knowledge of diverse worldviews.	Candidate occasionally demonstrates open-mindedness, intermittently or selectively values differences, or possesses rudimentary knowledge of diverse worldviews.	Candidate consistently demonstrates open-mindedness and a willingness to respect different points of view, and reliably values differences.	Candidate displays extraordinary open-mindedness by routinely honoring and valuing differences while actively seeking to attain substantial knowledge of diverse worldviews.
c. Effectively applies skills in a multicultural context	Candidate has difficulty applying skills in a multicultural context.	Candidate sporadically applies effective skills in a multicultural context.	Candidate intentionally applies effective skills in a multicultural context.	Candidate proactively applies effective skills in a multicultural context.
Personal Reflection and Growth				
a. Displays self-awareness	Candidate consistently avoids introspection or displays little understanding of impact of personal issues within the therapeutic relationship.	Candidate occasionally is able to demonstrate a commitment to personal growth by displaying basic introspection, or displays some understanding of impact of personal issues within the therapeutic relationship.	Candidate consistently displays accurate introspection, awareness of own strengths and weaknesses, and understanding of the impact of personal issues within the therapeutic relationship.	Candidate displays an extraordinary commitment to personal growth and meaningfully active introspection, and reliably reflects upon the impact of personal issues within the therapeutic relationship.

(continued)

EXHIBIT 3.2 • Professional Counseling Development Evaluation (*continued*)

Component	Not observed 0	Unsatisfactory 1	In Progress 2	Proficient 3	Exemplary 4
b. Shows commitment to personal growth and goals		Candidate lacks ability or initiative to develop personal goals or seek personal growth or does so in a superficial manner; or lacks ability to visualize appropriate personal and professional identity and to create goals to achieve this vision.	Candidate occasionally initiates personal and professional growth; or at times is able to develop long- and short-term personal and professional goals, taking some steps to achieve them.	Candidate actively seeks personal and professional growth; develops significant long- and short-term personal and professional goals and takes reasonable steps to achieve them; demonstrates an openness to take personal risks.	Candidate proactively seeks personal and professional growth; displays exceptional adeptness in developing and achieving significant long- and short-term personal and professional goals; confidently takes appropriate personal and professional risks.
c. Shows emotional stability and willingness and ability to balance personal and professional commitments		Candidate displays inappropriate boundaries by sharing too much or too little about self; or regularly appears stressed; or does not successfully balance personal and professional responsibilities.	Candidate occasionally is able to regulate and display appropriate emotions and empathy; or occasionally is able to successfully balance personal and professional responsibilities; or at times appears stressed.	Candidate displays adherence to a wellness philosophy, is consistently able to regulate and display appropriate empathy without overidentifying, and is able to manage life experiences appropriately and in a professional manner.	Candidate demonstrates a daily wellness philosophy with exemplary personal and professional behaviors, and displays exceptional forethought in successfully balancing personal and professional responsibilities.

of the counseling process. This process of defining and clarifying the counseling experience is related to the concept of *informed consent*. This right to know what to expect is equally integral to supervision. Supervisees should be informed of how the process of supervision will proceed.

According to the ACA *Code of Ethics* (2014), "supervisors are responsible for incorporating into their supervision the principles of informed consent and participation" (Section F.4.a, p. 13). Here, supervisors must detail the process of supervision, including aspects related to roles, responsibilities, and expectations inherent in the process of supervision. Additionally, the ACA *Code of Ethics* (2014) states that supervisees should be informed of how they will be evaluated during the process of supervision. In the process of informed consent, "supervisors inform supervisees of the policies and procedures to which supervisors are to adhere and the mechanisms for due process appeal of individual supervisor actions" (ACA, 2014, p. 13). In this manner, it is crucial that the supervisee is aware of how the evaluation process will affect his or her performance and ability to work as a counselor. Additionally, supervisees should be aware of the specific factors by which they will be evaluated and should know the possible courses of action that would need to be conducted in order to respond to any unsuccessful evaluations. This notion of understanding how to appeal any unsuccessful evaluations or actions is related to the notion of *due process*. Sometimes a supervisee may disagree with the evaluation of the supervisor. The supervisee has the right to disagree. In this case, it is essential to understand the ways in which supervisees can dispute evaluations in a systematic manner. In essence, the supervisee must know the rights inherent within the notion of due process. This opportunity to justify behaviors and performance allows the supervisee to have significant input regarding the process of evaluation. In sum, the notions of informed consent and due process underscore the importance of the supervisor and supervisee working collaboratively in the entire process of supervision. Last, it seems significant to consider a new and notable inclusion in the *Code* related to technology in terms of informed consent and due process. The current *Code* continues to state that it is important for the supervisor to discuss any issues "unique to the use of distance supervision" (2014, p. 13) as they relate to informed consent and due process. Therefore, it is imperative for the supervisor and supervisee to consider any limitations when supervision is conducted via electronic means.

ETHICAL DECISION MAKING

The ACA *Code of Ethics* (2014) includes clear rhetoric related to ethical decision making for counselors. Therefore, it is necessary to discuss ethical decision making as it applies to supervisees. At times, supervisees encounter ethical dilemmas that may be challenging to resolve. In order to choose an acceptable course of action, the supervisees must consider "professional values, professional principles, and ethical standards" (p. 3). In fact, the ACA *Code of Ethics* (2014) "Purpose" section describes the resolution of ethical decision making as a process of contemplation, evaluation, collaboration, and consultation. In this manner, the supervisee must reflect on possible actions, evaluate consequences of actions, collaborate with the client, and consult with supervisors.

In doing so, the supervisee is expected to "use a credible model of decision making that can bear public scrutiny of its application" (p. 3). Providing a comprehensive overview of possible decision-making models is beyond the scope of this chapter. However, the authors of this chapter propose one possible model that can be used to effectively determine ethical decisions and courses of action.

One possible ethical decision-making model that might prove useful for supervisees has been adapted from Remley and Herlihy (2010). This model includes 11 steps that can be easily addressed by the supervisee. *Step I* includes identifying and defining the problem. Here, the supervisee gathers as much information related to the dilemma as he or she can find. *Step II* entails careful consideration of the ethical principles inherent in the dilemma (autonomy, nonmaleficence, beneficence, justice, veracity, and fidelity). In this step, the supervisee should outline how the dilemma affects the ability to uphold the principles. *Step III* includes personal reflection on the part of the supervisee. Here, the supervisee must tune in to his or her own feelings and values regarding the dilemma. Also, the supervisee must consider how personal feelings and values might be impacting the dilemma and decision-making process. *Step IV* includes a review of relevant ethical codes and any applicable laws and regulations regarding the dilemma. *Step V* involves researching the situation to review how others may have approached similar situations. This step should include any possible literature or research related to the dilemma. *Step VI* entails consulting with colleagues or experts. In many instances, this could include a supervisor, faculty member, or other mental health professionals. *Step VII* discusses the importance of involving the client in the decision-making process if possible. In some cases, this can be an illuminating experience. *Step VIII* involves identifying any desired outcome and considering possible courses of action. Here, the supervisee can imagine any obstacles or challenges in terms of achieving desired outcomes or courses of action. *Step IX* includes choosing a course of action. In *Step X*, supervisees document their actions and the process by which they determined these actions. This step is an essential component. It is recommended that supervisees always document aspects related to ethical decision making. Last, *Step XI* involves evaluating the course of action taken. Here, the supervisee should follow up with the client and situation in order to assess the impact of the entire decision-making process.

If these steps are used in a reflective manner, the supervisee can better attend to the needs of the client in a systematic manner. This ethical decision-making model (Remley & Herlihy, 2010) offers a useful tool by which supervisees can approach challenging ethical situations in a more manageable manner.

CONFIDENTIALITY

Clearly, the notion of confidentiality is a cornerstone of the counseling profession. Indeed, it is essential when building a trusting therapeutic relationship with clients. Yet, Bernard and Goodyear suggest that "the most sacred trust in mental health practice is also the most vulnerable to insult" (2014, p. 269). The dynamics involved in a counseling relationship change due to the process of supervision. As a result, the issue of confidentiality becomes increasingly complex as it relates to the client and supervisee. Therefore, it seems crucial to address confidentiality as it relates to supervision in this chapter.

Client Confidentiality

Overall, the majority of language concerning confidentiality and supervision cited by the ACA *Code of Ethics* (2014) involves discussion related to client confidentiality. The process of supervision adds a third party to the counseling relationship. As a result, the transmission and storage of information is also affected. Therefore, it is necessary for supervisees to understand this dynamic related to third-party information. Supervisors are required to "make supervisees aware of client rights, including the protection of client privacy and confidentiality" in the counseling and supervisory relationship (ACA, 2014, p. 13). Meanwhile, supervisees are required to inform clients of any limits of confidentiality due to the supervisory relationship and how it might affect the counseling relationship (Section E.1.c). Furthermore, supervisees are required to seek client consent prior to sharing any information within supervision (Section F.5.c).

Many times, supervision is provided in triadic or group formats. In these instances, the unique dynamics related to confidentiality within triadic and group supervision will need to be discussed with the supervisee. Furthermore, it is the responsibility of the supervisee to discuss these dynamics and related limitations of confidentiality with the client(s). It is imperative that the unique issues related to confidentiality in these instances are conveyed to the supervisee in order for the supervisee to ensure that the supervisee presents these limitations to the client(s).

The ACA *Code of Ethics* (2014) contains a noticeable increase in language regarding confidentiality and technology. Because counseling and supervision can be provided via electronic means, the issue of confidentiality is essential to discuss with clients and supervisees. One addition to the *Code* (Section F.2.c) states, "Supervisors take the necessary precautions to protect the confidentiality of all information transmitted through any electronic means" (p. 13). This newly added standard suggests that all client *and* supervisee information discussed in online supervision should be protected. Meanwhile, considering the technological advancements related to data storage and transmission, the *Code* includes reference to this aspect of confidentiality as well. As such, supervisees are required to inform clients about who will have access to client records and "how these records will be stored, transmitted, or otherwise reviewed" (p. 13). Therefore, the supervisor and supervisee should be aware of and discuss any limitations to confidentiality when services are stored in or conducted via any electronic source.

Supervisee Confidentiality

Although the ACA *Code of Ethics* (2014) clearly outlines issues related to confidentiality and clients, it seems unclear whether or not the same issues of confidentiality pertain to personal information shared by the supervisee. Bernard and Goodyear (2014) state that this aspect of confidentiality is conspicuously absent in the *Code* but suggest that it is an essential element to be discussed within supervision. Indeed, the process of supervision is a growth-oriented experience and can be highly personal for the supervisee. As such, supervisors should clearly discuss how sensitive personal information will be kept confidential as much as possible. This same spirit of treating personal information as confidential is also essential for supervisors to consider in triadic and group supervision formats. In fact, these supervision settings present additional limitations due to the increase of persons involved. Therefore, it is critical for the supervisor to continuously monitor and remind supervisees of this integral notion of confidentiality and its limitations within dyadic supervision, triadic supervision, group supervision, and consultation.

MULTIPLE RELATIONSHIPS

Sometimes, the relationship between the supervisor and supervisee evolves and/or changes. Changes within the relationship may occur prior to, during, or after the supervision has been initiated. In this manner, the supervisor and supervisee may experience multiple relationships. Therefore, it is imperative to review and assess the appropriateness of multiple relationships. The ACA *Code of Ethics* (2014) specifically addresses the issue of multiple relationships. According to the *Code,* supervisors are responsible for clearly defining and maintaining "ethical professional, personal, and social relationships with their supervisees" (Section F.3.a, p. 13). Sometimes, supervisors may be former faculty for the supervisee. At other times, the supervisor and supervisee may have been colleagues in a particular setting. Regardless of the situation, the supervisee and supervisor must discuss the new roles, responsibilities, and expectations involved in the new supervisory relationship. This discussion should be addressed prior to forming the supervisory relationship. Meanwhile, once the supervisory relationship is formed, the supervisor and supervisee must "consider the risks and benefits of extending current supervisory relationships in any form beyond conventional parameters" (Section F.3.a, p. 13). Therefore, it is necessary to discuss the implications of any multiple relationships after establishing the supervisory relationship. Clearly, it is strictly prohibited to engage in "sexual or romantic interactions or relationships with current supervisees" (Section F.3.b, p. 13). Additionally, a new and notable inclusion in the *Code* discusses the prohibition of "both in-person and electronic interactions or relationships" (p. 13). Meanwhile, the *Code* also prohibits friends or family members from engaging in supervisory relationships as well. Therefore, there are clear instances when multiple relationships are prohibited.

At times, multiple relationships cannot be avoided and are quite common. Bernard and Goodyear (2014) state that these instances are not always unethical. Bernard and Goodyear suggest that multiple relationships "become problematic when (a) there is a power differential between the two parties and (b) the multiple roles they have in relationship to each other puts the person with less power at risk for exploitation or harm" (p. 259). Therefore, considering these two components offers a means by which supervisors and supervisees can examine the possible consequences of engaging in multiple relationships. After carefully considering the benefits and risks of multiple relationships, the supervisor and supervisee can make an informed decision about the relationship and proceed with the appropriate caution.

In the case of Amy, this is an area worthy of ethical consideration. Apparently, Amy is a friend to at least one of the new counselors who were recently hired by the agency. In this case, it may not be ethical to provide supervision to her friend because supervision of a friend is strictly prohibited by the ACA *Code of Ethics* (2014, Section F.3.d). Somehow, Amy and the agency will need to adapt to the situation because the new counselor cannot receive supervision from Amy. Additionally, Amy will need to examine her relationships with the interns with whom she will work. Because she is enrolled in classes in the same counseling program, she may attend the same classes. If so, she will need to assess how her relationship can or will affect the supervisory process. Amy may discover that clearly addressing and defining supervisory roles, responsibilities, and expectations may be beneficial. In this manner, Amy can pay close attention to the ethical principles within informed consent and due process in order to enhance the supervisory relationships. Regardless of outcomes, Amy can rest assured that she is attending to these ethical responsibilities inherent within the role of supervisor.

LIABILITY

Examining all of the legal issues involved in the counseling relationship is beyond the scope of this chapter. Instead, it is necessary to discuss the main legal tenets inherent within supervision. Of course, issues related to malpractice and duty to warn (and protect) are salient components to consider within the counseling relationship. As such, these issues are still applicable to supervision. Indeed, a major portion of the supervisory process will involve a discussion of appropriate and effective services provided to the client. In doing so, supervisors must adhere to the ethical and legal issues related to the ACA *Code of Ethics* (2014), state licensing and accreditation boards, and state laws in which the supervisor is conducting services.

After considering the above-mentioned legal issues, one must reflect on the legal issue of *liability* when engaging in the process of supervision. This is an essential and distinctly unique legal issue related to supervision. When discussing liability, Bernard and Goodyear (2014) state that there are two main components to be considered: *direct liability* and *vicarious liability*. Each of these unique legal terms warrants further discussion.

Direct Liability

As stated previously, the supervisor is responsible for providing competent services for the supervisee. Additionally, the supervisor must consider the competency of the supervisee as services are rendered to the client. In this sense, the supervisor is responsible for continually evaluating whether or not the supervision process is benefitting the client and supervisee. An essential element in this evaluation involves the concept of *direct liability*. The supervisory services provided by the supervisor may directly impact the services provided to the client. For instance, if the supervisor encourages the supervisee to use an unrecognized or unreliable form of therapy that damages or harms the client in some manner, the supervisor is directly liable for the services rendered. In this case, the services rendered are directly related to the competency of the supervisor. Also, the term *direct liability* involves the notion of any supervisory services that negatively affect or harm the supervisee. If a supervisor denies the rights of informed consent or due process, and unfairly criticizes the supervisee in a degrading manner, the supervisor would demonstrate direct liability. Therefore, the issue of direct liability is an essential factor within the supervisory relationship that needs to be addressed and considered by the supervisor and supervisee.

Vicarious Liability

As stated previously, the supervisor is responsible for evaluating the services provided by the supervisee in order to ensure effective services are rendered to the client. Therefore, the services provided to the client are indirectly related to the supervisor. In this manner, the supervisor is *vicariously liable* for the services rendered to the client. The supervisor is required to monitor the effectiveness of treatment and to assess any pertinent ethical issues involved in the counseling relationship. As such, the supervisor must evaluate any ethical concerns related to ethical principles as well as any infractions of the ACA *Code of Ethics* (2014). Therefore, it is crucial for the supervisor and supervisee to discuss the issue of vicarious liability because it affects both participants.

In the case of Amy, the issue of liability is vital to consider. If Amy becomes the supervisor of counselors and trainees, she becomes *vicariously liable* for their actions. As she navigates competencies related to supervision, she will also become *directly liable* for any services provided during supervision. Therefore, Amy will need to approach the situation with caution because she has not been able to obtain supervisory training. Most likely, Amy will already have professional liability insurance. This should provide some protection in terms of malpractice and liability. However, if she does not have professional liability insurance, she will definitely need to consider this option because liability expands once supervision is provided. Regardless of having insurance, Amy is ethically obligated to enhance her professional development in order to increase her competency as a supervisor. Ultimately, she will be responsible for the clients with whom her supervisees work.

REFLECTION QUESTIONS

1. Amy is clearly confronted with ethical dilemmas. Consider these dilemmas in reference to the steps outlined in the ethical decision-making model adapted from Remley and Herlihy (2010). Be sure to reflect on each step in a meaningful manner.
   a. Which ethical principles are involved in Amy's situation?
   b. Which ethical codes are involved in Amy's situation?
   c. How would you feel if you were in Amy's situation?
   d. How might you choose to act in this situation?
   e. Was your choice in action different than your initial reactions? If so, how?
   f. Which steps are most challenging for you?

g. Which steps seemed most clear to you?
h. What obstacles or challenges does Amy face in terms of possible outcomes?

2. The ethical standard regarding confidentiality seems uncertain as it relates to personal information shared by the supervisee. As a supervisor, how would you approach the issue of personal information shared by the supervisee? As a supervisee, how might you plan to address this issue with your supervisor?

SUGGESTED RESOURCES

American Counseling Association (ACA), Knowledge Center—Ethics: www.counseling.org/knowledge-center/ethics

Association for Multicultural Counseling and Development (AMCD), Multicultural Competencies: www.counseling.org/Resources/Competencies/Multcultural_Competencies.pdf

American Psychological Association (APA), Ethics Office: www.apa.org/ethics/index.aspx

National Association of Social Workers (NASW), Office of Ethics and Professional Review: www.naswdc.org/nasw/ethics/ethicsoepr.asp

REFERENCES

Acker, G. M. (2010). The challenges in providing services to clients with mental illness: Managed care, burnout and somatic symptoms among social workers. *Community Mental Health Journal, 46*, 591–600.

Acker, G. M. (2012). Burnout among mental health care providers. *Journal of Social Work, 12*, 475–490.

American Counseling Association. (2005). *Code of ethics.* Alexandria, VA: Author.

American Counseling Association. (2014). *Code of ethics.* Alexandria, VA: Author.

American Psychological Association. (2010). *American Psychological Association ethical principles of psychologists and code of conduct.* Washington, DC: Author.

Bernard, J. M., & Goodyear, R. K. (2014). *Fundamentals of clinical supervision* (5th ed.). Upper Saddle River, NJ: Pearson Education.

Lent, J., & Schwartz, R. C. (2012). The impact of work setting, demographic, characteristics, and personality factors related to burnout among professional counselors. *Journal of Mental Health Counseling, 34*, 355–372.

Myers, J. E. (1991). Wellness as the paradigm for counseling and development: The possible future. *Counselor Education and Supervision, 30*, 183–193.

National Association of Social Workers. (2008). *Code of ethics of the National Association of Social Workers.* Washington, DC: Author.

National Board for Certified Counselors. (2013). *NBCC policy regarding the provision of distance professional services.* Retrieved from http://www.nbcc.org/Assets/Ethics/NBCC PolicyRegardingPracticeofDistanceCounselingBoard.pdf

Pederson, P. B. (1990). The constructs of complexity and balance in multicultural counseling theory and practice. *Journal of Counseling & Development, 68*, 550–554.

Remley, T., & Herlihy, B. (2010). *Ethical, legal, and professional issues in counseling* (3rd ed.). Upper Saddle River, NJ: Pearson Education.

Sue, D. W., Arredondo, P., & McDavis, R. J. (1992). Multicultural counseling competencies and standards: A call to the profession. *Journal of Counseling and Development, 70*, 477–486.

F • O • U • R

Theories of Supervision

Lisa Aasheim

Entering the role of supervisor may be a thrilling, yet daunting task. Amy, a new supervisor, is especially eager to provide her supervisees with support and adequate amounts of challenge to ensure their success and continued development. However, she is not certain about how to best engage them in the process other than doing supervision as she herself experienced it: a supportive, engaged discussion about clients. Although this may, on the surface, seem sufficient, Amy felt certain that it was not enough to be able to really help her supervisees' progress in the manner she hoped for. Amy was seeking a framework, a model, to help her conceptualize the task at hand. She took a training course in supervision, did some further reading, and settled on a model of supervision that felt most aligned with her philosophy about how counselors develop.

Amy adopted a model of supervision so that she could conceptualize her supervisees' development and progress in a clear, concise manner. Her model allows her to identify the supervisees' strengths and improvement needs, and also informs her about how and when to intervene. Amy appreciates that her use of the model allows her to streamline her thinking and her attention so that she can focus on the most important aspects of the supervisees' performance and experience. Prior to settling on a model, Amy was concerned that she would not be able to effectively track the voluminous amount of information her supervisees would provide. Now, with the use of a supervision model, she has found that she is more easily able to distill the important aspects from the less important. This has provided Amy with a sense of purpose and direction in her work. Her supervisees take comfort in the intentional, purposeful conversations, and they understand that supervision is a purposeful, meaningful activity that far exceeds mere conversation among colleagues. With the use of a supervision model, Amy has found a way to effectively guide her supervisees in a way that she would not have been able to otherwise.

INTRODUCTION

The Role of Theory in Counseling and Supervision

Clinical supervision is a core function of counselor training and development. In early stages of the supervision process, counselors use supervision to become more fully competent in all areas of professional practice, which includes theory development and utilization (Falender & Shafranske, 2004). In later stages, supervision assists a counselor in becoming increasingly proficient and efficient in his or her practice while dealing with more complex phenomenon. The supervisee's increased efficiency and competence can be attributed in part to an ability to more skillfully use counseling theory (or theories) to conceptualize and make sense of the complex features of one's work.

Supervisors use models of supervision in a manner similar to the way counselors use counseling theories. Research in the supervision field reveals that a model for practicing supervision is equally necessary and that supervisors should select, develop, and practice from a supervision model rather than practice without one (Bradshaw, Butterworth, & Mairs, 2007; Haynes, Corey, & Moulten, 2003). Effective supervisors, according to Haynes et al. (2003), clearly articulate their chosen model of supervision and, because of that model, know where they are going with the supervisee and what they need to do to get there. Supervision models provide a road map that gives the supervisor and supervisee a sense of direction, purpose, and intention. Without such a map, supervision may feel like a rich discussion but one that does not necessarily provide the structure and organization necessary to help the discussion generalize and carry forward in a sensible, optimally effective manner.

According to Haynes et al. (2003), a supervision theory is adequate when it contains six main components. First, the model should describe clearly how learning and development occur. Second, the model explains the role of individual and cultural differences in the supervision process. Third, the model should provide guidance about how to structure the goals of supervision. Next, the model should make clear the role of the supervisor. Then the model should provide guidance regarding intervention strategies. Finally, the model should provide information about evaluation and its function in the supervision process.

In this chapter, the terms *model* and *theory* are used interchangeably. Although the terms *model* and *theory* are not technically synonymous, the models of supervision typically function in the same manner as theories do, so the terms are used interchangeably in the literature (Aasheim, 2011; Watkins, 1997).

To Have or Not to Have? Why a Supervision Model Matters

Supervisors ultimately have the choice about how to conduct their practice. Some supervisors opt to practice from a no-model model in which they engage in conversation without a conceptual framework. Some supervisors emulate the supervision they have been provided without understanding the theoretical underpinnings that may have guided the work of their supervisors (if their supervisors practiced from a model at all). However, to be maximally effective, supervisors will select a supervision model because they understand that supervisors who practice without a model are less effective than supervisors who learn and use a supervision model (Haynes et al., 2003; Holloway, 1995).

When counselors first learn their craft, many feel intimidated by the complexity of the process and the sheer amount of information that must be attended to. Similarly, when supervisors transition into a supervision role, many may recognize that they are facing a complex and multifaceted experience that requires additional skills and competence beyond those acquired in prior practice. Identifying and practicing from a supervision model may prove useful to someone who is transitioning into this new role (Aasheim, 2011). Having a clear supervision model helps a supervisor develop and maintain role clarity and helps with professional identification as a supervisor (Borders, 1992). Further, a supervision model helps a supervisor act with clarity, intention, and organization. A supervisor acting in such a manner will undoubtedly earn more professional credibility than a supervisor who approaches supervision from a no-model model—that is, responding to material in a list form or disorderly fashion. In such a case, the supervisor is probably engaging in collaborative problem solving that does not attend to the counselor's developmental needs or, in some cases, the supervisor is simply providing the counselor with action advice, which creates a dependence on the supervisor for professional guidance. In these cases, supervision not only stifles the counselor's growth, it leads the counselor away from the autonomy that supervisors seek to develop in their supervisees. In its most effective form, supervision helps supervisees develop and use theories and subsequent practice styles that ultimately lead the supervisee to optimal professional autonomy.

Counselors and supervisors alike approach their work with certain ideas and assumptions that guide, influence, and inform their practice. When these ideas are organized into a clear framework, the practitioner is more readily able to conceptualize the situation, select and discard intervention options, and engage in the change process. Theories provide supervisors with a clear framework that allows them to decide where and how to focus their attention and how to make sense of complex phenomena (Holloway, 1995).

In any given supervision encounter, a supervisor faces a multitude of situations and features that call for attention. Supervision is a process of deciding which situations and features should be addressed foremost, and supervisors must use a great deal of immediacy and efficiency to be able to cover the most material in a comprehensive and timely manner. Further, supervisors ensure that growth and development progress over time and that particular themes and skills are addressed continually. Theories help supervisors organize and make long-term sense of these themes and return to these as needed to ensure supervisee growth. Additionally, in order to help a supervisor make content decisions, a supervision model influences a supervisor's behaviors, roles, attitude, and approach (Goodyear, Abadie, & Efros, 1984).

Regardless of which model one subscribes to, the supervision literature reveals a consensus that the supervision relationship continues to be the cornerstone of any supervision experience (Aasheim, 2011; Holloway, 1995). Supervision models provide the conceptual framework with which to approach supervision, and the supervision relationship creates the atmosphere for the supervisor and supervisee to each do their best work.

THEORY AND THE SUPERVISORY ALLIANCE

In recent decades, the counseling profession has paid increasing attention to the importance of the therapeutic alliance in creating effective treatment outcomes between counselors and clients (Safran, Muran, Samstag, & Stevens, 2001). Similarly, the supervision field readily embraces the importance of the supervisory alliance in creating positive supervision outcomes (Ramos-Sanchez et al., 2002). The supervisory alliance may be considered the most important component of the supervision relationship (Holloway, 1995), and supervisors may find that using a specific and well-defined supervision model helps build trust, safety, credibility, and mutual understanding in the supervisory alliance.

SUPERVISION MODELS: CATEGORIES

Supervisors have several models of supervision to select from, and these models can be categorized based on similar underlying principles and core beliefs about how to conceptualize supervisees and the supervision process. These categories include developmental models, counseling theory-based models, and social role models. This chapter addresses these three categories of supervision models, which may be particularly useful in agency practice, beginning with developmental models, including Loganbill, Hardy, and Delworth's (1982) step-by-step process model and the integrated development model. Next, cognitive behavioral supervision, a counseling theory-based model, is examined. Finally, the chapter concludes with the discrimination model of supervision, a social role model of clinical supervision.

DEVELOPMENTAL MODELS OF SUPERVISION

Developmental models of supervision center around the belief that change occurs over time and that supervision will adjust supervisory interventions to align with the counselor's evolving performance (Stoltenberg & McNeill, 1997). Supervisors conceptualize a supervisee in terms of knowledge, competence, and experience and adjust the supervision climate to meet the supervisee's changing needs (Worthington, 1987).

In the past six decades, over 20 developmental models of supervision were introduced that carry similar underlying assumptions and ideas but differ in application and structure (Bernard & Goodyear, 2008). These models all conceptualize counselor development as a progression through developmental stages during which supervisees develop and solidify certain skills and competencies. The supervisee's needs are different with each stage, and supervisors must adjust the supervision process accordingly (Ladany & Bradley, 2010). One core underlying assumption is that supervision influences the supervisee toward change and progression through these developmental phases (Loganbill et al., 1982). Supervision must be adjusted to include greater complexity and sophistication as the supervisee gains additional mastery over initial skills until, eventually, the supervisee develops a sufficient level of competence and a secure understanding of the intersection of professional and personal identities (Borders & Brown, 2005).

Prior to selecting a model, supervisors should examine the developmental models in terms of their underlying assumptions about how counselors develop. The developmental models may be categorized in accordance with their underlying beliefs about how growth and development occur over time. The categories are (1) step-by-step process models (Loganbill et al., 1982), (2) stages-of-development models (Russell, Crimmings, & Lent, 1984; Stoltenberg & McNeill, 2009), and (3) life-span developmental models (Bernard & Goodyear, 2008).

Step-by-Step Process Models: The Loganbill et al. Model of Supervision

One foundational model of supervision is a step-by-step process model introduced decades ago by Loganbill et al. (1982). The Loganbill et al. model introduces a supervision framework that is heavily influenced by Erik Erikson's developmental stages and overall sense of optimism that humans are capable of mastery, especially in supportive conditions (Loganbill et al., 1982). Further, the model embraces Erikson's view that identity development is a central task, and, in this model, professional identity development is a key construct that is embraced throughout the supervision experience.

This model posits four key elements of the supervision experience, elements that continue to hold central positions of importance in the supervision field today: (1) the supervisee and all the variables the supervisee possesses; (2) the supervisor, similarly laden with numerous personal and professional variables; (3) the supervision process; and; (4) the relationship between the supervisee (counselor) and client (Loganbill et al., 1982). All of these elements must be acknowledged and readily attended to throughout the supervision experience.

Next, this model hypothesizes three stages of supervisee development. These three stages of development are then applied to the model's eight key practice areas. The model posits that a supervisee might be in one stage of development within one practice area, and a different stage of development within another practice area. It is uncommon for a supervisee to advance through the stages of development at the same pace in all eight practice areas. So, a supervisor can learn these practice areas and then assess a supervisee's development in each of the eight domains. The practice areas, referred to in this model as *key issues*, are as follows:

1. Issues of competence
2. Issues of emotional awareness
3. Issues of autonomy
4. Issues of theoretical identity
5. Issues of respect for individual differences
6. Issues of purpose and direction
7. Issues of personal motivation
8. Issues of professional ethics

When using this model, supervisors examine each of these issues in relationship to three developmental stages: stagnation, confusion, and integration. Stage 1, *stagnation*, is characterized by inertia and unawareness wherein a supervisee is relatively unaware of areas of deficiency. Supervisees in this stage also have more trouble deciphering the important concerns and may overlook areas of concern altogether. The supervisee might also appear to be stuck and unable to make adequate progress in regard to a particular area of functioning and is considered to be experiencing stagnation. During this period of unawareness, the supervisee might feel as if he or she is functioning well enough because he or she is not yet aware of the greater complexity involved in the situation(s). This supervisee may feel somewhat content, although he or she exists with the knowledge that the work could probably be better. Stage one is a period of stability and energy for the supervisee. The supervisor is well advised to provide the supervisee with structure, guidance, and plenty of input, as the supervisee's blind spots remain profound at this stage and the supervisee is unlikely to have great awareness about what he or she should be attending to and improving (Loganbill et al., 1982).

Stage 2, *confusion,* represents a distinct shift away from the characteristics of the first stage. This stage is often characterized by instability, conflict, and a general sense of disruption (in organization, conceptualization, and other areas of key functioning). The supervisee in this stage is attempting to rebalance and find equilibrium, yet at once is finding him- or herself free from the more rigid thinking found in stage 1. This is the stage in which a supervisee starts to recognize the complexity of the work, and realizes that the solutions are not as accessible as previously thought. The supervisee may feel threats to his or her sense of competence and skill, yet at other times will find him- or herself feeling masterful and confident. The supervisee gains a greater sense of his or her ability to contribute, yet has a low sense of awareness about how others perceive or experience those abilities. Although this is a disruptive and potentially highly stressful stage for the supervisee, this is also a stage that presents tremendous opportunity for growth and challenge. This is best enhanced by a supervisor who acknowledges the benefit of the disruption and does not join in the crisis. A supervisor who understands the potential for growth that can emerge from the chaos will be the most beneficial supervisor to this supervisee as the transition to stage 3 occurs (Loganbill et al., 1982).

Stage 3, *integration,* provides the supervisor and supervisee with great relief. The turbulence of the confusion stage has led to a calm, reorganized experience. The supervisee now has the ability to integrate material in a manner that makes better sense than before. The supervisee feels more secure in his or her role and performance, and is better able to decipher the important material from the less important. The supervisee gains help from the supervisor on the more critical issues, and feels more competent to autonomously manage the less critical issues. The supervisee feels better able to manage the inevitable challenges of the work and has a sense of predictability and confidence about the future.

Finally, the model introduces five categories of intervention types that supervisors use to help advance supervisees to further development. The first category is *facilitative interventions,* which are steeped in Rogerian principles wherein the supervisor uses unconditional positive regard, warmth, and empathy to help the supervisee gain a sense of security. These interventions are designed to manage anxiety, allow time for thoughtful reflection, and foster the supervisee's sense of psychological safety in the supervision experience.

The second category is *confrontive interventions,* which are designed to help the supervisee examine discrepancies. A supervisor may highlight a discrepancy so that the supervisee can examine and make meaning of the discrepancy. These discrepancies may include feelings and emotions, attitudes and beliefs, or behaviors and actions. The third category is *conceptual interventions,* which are interventions designed to help the supervisee understand and apply pertinent conceptual knowledge. This category highlights the interplay between theory and practice, and is especially useful in moving a supervisee from developmental stage 2, *confusion,* to stage 3, *integration.* The fourth category is *prescriptive interventions,* which are especially necessary when dealing with issues of client welfare. These interventions usually consist of the supervisor directing the supervisee to engage in a particular action or set of actions, and this type of intervention is used with caution. When a supervisor uses a prescriptive intervention, the supervisee is inhibited from developing autonomy and independent problem solving. So, the supervisor limits the use of this type of intervention and saves it for times when a certain outcome is needed quickly for the protection of client welfare. The final intervention type is *catalytic interventions,* which are interventions designed to promote movement and change in the supervisee's thoughts, feelings, or actions. Although all interventions may be catalytic in nature, this distinct category references interventions that highlight aspects of the supervisee's work for the purpose of helping the supervisee find additional meaning or understanding. Supervisors constantly stay on the lookout for signs of change or progress in the supervisee. When those signals of change are evident, the supervisor may highlight the phenomenon and engage in catalytic interventions to facilitate further or deeper change than what is already occurring.

The Loganbill et al. (1982) model provides supervisors with a conceptual framework with which to describe the supervisee's experiences and provides supervisors with guidance about supervisory intervention. The interventions found in this model were absorbed into a later model, the integrated developmental model (IDM), which expanded on this initial model using a stage-based approach to supervisee development (Stoltenberg & McNeill, 2009).

Stages-of-Development Models: Integrated Developmental Model

Stages-of-development models assert a linear approach wherein supervisees move through stages of development in a fairly defined and clear fashion (e.g., Blocher, 1983; Stoltenberg & McNeill, 2009). The most widely appreciated and cited stage-of-development model is the IDM (Stoltenberg & Delworth, 1987). Although there are other stages-of-development models in the literature, this model is particularly adaptable for use in agency settings with counselors of varying skill and development levels. To effectively use this model, supervisors need to study it and gain a clear understanding of the individual stages and the characteristics of each stage.

The IDM centers on the idea that a supervisee functions at different levels in different domains of practice and needs supervision that aligns with that functioning in each area (Stoltenberg & McNeill, 2009). For example, a supervisee might be well functioning in areas he or she practices often and has a strong educational background in, such as couples counseling. However, when a couple with an evident substance abuse issue present for counseling, the counselor might be much less skilled because of a lack of knowledge about how to work with couples who are contending with substance abuse problems. The supervisor must examine how competent a supervisee is in all relevant practice areas (domains) so the supervision experience can be customized to meet the supervisee's specific developmental needs.

Developmental Levels

In this model, supervisees are conceptualized in terms of linear development in relationship to practice domains. Supervisees are considered to be Level I, Level II, Level III, or Level IIIi, which is reserved for the most advanced and integrated practitioner. Supervisors try to accurately conceptualize a supervisee's level so that the supervision activities and interventions best align with the supervisee's developmental needs. Supervisors should take care to avoid biased assumptions that are not steeped in observation, such as the assumption that years of practice equals stage of development. A supervisee who has practiced many years is not necessarily more advanced in these stages than emerging counselors, especially if that supervisee lacked supportive training and supervision. Supervisors understand that accurate conceptualization is important to creating the most optimal supervision environment. If supervisors do not accurately identify the stage of development, interventions and attempts at challenge will likely go awry. If interventions are not appropriate for the developmental stage, the supervisory relationship may suffer a series of irreparable strains or ruptures. Following is a description of each of the developmental levels.

LEVEL I. The Level I supervisee is still uncomfortable in the counseling role, although he or she may have some background as a helping professional. This fledgling supervisee typically does not like the feeling of incompetence or discomfort with the process, so is typically very motivated to learn and improve quickly (Stoltenberg & McNeill, 1997). Level I supervisees may engage in efforts to copy practitioners whose work impresses them, and these supervisees oftentimes identify as "wanting to be like . . ." while he or she waits to uncover his or her own professional identity and style. Level I supervisees appear very dependent and often recognize that it is too early for independent work. Supervisors at this stage provide supervisees with oversight, skills training, honest and evaluative feedback, and positive feedback wherever warranted (Stoltenberg & McNeill, 2009).

Level I is characterized by high self-focus, high motivation, and low autonomy. Once the supervisee starts to master initial counseling skills and early conceptual understanding, the supervisee's self-efficacy will increase and he or she may be ready to develop some independence and increase risk taking and the use of challenging skills. At this point, the supervisor and supervisee work together to ensure that the supervisee is striving toward autonomy at an appropriate pace. Supervisees should not have more autonomy than they are ready for at this stage, yet some supervisees strive too eagerly for autonomy and independence. Conversely, some supervisees refrain from building independence and might benefit from a bit of additional challenge from the supervisor. When assessing a supervisee's readiness for autonomy, the supervisor examines features such as ability to manage and minimize risk to the client as well as the ability to utilize challenges and address interpersonal dynamics effectively. Supervisors should not determine that supervisees are ready for increased autonomy solely because the supervisee feels confident or ready; rather, demonstrable skills in the key practice areas should be present (Aasheim, 2011).

Level I supervisees are often still early in pre degree training programs, but a supervisee may appear to be Level I when beginning work in the counseling field as a post degree professional. Oftentimes, early professionals might be in later levels in some practice domains, but still Level I in areas that were not solidified during earlier training.

Level II. The Level II supervisee has likely mastered most initial counseling skills and has proven at least moderately effective in working with clients (Stoltenberg & McNeill, 2009). This supervisee now spends more time examining variable levels of effectiveness with different clients rather than concerning him- or herself with his performance as a whole. The supervisee at this stage might find that he or she is having ongoing struggles with particular skills or limitations, or may learn that the field or various systems have limitations that negatively impact the effectiveness of the work. The counselor is finding out at this point that he or she does not have the power to "fix" everyone and may be frustrated by this discovery. Motivation and confidence may drop as the supervisee realizes that perhaps he or she was not ready for the autonomy that has been recently earned. The supervisee may experience crisis as he or she struggles with autonomy versus independence, and some supervisees at this point may even question goodness-of-fit to the profession or, in some cases, the agency or work setting (Aasheim, 2011; Stoltenberg & McNeill, 1997).

The Level II supervisee has gained other-awareness and has become less self-focused over time. With this shift to other-awareness, the supervisee may start to lose objectivity and might have trouble dealing with some common phenomena that increase at this stage (e.g., countertransference, enmeshment, overidentification, and strains in the therapeutic alliance). The supervisee may need the supervisor to infuse objectivity until skills to monitor and maintain objectivity are more fully developed.

At this point in the supervisee's development, a supervisor will focus on providing oversight and professional distance simultaneously. The supervisor uses supervision to facilitate the supervisee in his or her own exploration and conceptualization process, and will provide the supervisee with less direct guidance than in Level I. The supervisor will encourage the supervisee to take initiative and to take well-considered risks. The supervisor understands that with more risk taking comes more risks and does not falter in oversight. Direct intervention and directives are provided when client safety is compromised, yet supervisees are provided with opportunities to generate solutions and options alongside the supervisor.

Supervisors should maintain awareness that this stage has been dubbed the "trial and tribulation" stage (Stoltenberg & Delworth, 1987) because of the amount of experimentation and turbulence that occurs during this stage.

Supervisors may feel tempted at times to alleviate their supervisees of oversight and reduce supervision; however, this is ill advised. Supervisors should understand that greater autonomy and experimentation mean greater risk, and supervisors should increase oversight and feedback through the use of raw data (e.g., videotapes, audiotapes, or direct observation). Self-report is not to be relied on because the work now carries increased complexity and the supervisee may not be able to accurately describe the problem areas (especially in the case of blind spots or undiscovered biases). The supervisor will continue to lead and guide the content of the supervision sessions in collaboration with the supervisee, but should not allow the supervisee to direct the content of the sessions.

Level III. The Level III supervisee has emerged from the trials and tribulations of Level II and is stabilizing in his or her practice style and approach. This supervisee is likely back to feeling eager and excited about the work, and is identifying more fully as a professional with a stable set of skills and abilities that remain consistently strong over time. This supervisee is comfortable acting with considerable autonomy and will make decisions and initiate interventions without feeling a need for supervision consult beforehand. This supervisee has developed a wide range of techniques to draw from and is no longer trying to emulate others but has instead found a style and approach that is more authentic to his or her own ideas and beliefs.

Supervisors should remember that Level III supervisees will likely still have some practice domains that are Level I or II, and supervisors now spend their time and energy focusing on those lesser developed domains to optimize functioning in all areas. Supervisors provide support and challenge to maintain growth and development in the supervisee who now has greater comfort than ever before with his or her work. Most counselors experience Level III as the pinnacle of their development, but some proceed to the final stage of integration, Level IIIi.

Level IIIi. Level IIIi is reserved for the supervisees who have mastery in a wide enough range of skills and practice domains that they can move easily and flexibly from one practice domain to another (Stoltenberg & Delworth, 1987). Level IIIi counselors are typically interested in increasing the complexity of their practice and their understanding of their practice, and they typically prefer not to rest or become complacent. Instead, they rely on their supervisors to help them further deepen their exploration of their practice across all domains, and at this stage, staying the same is seen as regression (Stoltenberg & McNeill, 2009).

Overarching Structures

In addition to the emphasis on customizing supervision to meet developmental needs, this model contains three overarching structures to monitor supervisee development through three levels across various practice domains (Stoltenberg & Delworth, 1987; Stoltenberg & McNeill, 2009). These structures are *self- and other-awareness, motivation,* and *autonomy*.

Self- and other-awareness refers to the supervisee's preoccupation and focus on him- or herself and awareness of the client's experiences, both cognitively and affectively. In the early phases, supervisees are likely to have greater self-focus than focus on their clients (other-focus). These supervisees are often motivated and eager and will avoid the insecurities of this phase by leaning on their supervisors for answers, guidance, or advice (Aasheim, 2011). These supervisees are attempting to impress others with a good performance and often keep careful track of their own skills and abilities during this phase. These supervisees are often tuning so well into themselves that they may not be wholly tuning in to their clients' experiences, so empathy and authentic understanding may be compromised. These supervisees are in Level I of their training, and as they transition to the next developmental stage, Level II, supervisors can expect to witness a greater capacity for empathy, authentic connection, and empathic listening. By Level III, the supervisee can maintain an awareness of internal processes, the client's processes, and the relational features between counselor and client. The supervisee can monitor his or her own reactions and uses countertransference and internal reactions as useful therapeutic information.

Motivation refers to the supervisee's level of interest and the effort that the supervisee is willing to expend on clinical training and practice activities (Stoltenberg, McNeill, & Delworth, 1998). Supervisees experience changes in motivation over time, and early supervisees typically have high motivation that fluctuates when they enter Level II. Supervisees, once they reach the challenge of Level II, often experience periods of lower motivation as the work becomes more challenging and complex (Stoltenberg & McNeill, 2009). Level III supervisees tend to experience more stable, consistent levels of motivation with an occasional bout of self-doubt or insecurity, which they are able to push through with relative ease.

Autonomy is the degree of autonomy and independence a supervisee demonstrates (Stoltenberg & McNeill, 2009). Supervisors examine whether the level of autonomy is appropriate considering the supervisee's skill and development level. Autonomy levels vary over time, and supervisees demonstrate independence, dependence, or counterdependence at different stages of development. A Level I demonstration of autonomy is highly dependent, and this supervisee is not demonstrating eagerness to act autonomously. When the supervisee reaches Level II, that supervisee struggles between autonomy and dependence and may not have a clear understanding of how much autonomy should be exercised at each point in time. By Level III, the supervisee feels a more solid sense of competence and is ready to work with autonomy and maintains an appropriate interdependence on other colleagues for consultation as needed.

COUNSELING THEORY-BASED MODELS: COGNITIVE BEHAVIORAL SUPERVISION

Cognitive behavioral supervision (CBS) models represent the convergence of cognitive theories, behavioral theories, and counselor supervision. Cognitive and behavioral theories did not emerge as a unit; rather, they converged in practice (Barlow, 2001). This blended cognitive behavioral approach appears more common in modern counseling practice than either of the approaches individually, so this section of the chapter presents a general model of cognitive behavioral supervision that integrates the principles and practices of each theory as applied to supervision.

Cognitive behavioral models are model-based approaches that have grown in popularity and acceptance over time, primarily because of several key factors (Aasheim, 2011; Rosenbaum & Ronen, 1998). First, cognitive behavioral approaches have become increasingly manualized. Instead of simply using cognitive behavioral techniques, many practitioners are using manualized protocols that implore them to follow a specific set of instructions and guidelines. So, agencies are utilizing these approaches more commonly and need supervisors who can role model such approaches in the supervision process. Consequently, many of these manualized cognitive behavioral approaches include specific supervision instructions. Supervisors are called on to oversee treatment fidelity and ensure treatment protocols are followed skillfully and carefully. Finally, cognitive behavioral theories have deep roots in the helping professions and many supervisors may be well seasoned in their cognitive behavioral therapy (CBT) practice. They may readily find cognitive behavioral supervision to be a natural extension of their well-developed skill set.

Theory Tenets

There are several models of CBS, all of which share a common set of core tenets. First, CBS models subscribe to the idea that cognitive and behavioral factors carry importance in the supervision process. The models differ in the proportion of importance they place on each of these factors, though. Some models contend that supervisees' behavior and affective responses are influenced by their cognitions, and a pattern of reinforcers can serve to decrease or increase a supervisee's behaviors (Bradley & Gould, 2001). Other models contend that cognitive experiences outweigh the importance of behavioral experiences (Kindsvatter, Granello, & Duba, 2008). Regardless, cognitive behavioral models of supervision all recognize the importance of both cognitive experiences and supervisee behaviors as central factors in the supervision experience.

Second, CBS models typically use a circular problem-solving approach (Milne, 2009). The supervisor and supervisee work together to specify problems in specific, concrete terms. Next, problems are discussed and solutions are generated. Finally, solutions are implemented and tested for effectiveness. The supervisor and supervisee then return to discussion about whether the solutions effectively addressed the problems.

Third, CBS models typically emphasize the training aspects of the supervision experience. Supervisors provide specific training to supervisees so that supervisees are employing relevant skills correctly and with fidelity to the treatment model. In this sense, there is a strong emphasis on the supervisee's ability to learn and adjust behaviors accordingly. Supervisees continue to receive feedback about their behaviors until the supervisee determines that the counselor's delivery skills are maximally useful to the clients.

Fourth, CBS models focus on brief interventions rather than long-term psychotherapeutic approaches to problem solving. The interventions used and generated in supervision focus on unhelpful behaviors and thoughts, and may include an exploration of problematic patterns. Supervisors and supervisees work together to explore the supervisee's unhelpful thoughts and actions, as well as a client's unhelpful thoughts and actions. The interventions focus largely on the here-and-now rather than the past (e.g., causes of the unhelpful thoughts and behaviors). The supervisor and supervisee aim to work with brevity and efficiency to facilitate noticeable change.

Next, CBS models use case conceptualization as a key focus during supervision sessions (Liese & Beck, 1997; Townend, Iannetta, & Freeston, 2002). Supervisors work with their supervisees to create case conceptualizations that align with CBT principals. Much of the supervision session is often dedicated to formulating clear, accurate conceptualizations, which then inform the subsequent discussion and decisions about intervention (Milne, 2009).

Finally, cognitive behavioral theories of supervision embrace the training and role-modeling aspects of supervision. One model of CBS (Schmidt, 1979) provides direction to supervisors who are training their supervisees to reduce anxiety so that they have cognitive clarity while they engage in new treatment actions and techniques. The training aspect covers cognitive, behavioral, and affective elements of the supervisee's experience. The supervisor's role is to educate, encourage, act as role model, and challenge the supervisee to continually practice anxiety-reduction techniques for the betterment of the cognitive and behavioral skill sets.

Putting the Theory to Work

Those familiar with the therapeutic practice of CBT are often familiar with at least one of the many manualized forms of the theory. Similarly, Milne and Dunkerley (2010) published a set of guidelines in an effort to operationalize an evidence-based approach to CBS. These four guidelines address the supervision cycle itself from a CBT perspective.

The authors contend that the supervision cycle begins with assessing learning needs and engaging in a process of collaborative agenda setting. Once these tasks are satisfactorily complete, supervision involves the process of facilitating learning and the use of evaluation throughout. This cycle mirrors CBT's typical cycle, wherein a client and counselor clarify goals, facilitate learning and skills training, and then evaluate progress toward treatment goal satisfaction.

Milne and Dunkerley (2010) highlight the importance of four key elements in CBS: (1) developing the supervision contract, (2) methods of facilitating learning, (3) evaluation in supervision, and (4) the supervisory alliance. The supervision contract is a tool commonly encouraged in supervision literature (Aasheim, 2011; Osborn & Davis, 1996) and is intended to ensure clarity and mutual understanding regarding many key elements of the supervision process. This is a particularly useful endeavor in the context of CBS because it allows the supervisee to experience the process of a helper (the supervisor) and helpee (the supervisee) engaging in a dialogue about creating clear, concrete agreements at the onset of the working relationship. Further, the contract should include clear verbiage regarding the type and frequency of evaluation in the supervision relationship, a direct parallel to the CBT process of consistently assessing progress in relation to presenting symptoms. Finally, the supervision relationship is deemed to be as critically important as claimed by other models of supervision discussed earlier in this chapter. Without a supportive relationship, the supervisee is likely going to experience hesitance to try new skill sets and techniques, which are important in building CBT skills.

Structuring a CBS Session

Cognitive behavioral practices typically involve a structured approach that yields a predictable and consistent session format. Keeping with this typical mode of practice, Liese and Beck (1997) and Liese and Alford (1998) propose a CBT supervision structure involving multiple key components. Each session begins with a check-in followed directly by setting the session's agenda. Next, the supervisory dyad bridges from the prior session and reviews any outstanding information from the prior session, including a review of cases from the prior session. Next, the supervisee produces homework to be reviewed and discussed. Together, the supervisory dyad then prioritize additional agenda items and discuss those items. The supervision session may include review of a recorded session, and direct instruction and guided discovery methods may be used alongside recording reviews. Homework assignments will emerge from the session's content, and the session will conclude with a summary.

The supervisor, during the session, keeps a range of learning goals in mind. These goals include problem identification and diagnosis, associated cognitive models, case conceptualization, counseling skills (and counseling delivery), therapy structure, and cognitive and behavioral techniques (Liese & Alford, 1998).

CBS Practices

In CBT supervision (a term used interchangeably with CBS), supervisors attend to cognitive and behavioral phenomena in a manner very similar to that of a CBT counselor. Cognitive phenomena include case conceptualization, dysfunctional beliefs, and overall cognitive schema (Pretorius, 2006). Dysfunctional or distorted beliefs must be addressed early, as close to their time of emergence as possible (Yogev, 1982). Some dysfunctional beliefs might include "If I don't say the exactly right thing, my client will not feel better" or "If I ask about suicide, my client will feel more suicidal." Supervisors are constantly monitoring for statements that are false, distorted, or representative of an unhelpful belief system and will challenge these statements in a supportive manner. Supervisors recognize that many of these statements and beliefs are emerging from the supervisee's anxiety, and many help perpetuate further anxiety. A supervisor is interested in helping supervisees both manage their anxiety as well as create more accuracy and adaptability in how they view their work and the processes therein.

Although all supervisors readily examine a supervisee's behavior, CBT supervisors may use techniques that align with behavioral therapy techniques with a significant emphasis on skill proficiency. For instance, supervisors may have supervisees video or audio record their sessions, then examine the sessions for behavioral patterns, particularly those that are interfering with progress.

A CBT supervisor may use techniques commonly used in CBT to help a supervisee learn and practice relevant skills. For instance, a CBT supervisor may use role modeling and demonstrations. The supervisor may demonstrate a particular skill or behavior for the supervisee. The supervisor may then ask the supervisee to practice that skill delivery right there in the supervision session. This may be part of a role-play strategy, or may be done using an empty chair to represent the client. Either way, the supervisee is practicing new skills with the guidance of a more skilled facilitator, just as in CBT.

Cognitive behavioral supervisors will typically assign homework in the same fashion as a CBT practitioner. The homework often emerges from the identified skill deficits or cognitive malfunctioning revealed during the course of the session. The supervisor works with the supervisee to create homework that will aptly help the supervisee address and correct skill deficits. The dyad then examines the progress during the next supervision session, and the supervisor determines whether additional attention should be paid to the target skill or cognition.

CBS is often an ideal fit for agency practitioners who work in agencies that maintain a strong cognitive behavioral orientation. Others may find this approach a misfit for their agencies or supervisees, especially if CBT is not a commonly used or appreciated modality. In these cases, a social role model of supervision may be more suitable.

A SOCIAL ROLE MODEL OF SUPERVISION

Social role models of supervision tend to focus primarily on the role a supervisor engages in during the supervision process (Holloway, 1995) as well as the areas of focus selected during the supervision experience (Bernard, 1997). Clinical supervisors hold many different roles within any given supervision experience. A supervisor may be a trainer, consultant, teacher, encourager, and so forth. Social role models posit that roles are selected purposefully and strategically to further the goals of supervision. When a supervisor selects a role, that supervisor engages in the behaviors that align with that role (Holloway, 1995). The supervisor additionally selects a focus area based on the perceived needs of the supervisee at any given time. So, social role models may be conceptualized as the combination of a carefully selected role and an intentional focus on a specific area. This combination is flexible and changes and adapts to the needs of emerging situations. This chapter includes an examination of the discrimination model of supervision (Bernard, 1997), a well-regarded social role model.

The Discrimination Model

The discrimination model developed by Bernard (1997) involves a two-step process in which the supervisor firsts determines which focus area to attend to during supervision. Once the supervisor determines the focus area, the supervisor then selects a role that he or she determines will best facilitate growth in the selected focus area. To most effectively use this model, the supervisor needs to be familiar with the three separate foci as well as the three roles described in this model.

Focus Areas

The supervisor, according to this model, selects from three focus areas: intervention skills, conceptualization skills, and personalization skills. *Intervention skills* deal specifically with the supervisee's behaviors and choices during the course of his or her work. This may include the supervisee's interventions, specific skill sets, or use of techniques. These skills are observable by the supervisor (and the client), and supervisors who use raw data (e.g., video recordings) are better positioned to most accurately assess these skills based on direct observation (Aasheim, 2011).

Conceptualization skills refer to the supervisee's cognitive processes with regard to his or her work. These skills might include case conceptualization, understandings of therapeutic phenomena (e.g., countertransference), pattern identification, identification of factors that enhance or inhibit therapy, and understandings of dynamics between counselor and client. These skills are revealed through behaviors and, more commonly, through discussion about the work and clients.

Finally, *personalization skills* refer to the intersection of a supervisee's personality and personal features with the professional therapeutic process and service delivery. These skills may be revealed through behaviors and discussions or may be hidden from plain view; however, they may greatly affect the supervisee's development or work with clients. For instance, a supervisee may experience strong emotional reactivity to clients who engage in a particular set of behaviors. The supervisee might attempt to reduce the impact of this reactivity by ignoring his or her feelings, and in the process might present to the client as judgmental, cold, or stoic. The supervisor is tasked with assisting the supervisee to engage in a discovery process during which this dynamic can be identified and ultimately resolved so that the supervisee's personal beliefs do not unnecessarily cloud his or her ability to provide an objective, empathic experience for the client.

Roles

The supervisor, after determining which focus area seems the most important, will then select the role that he or she believes will best facilitate professional development and movement in the supervision session. This model presents supervisors with three roles to select from: teacher, counselor, and consultant.

The teacher role is used when a supervisor determines that a supervisee needs to learn additional information or skills for effective practice. The teacher will assist the supervisee in accessing further information and practicing new or fledgling skills. The teacher will also use feedback and evaluative processes to ensure that supervisees understand how well they are progressing and where they need to continue to learn and focus.

The counselor role involves the supervisor addressing the supervisee's inter- or intrapersonal experiences. The supervisee and supervisor explore the meaning of various elements of the work, and the supervisor facilitates reflection and a deeper understanding of aspects of the work or incidents therein.

The consultant role is used when the supervisor wants to ensure a shared responsibility for learning with the supervisee. The supervisor challenges supervisees to develop trust in their own processes, including understandings, insights, and feelings about their work. The supervisor is present as a sounding board but will refrain from taking on the majority of the responsibility for supervisees' learning processes, and will instead challenge supervisees to trust themselves with regard to a specific issue, circumstance, or process.

Using the Model

Supervisors using the discrimination model are thoughtful and strategic in their foci and role selection. Supervisors should ask themselves what they are hoping to accomplish at this point in supervision. Supervisors might wonder "which area should I focus on first at this time?" then, once that is decided, ask themselves "which role is going to be the most advantageous here given what I know about the situation and the supervisee?" Supervisors learn, over time, which roles might best facilitate growth for their supervisees in particular contexts. For instance, a supervisee might find the counselor role particularly useful when facing countertransference that feels daunting or shameful. The supervisor can help the counselor make sense of the phenomenon so that the supervisee's reaction to it is not inhibiting client care or supervisee development. However, a supervisee who appears to lack knowledge about countertransference might be best served by a supervisor who takes on a teaching role first. When the supervisee has sufficient understanding of the phenomena, the supervisee can make better sense of the meaning of it in his or her work. A supervisee who has a strong understanding of countertransference and understands what it means in a particular context might be best served by a supervisor in the consultant role. In this case, the supervisor might help the supervisee feel confident in his or her ability to manage countertransference as a useful source of information. The other two roles might feel ineffective to the supervisee, and the supervisor will intentionally aim to select the role that will be the most effective.

SUMMARY

Supervisors have an important decision to make when considering which model of supervision best suits their purposes and the needs of their supervisees. The supervisor must consider the work setting (of both the supervisor and the supervisees), the therapeutic models the supervisees use, and the supervisor's own views about how supervisee development is best facilitated. Supervisors who are dedicated to a belief that supervisee developmental needs are foremost in the supervision process might be best suited for developmental models. Supervisors practicing in settings that use consistent adherence to one counseling theory might find a theory-based model to be the best fit. Conversely, supervisors who need to integrate multiple approaches and theories among supervisees might find a social role model, such as the discrimination model, to be the most effective and feasible.

REFLECTION QUESTIONS

1. What are some ways the different theoretical orientations influence the role of supervision?
2. What are some of the professional characteristics and personal traits of an effective supervisor?
3. What are some of the essential ethical standards supervisors will need to implement in supervision?
4. What might the ideal supervisor–supervisee relationship look like?

REFERENCES

Aasheim, L. L. (2011). *Practical clinical supervision for counselors: An experiential guide*. New York, NY: Springer Publishing Company.

Bernard, J. M. (1997). The discrimination model. In C. E. Watkins (Ed.), *Handbook of psychotherapy supervision* (pp. 310-327). New York, NY: John Wiley & Sons.

Bernard, J. M., & Goodyear, R. K. (2008). *Fundamentals of clinical supervision* (4th ed.). Upper Saddle River, NJ: Merrill/Pearson.

Blocher, D. H. (1983). Supervision in counseling: II. Contemporary models of supervision: Toward a cognitive developmental approach to counseling supervision. *Counseling Psychologist*, *11*(1), 27–34.

Borders, L. D. (1992). Learning to think like a supervisor. *Clinical Supervisor*, *10*(2), 135–148.

Borders, L. D., & Brown, L. L. (2005).*The new handbook of counseling supervision*. Mahwah, NJ: Lawrence Erlbaum.

Bradley, L. J., & Gould, L. J. (2001). Psychotherapy-based models of supervision. In L. J. Bradley & N. Ladany (Eds.), *Counselor supervision; principles, process and practice* (3rd ed., pp. 147–180). New York, NY: Routledge.

Bradshaw, T., Butterworth, A., & Mairs, H. (2007). Does structured clinical supervision during psychosocial intervention education enhance outcome for mental health nurses and the service users they work with? *Journal of Psychiatric and Mental Health Nursing*, *14*(1), 4–12.

Falender, C. A., & Shafranske, E. P. (2004). *Clinical supervision: A competency-based approach*. Washington, DC: American Psychological Association.

Goodyear, R., Abadie, P., & Efros, F. (1984). Supervisory theory into practice: Differential perception of supervision by Ekstein, Ellis, Polster, and Rogers. *Journal of Counseling Psychology*, *31*(2), 228–237.

Haynes, R., Corey, G., & Moulton, P. (2003). *Clinical supervision in the helping professions: A practical guide*. Pacific Grove, CA: Brooks Cole.

Holloway, E. L. (1995). *Clinical supervision: A systems approach*. Thousand Oaks, CA: Sage.

Kindsvatter, A., Granello, D. H., & Duba, J. (2008). Cognitive techniques as a means for facilitating supervisee development. *Counselor Education and Supervision*, *47*(3), 17–192.

Ladany, N., & Bradley, L. J. (2010). *Counselor supervision*. New York, NY: Routledge.

Liese, B. S., & Alford, B. A. (1998). Recent advances in cognitive therapy supervision. *Journal of Cognitive Psychotherapy*, *12*(2), 91–94.

Liese, B. S., & Beck, J. (1997). Cognitive therapy supervision. In E. Watkins Jr. (Ed.), *Handbook of psychotherapy supervision* (pp. 184–202). New York, NY: John Wiley & Sons.

Loganbill, C., Hardy, E., & Delworth, U. (1982). Supervision: A conceptual model. *Counseling Psychologist*, *10*, 3–42.

Milne, D. (2009). *Evidence-based clinical supervision: Principles and practice*. Chichester, UK: BPS/Blackwell.

Milne, D., & Dunkerley, C. (2010). Towards evidence-based clinical supervision: The development and evaluation of four CBT guidelines. *Cognitive Behaviour Therapist*, *3*(2), 43–57.

Osborn, C. J., & Davis, T. E. (1996). The supervision contract: Making it perfectly clear. *Clinical Supervisor*, *14*(2), 121–134.

Pretorius, W. M. (2006). Cognitive behavioural therapy supervision: Recommended practice. *Behavioural and Cognitive Psychotherapy, 34*(4), 413–420.

Ramos-Sanchez, L., Esnil, E., Goodwin, A., Riggs, S., Osachy, T. L., Wright, L. K., . . . Rodolfa, E. (2002). Negative supervisory events: Effects on supervision satisfaction and supervisory alliance. *Professional Psychology: Research and Practice, 33*(2), 197–202.

Rosenbaum, M., & Ronen, T. (1998). Clinical supervision from the standpoint of cognitive-behavior therapy. *Psychotherapy: Theory, Research, Practice, Training, 35*(2), 220.

Russell, R. K., Crimmings, A. M., & Lent, R. W. (1984). Counselor training and supervision: Theory and research. In S. D. Brown & R. W. Lent (Eds.), *Handbook of counseling psychology* (pp. 625–681). New York, NY: John Wiley & Sons.

Safran, J. D., Muran, J. C., Samstag, L. W., & Stevens, C. (2001). Repairing alliance ruptures. *Psychotherapy: Theory, Research, Practice, Training, 38*, 406–412.

Schmidt, J. P. (1979). Psychotherapy supervision: A cognitive-behavioral model. *Professional Psychology, 10*(3), 278–284.

Stoltenberg, C. D., & Delworth, U. (1987). *Supervising counselors and therapists: a developmental approach*. San Francisco, CA: Jossey-Bass.

Stoltenberg, C. D., & McNeill, B. W. (1997). Clinical supervision from a developmental perspective: Research and practice. In E. Watkins Jr. (Ed.), *Handbook of psychotherapy supervision* (pp. 184–202). New York, NY: John Wiley & Sons.

Stoltenberg, C. D., & McNeill, B. W. (2009). *IDM supervision: An integrative developmental model for supervision counselors and therapists*. New York, NY: Routledge.

Stoltenberg, C. D., McNeill, B. W., & Delworth, U. (1998). *IDM supervision: An integrated developmental model for supervising counselors and therapists*. San Francisco, CA: Jossey-Bass.

Townend, M., Iannetta, L., & Freeston, M. H. (2002). Clinical supervision in practice: A survey of UK cognitive behavioural psychotherapists accredited by the BABCP. *Behavioural and Cognitive Psychotherapy, 30*(4), 485–500.

Watkins, C. E. (Ed.). (1997). *Handbook of psychotherapy supervision*. New York, NY: John Wiley & Sons.

Worthington, E. L., Jr. (1987). Changes in supervision as counselors and supervisors gain experience: A review. *Professional Psychology: Research and Practice, 18*(3), 189–208.

Yogev, S. (1982). An eclectic model of supervision: A developmental sequence of beginning psychotherapy students. *Professional Psychology, 13*(2), 236.

F • I • V • E

Evaluation

Michael A. Hauser

The boss called Amy into his office for a conversation one afternoon. When she left his office, she was overwhelmed and felt a great deal of trepidation. So much so that she felt physically ill. The boss handed Amy a nicely bound document. After Amy read the executive summary in the document, she understood that a firm hired by the state to randomly evaluate agencies receiving state funding had recently evaluated her current employer. The evaluation was completed about 18 months ago and to date little has been done to correct the deficiencies listed in the report. When the boss hired Amy, he had suggested that if she performed well he would consider her for a supervisory position at some point. Because she was one of the newest people on staff, she was the most available person the boss had for this task.

Amy was given the task of correcting the deficiencies noted in the evaluation. The boss was notified that the evaluating firm would return approximately 6 months from the date of notification to determine how well the agency had complied with the shortcomings noted in the evaluation summary. Amy had asked what authority she had to fulfill the requirements dictated by the evaluation. The boss was unable to answer Amy's question, but he said he would like to meet with Amy regularly to see what she thought would be the best way to fix the problems. At those meetings, he would tell her what she had for resources. Even though she believed the boss would be supportive, Amy knew she would face significant challenges and her feeling of trepidation persisted. She had little idea about how to proceed and knew she had a lot of work to accomplish in the intervening 6 months.

INTRODUCTION

The very word *evaluation* causes some people to get heartburn or other unappealing reactions. Some have endured endless exasperation while preparing for, or enduring, an evaluation. Nonetheless, if you stay in the mental health profession for any significant period you will experience an evaluation of some sort, whether it is formal or informal, whether you are the subject or the one doing the evaluation. Although evaluations can be demanding, they are common in a society that seeks to deliver quality health care and one that demands the delivery of best practices. This chapter discusses the evaluation process from very specific perspectives. Specifically, this chapter addresses how to evaluate a therapist's performance and how to evaluate the client's experience in therapy, and then provides a more broadly based approach to evaluating a program or agency.

The Council for the Accreditation of Counseling and Related Educational Programs (CACREP) standards for 2009, as described in Chapter 1, are very specific regarding the types of knowledge required. Those standards make it clear that to be fully capable or qualified as a professional counselor one must be knowledgeable about management and evaluation. This author believes that management and evaluation, if considered at all, are only taught in superficial ways in most counseling programs. It is probably safe to assume that few counselors who are just finishing their academic programs are capable of assuming a leadership or evaluation role unless they came into the program with those skills. With that in mind, this chapter will introduce evaluation and then discuss specific applications. It would be impossible to teach everything that one needs to know about evaluation in the space allowed; this chapter will only provide a broad-based approach to the topic of evaluation.

For all of those who see evaluation as something to be feared, take heed,

> However, personnel do not have to be experts . . . to carry out a useful program evaluation. . . . It's better to do what might turn out to be an average effort at evaluation than to do no evaluation at all. (McNamara, 2006, p. 1)

That message should resonate with and encourage many who have misgivings about the value of an evaluation. In essence, evaluations are taking place daily in the work environment. There is significant information readily available in any program that, when placed in the proper context, could be profitable in terms of understanding the relative worth or merit of the program. A formal evaluation attempts to place all of the available data into a proper context and then give it a presentation that answers the primary question that was asked in order to enhance the function of any organization.

Before we go much further it seems prudent to narrow the focus of this chapter somewhat. Evaluation in general can take many forms. Therefore, in this chapter we will focus our attention on the evaluation of social programs. Furthermore, we can narrow the scope by eliminating such programs as may provide for education, or programs designed for meeting physical needs such as providing shelter for the homeless. This chapter focuses on social programs designed to provide for the mental health needs of their clientele. Many of the methods discussed in this chapter are useful in a variety of settings, but for the sake of clarity, only social programs focused on mental health will be discussed herein.

Definition of *Evaluation*

Defining the term *evaluation* for the purpose of this chapter is a matter of choosing a singular definition from the myriad of definitions now promulgated in a large number of textbooks and other writings on the subject. The problem comes in narrowing it down to one that works well without being overly broad, or, on the converse, overly restrictive. However, to make any definition meaningful there must be a context. The context here provides for the incorporation of matter peculiar to professionals who have to make nuanced judgments regarding the soundness of any program or operation. Furthermore, the target audience includes those professionals working in a mental health environment providing services to the public.

As more variables are added to the context, the ability to define *evaluation* becomes more complicated. The definition suggested for this work is the one used in the *Evaluation Guidebook for Small Agencies* (Treasury Board of Canada Secretariat, 2010):

> Evaluation can be defined as the systematic collection and analysis of information on the performance of a policy, program, or initiative to make judgments about relevance, progress or success and cost-effectiveness, and/or to inform future programming decisions about design and implementation. (p. 8)

As the chapter develops, the particulars of this definition should unfold such that parsing this particular definition seems unnecessary. This definition emphasizes several key points of evaluation that are worth noting. Evaluations are systematic and may cover policies, programs, initiatives, or any combination of elements within the agency. Evaluations will seek to determine the worth or merit of the agencies, policies, programs, or initiatives. In addition, any evaluation should ask about the "how" and "why" of an agency's results (or lack thereof) and address suggestions or recommendations for improvements as well as minimizing both expense and impact.

Often the terms *evaluation* and *research* are used interchangeably. Despite the similarities between the two terms, there are differences. In practice, evaluations and research are conceptually different and may have widely divergent stakeholders and audiences. Stufflebeam (1983) may have made the clearest, and by far simplest, distinction between evaluation and research when he said, "The purpose of evaluation is to improve, not prove" (p. 119). That is the sense with which *evaluation* will be used throughout the remainder of this chapter.

History of Evaluation

A great many amazing and wonderful human-fabricated items exist in this world. It is not hard to imagine that for most of the world's great accomplishments there has been some degree of oversight, some supervision, and at least some rudimentary evaluation taking place. Imagine the craft guilds of Europe, or the makers of weaponry in Asia. There are countless examples wherein master artisans taught, trained, and oversaw the work of their protégés. Many of the monuments and cathedrals throughout the world could not have existed without some form of evaluation going on. The patrons of such projects, whether institutions, such as the Church, or an individual, such as a monarch, must be satisfied that the project will produce what it set out to accomplish and be an improvement over previous similar projects. The term *evaluation* is often defined as judging the worth or merit of something, or finding the value in a product. Surely, the patrons evaluated the merits and worth of their projects before, during, and after they were completed.

However, to meet the previously offered definition of evaluation, the assessments in question must be systematic—that is, the evaluation should be reliant on a codified system or process. With that idea in mind, it is probably safe to say that systematic approaches to program evaluation in the United States were not commonplace until the time of the "New Deal," the series of domestic programs enacted in the United States between 1933 and 1938. Then-president Franklin D. Roosevelt and the U.S. Congress passed a series of laws aimed at relief of the Great Depression, which had reached its economic low point in 1933.

The new programs presented a challenge, and that challenge was to determine whether the huge investment by the U.S. government was actually providing benefits, or whether the government was just squandering huge amounts of money. If the outlay of cash for these programs was going to continue, the program had to prove that it was eliminating the original problem. Social research was not entirely new, but it came of age due to the extent of its use during this period. According to Freeman (1977), the contemporary understanding and usage of *evaluation* (he called it *evaluation research*) can be dated back to the Great Depression. Since then it has steadily evolved as a scientific endeavor.

Indeed, Hogan (2010) describes five periods since 1930 through which the science of program evaluation has progressed. During these five periods, program evaluation became a distinct academic discipline, with increasing numbers of dedicated publications (e.g., according to UlrichsWeb.com [R. R. Bowker & Serial Solutions, 2015], as of January 2015, there were over 65 periodicals dedicated to evaluation or assessment appropriate to the mental health professional) and associations for those in the discipline. In the writings of various authors (e.g., Stufflebeam, 2001; Worthen, 1990) the approaches to evaluation have been listed, with one author championing as few as five approaches and another noting as many as 22 approaches. When an evaluation takes place, evaluators, for all practical purpose, probably do not use a specific "model" but more likely use specific elements from the many approaches that allow them to tailor their work to specific needs. Just like a conversation about theoretical orientation among counselors, it is fair to say that there are few evaluators who are truly purists in terms of the methodology they use.

Purpose of Evaluation

When writing this section I fear that *purpose* may be confused with *reason*, or even type of evaluation. It is true that when starting to decide on the process for any given evaluation there may be a time when reason, type, and purpose may have bearing on, and be virtually indistinguishable from, each other, much like a Venn diagram with significant overlap. However, it should become clear in this chapter that the three terms are different in description and application, and in the evaluation literature they have distinct meanings, even if not everyone agrees on the precise definition.

The *Evaluation Guidebook for Small Agencies* (Treasury Board of Canada Secretariat, 2010) suggests that the main purposes for evaluation can be reduced to two: (1) improvement and (2) accountability. In one sense an evaluation tends to lead to a new or revised program that seeks to meet needs similar to those met by the old program. From the ashes of one program, a new one arises.

Posavac (2011) states that there is only one purpose for the conduct of evaluation, "contributing to the provision of quality services to people in need"; he goes on to say that program evaluation "contributes to quality services by providing feedback from program activities and outcomes to those who can make changes in programs or who decide which services are to be offered" (p. 13). Feedback is the critical element of evaluation, although it can take many forms; feedback is why evaluations are performed.

With the acknowledgment that feedback is the primary purpose of evaluation, it may be proper at this point to make a distinction between evaluation and research. Many of the same techniques and methods are employed in both activities. Research is more likely to be an academic pursuit, whereas evaluation tends to be geared toward the facilitation of extant programs. Evaluation works with programs that are already functioning and seeks to understand the essence of the program to either improve or hold accountable with the intent of contributing to the provision of quality services. To make it clear for this chapter, the working definition of the purpose of evaluation is *the search to understand the essence of a program in order to either improve or hold accountable with the intent to contribute to the provision of quality services*. Accordingly, in order to improve or hold accountable, the evaluator must make judgments regarding the worth or merits of the program or elements of the program.

ETHICS IN EVALUATION

Ethics in evaluation is no small matter. As Posavac (2011) warns, "Evaluators often find themselves in ethical conflicts that are seldom experienced by social scientists engaged in basic research" (p. 91). Practically speaking, ethics can become the paramount concern in evaluation. An evaluation conducted without an ethical foundation renders the evaluation itself and any output from the evaluation essentially meaningless, and practically useless. When an evaluation is seen to have ethical flaws, the evaluators, the process, and virtually everyone involved becomes suspect, and for some it could be the end of a career. One need look no further than the financial crisis that hit Wall Street in 2008 to see how much confidence was lost in those who were supposedly involved in evaluating and regulating the financial institutions involved in the "Great Recession."

The American Evaluation Association (AEA) has developed a set of principles that are designed to guide evaluators in the conduct of their work (AEA, 2004). Those principles are divided into five basic components, all of which have some relation to common ethical concerns. The first principle is *systematic inquiry*, and the concern is that evaluators need to approach their business methodically, structuring their work with a logic that meets professional standards. The ethical concern here is that when evaluation is unstructured the stakeholders cannot possibly be assured of the quality of the work, and it is likely that some important aspects were overlooked. There can be no assurance of the quality of the work and certainly no belief in the output of the evaluation.

The second principle is *competence*. Everyone involved in the evaluation must have the competence required to do the job. This principle overshadows all of the other principles. An incompetent evaluator cannot be expected to complete an evaluation properly, thereby putting the entire process in jeopardy. The third principle is *integrity/honesty*, something that must be infused throughout the evaluation and an essential character asset of any evaluator. The entirety of any evaluation can be compromised by any hint of dishonesty or personal integrity issues. The fourth (*respect for people*) and fifth principle (*responsibilities for general and public welfare*) seem to this author to be of the same fabric. Respect for people in general leads to a greater respect for the welfare of others and the process as a whole. Again, to this author, the set of principles espoused by the AEA can be seen as a Venn diagram with significant overlap among the five principles, each affecting and having bearing on the others, such that one of the principles could not be extracted from the set without compromising the whole.

The American Counseling Association (ACA) and the National Board for Certified Counselors (NBCC) have sections in their respective *Codes of Ethics* (ACA, 2014; NBCC, 2013) that are dedicated to the ethics of conducting evaluations. Counselors, especially those who are considering participation in an evaluation, should become intimately familiar with the ethical binders inherent in their chosen profession. One of the interesting things regarding the ACA *Code of Ethics* (2014) is that Section G (Research and Publication) is probably more applicable to the conduct of the type of evaluation discussed in this chapter than is Section E (Evaluation, Assessment, and Interpretation).

Morris and Cohn (1993) surveyed members of the AEA regarding ethical concerns. Roughly 65% of those surveyed reported facing major ethical concerns in their work. There were four concerns that seemed to occur more often than others: (a) challenges in the contracting phase (e.g., stakeholders who thought they knew what the answer should be prior to the conduct of the evaluation; that is, that the stakeholders wanted the evaluators to reach a predetermined outcome), (b) challenges regarding the confidentiality of the participants, (c) concerns over the presentation of their findings, and (d) concern regarding the use of findings after the reporting was complete. This list is but a brief overview of the potential ethical concerns that one might encounter while evaluating. As Fitzpatrick, Sanders, and Worthen (2011) explain, "evaluators must be sufficiently sensitive to the potential ethical problems that can occur and have some sense for what to do about them" (p. 78). Only by forearming themselves can evaluators escape all of the potential ethical landmines that they may encounter.

Ethics in any evaluation scenario can result in particularly thorny predicaments. In that vein it may be appropriate to repeat Fitzpatrick et al. (2011) in their warning, "evaluators must be sufficiently sensitive to the potential ethical problems that can occur and have some sense for what to do about them" (p. 78). This simple statement should be a mantra often repeated during all evaluation processes.

SMART Goals

The acronym SMART serves as a model for outlining the constituent parts of viable and desirable goals helpful in focusing an evaluation. Credit is often given to Drucker (1954) for coming up with the acronym more than half a century ago. Since then the acronym has been expanded and modified by several authors; the acronym as used herein will be as follows: S = specific, M = measurable, A = achievable, R = relevant, and T = time oriented. "E" and "R" have often been added to the acronym to ensure that the goals are "evaluated" and "reviewed," calling to mind the essence of this chapter, which is that the original goals of any program can change over time, and evaluations are the best way to ensure that the program remains on track and focused on its goals.

SMART was intended to aid in the development of objective measures useful in the process of evaluation. Evaluators should be able to define commonly accepted criteria by which any program can be evaluated to determine mission compliance. If there is no agreement or understanding at this elementary level, no evaluation can be objective, and therefore cannot meet its intent. Without this understanding, it would become difficult to frame an evaluation that arrives at conclusions that are meaningful for all of the interested parties. An evaluation should clearly define a means to derive a measurement and comparison of the program's actual performance with the standards set in the program's statement of its mission.

The following definitions should be considered as goals that guide and focus, and are used to limit the reach of an evaluation so that the results are objective and reliable. If these constraints are not used the results may be contentious, lack empiricism, and stray significantly from the initial purpose defined by stakeholders.

1. S = Specific: Specific goals need to be clear and unambiguous. A specific goal should withstand any scrutiny that can be thrown at it. It should answer, at a minimum, the five interrogative questions of why, who, when, where, and what. The use of action verbs to describe definitive actions within a specified time frame by certain actors in a prescribed manner can hardly be misunderstood.
2. M = Measurable: This criterion emphasizes concrete means for measuring progress toward the goal. It is impossible to determine whether a goal has been measure if there is no empirical (quantifiable) means to measure the outcome. A measurable goal will determine when a process has crossed the finish line. Good descriptions of observable outcomes avoid confusion by delineating what is to be measured.
3. A = Achievable: This criterion places a premium on goals that are clearly attainable in a realistic and sustainable manner. If people know the end goal is not truly achievable, then the aspiration to achieve it dies. If the process is to be maintained over an indefinite period, it should be within the realm of daily performance, not something that requires a Herculean effort to attain, because it will not be sustained over time. A goal of this nature will require that all necessary skills be present within the staff members who are expected to achieve the goal (there should be no expectation that the staff will learn new skills in order to comply with the evaluation expectations). Staff should have sufficient control and resources to affect the goals.

4. R = Relevant: This criterion stresses the value of selecting evaluation goals that have significance. Relevance can become a source of support when the stakeholders can get behind the idea. There any number of things that can be evaluated in an agency, and choosing irrelevant goals can be distracting as well as disheartening. One way to determine relevance is to ask how the attainment of a particular goal will influence the overall mission of the program.
5. T = Time oriented: The last criterion underscores the importance of creating goals that have a logical, time-bound frequency and endpoint.

Goals framed by these constraints are likely to be influential in determining the merit and the worth of any program. The formulation of these types of goals will likely result in a comprehensive understanding of the program, such that stakeholders can use the information to take rational and thorough steps in transforming the program for the better. Evaluators will likely sidestep a multitude of concerns related to the merits and value of any reports based on goals that consider the SMART model.

Considerations Before Beginning an Evaluation

The following list notes 10 considerations one might make before beginning an evaluation. The list comes from a blog posted by Brad Rose (2014); for the sake of brevity, the commentary on each consideration has been removed, and only the list remains intact. These questions are concise and worthy of consideration, equally applicable and potentially profitable to virtually any evaluation worth undertaking.

1. Why is the evaluation being conducted? What is the purpose(s) of the evaluation?
2. What is the "it" that is being evaluated?
3. What are the intended outcomes that the program or intervention intends to produce?
4. What are the key questions to be answered by the evaluation?
5. Who is the evaluation for?
6. How will evaluation findings be used?
7. What information will stakeholders find useful?
8. What will be the "product" of the evaluation?
9. What are the potential sources of information and data?
10. What is the optimal design for the evaluation?

TYPES (MODELS) OF EVALUATION

Different types of evaluations are conducted, and the different models that are used to frame the process serve to help all of the participants envision the task ahead. In the social sciences, there has been much development in the creation of complex and refined methodologies for the conduct of evaluations. So much so that it is probably too much to expect that any one person could be an expert in each of the different types of evaluations. Therefore, it is the goal of this chapter to give a broad-based outline of some of the more common models, and then move to specific types of evaluation used when engaging in the evaluation of specific areas of interest in the three sections that follow.

For someone tasked to lead an evaluation there is much to do, and one of the most challenging and controversial areas to consider is the model of evaluation to be used. The question "why" will come from many different fronts, and from many of the stakeholders. The manager of any evaluation process must be able to answer the "why" questions that inevitably come, and perhaps defend "why not" questions such as "why not choose another model?" To aid in the defense of their model choice, evaluators must be sufficiently familiar with the common models to make an intelligent response. The provision of an intelligent and informed response takes a big step toward building the confidence that stakeholders will need during the evaluation process, including the use of the products that come forth well after the evaluation has concluded.

There are several decision points that one must make while deciding on an evaluation model. One must consider whether the evaluation will produce it results through qualitative, quantitative, or mixed means. The assumption, then, is that the output of the evaluation will also be reported in the same fashion. A quantitative evaluation will provide a statistics-based output.

Qualitative evaluations are conducted by collecting written or verbal narratives and other types of descriptors that, when compiled, produce free-form, open-ended narratives. The resultant data are difficult to generalize to any other sample or population. Qualitative evaluations are often more difficult to conduct but often provide a level of insight perhaps not available as compared with quantitative evaluations. The qualitative evaluation may provide significant detail and personal reasoning behind the observations.

In contrast, a quantitative evaluation conducts and reports information encoded in a numerical fashion. Quantitative evaluations are generally easier to conduct and have a larger sample size. In the end, they offer an aggregated, statistically valid conclusion that can be generalized to other samples or populations. Stake (1995) suggests that one way to understand the difference is that qualitative evaluations seek to *understand* the relationship between objects, peoples, and programs, whereas quantitative evaluations are seeking to *explain* relationships among objects, peoples, and programs. These are not the only distinctions that can be made between qualitative and quantitative evaluations, but they are helpful when trying to determine which type will prove most useful for any given demand.

Mixed evaluations combine both methodologies to produce both empirically valid and generalizable information that incorporates rich, descriptive, narrative-based information. This type of evaluation is by its very nature more difficult and resource intensive than either of the other two types. It is understandable that this type of evaluation is less often conducted, in part because the methods are so different that most evaluators clearly prefer one method over the other, and, as such, it is hard to find someone who is equally comfortable with, and knowledgeable regarding, how to combine both methods.

Scriven (1967) was presumably the first author to suggest that the two major functions (roles) of evaluation be divided into either *formative* and *summative* evaluation (Fitzpatrick et al., 2011). These two terms have become widely used in the discipline. Virtually all evaluations can be categorized into one of these types, or a third category that is a mixture of these two types.

Formative evaluations (also known as "internal") have the intent of judging the quality of a program or can focus on just one aspect of a program. Fitzpatrick et al. (2011) describe a formative evaluations as follows: "An evaluation is considered to be formative if the primary purpose is to provide information for program improvement" (p. 20). In part, the title is descriptive of the process; the evaluation is conducted while the program is in its formative stage, and it is intended to help the program comply with its stated mission. The intent is to monitor and reform programs by calling attention to deficiencies and then provide remedial training, education, instruction, knowledge, or insight that may be helpful. Another description that expands on the definition comes from the Treasury Board of Canada Secretariat (2010): "This type of evaluation examines the effectiveness of implementation for facilitating improvement. A formative evaluation may be conducted in mid-cycle of the program, policy, or initiative. Its intent is to provide information to improve the program, policy, or initiative" (p. 11).

On the other hand summative evaluations (also known as "external" evaluations) contrast with formative evaluations because they focus on determining how well the program has met its stated goals. These are generally done at the end of the program activities and are interested primarily in the outcome or output, the summation. Fitzpatrick and company (2011) describe summative evaluations as follows: "Summative evaluations are concerned with providing information to serve decisions or assist in making judgments about program adoptions, continuation, or expansion" (p. 21). The Treasury Board of Canada Secretariat (2010) provides additional insight into the distinctions between formative and summative evaluations by adding the following description: "This type of evaluation examines impacts in order to make a decision about overall effectiveness. They have primarily an accountability function and are generally conducted towards the end of the cycle" (p. 12).

Jen Harvey (1998) provides an interesting means of distinguishing between formative and summative evaluation. In her cookbook, she states that, "When the cook tastes the soup, it is formative evaluation; when the dinner guest tastes the soup, it is summative evaluation" (p. 7). As noted earlier, greater distinctions can be made regarding the typology of evaluation, but these simple distinctions can go a long way toward helping the novice understand which direction to take when confronted with the need to conduct an evaluation. Most of this section has discussed models and types of evaluations that are the most common. In the following three sections, the discussion turns to more specific areas of evaluation. How to evaluate these areas is not the topic in these sections; what to evaluate when considering these specific topics is the focus.

EVALUATION OF THE THERAPIST

A program that provides counseling to the public will have therapists. The term *therapist* is used here to highlight the fact that in many agencies or programs there may be mental health practitioners from a variety of disciplines. In light of the fact that many disciplines may peacefully coexist in any counseling program, this section acknowledges that a "therapist" may be a psychiatrist, counselor, social worker, or member of any number of other disciplines, such as rehabilitation or substance abuse specialists.

When evaluating a therapist's work, what are the characteristics that one might choose to look at? If the client is not satisfied with the performance of the therapist, little else is of true concern to management. From whose perspective do you want to look at the therapist in order to determine effectiveness? It should come as no surprise that clients look at therapist efficacy in a vastly different manner than the clinical director. The topic is far too vast to address in this chapter. From a pragmatic view, it is the client whose view is most important. If the customer is not satisfied, then the questions that management may have are in essence answered, or moot.

Suffice it to say that *client* as used here refers to the larger client base using a single therapist. There will always be clients who find it impossible to work with a particular therapist. However, if a large number of clients assigned to a therapist do not find the therapist helpful they will quit coming, and when enough quit, the agency will begin to suffer. If the agency is large enough it may survive financially. However, the record of client turnover should become evident to any competent manager, if, in fact, managers are looking for that type of information.

Another caveat is in order here: Just because clients like a therapist, that in and of itself presents no reason to assume that the therapeutic approach of the therapist is efficacious. However, clients who can establish a working alliance are far more likely to stay engaged long enough to reach their goals. In fact, according to Asay and Lambert (1999), the working alliance accounts for as much as 30% of therapeutic efficacy. With that in mind, this chapter will look at therapeutic efficacy from the mind-set of a client.

Most therapists are aware of the impact of Carl Rogers and his idea of *conditions for change*. In his writings, Rogers obligated the therapist to create the conditions for change. Here are the conditions as outlined by Rogers (1946, p. 417):

1. If the counselor operates on the principle that the individual is basically responsible for himself, and is willing for the individual to keep that responsibility.
2. If the counselor operates on the principle that the client has a strong drive to become mature, socially adjusted, independent, productive, and relies on this force, not on his own powers, for therapeutic change.
3. If the counselor creates a warm and permissive atmosphere in which the individual is free to bring out any attitudes and feelings which he may have, no matter how unconventional, absurd, or contradictory these attitudes may be. . . .
4. If the limits which are set are simple limits set on behavior, and not limits set on attitudes. . . .
5. If the therapist uses only those procedures and techniques in the interview which convey his deep understanding of the emotionalized attitudes expressed and his acceptance of them. . . .
6. If the counselor refrains from any expression or action which is contrary to the preceding principles.

Please note that the therapist is responsible for creating all of the listed conditions. At the time, Rogers challenged the status quo. Since their introduction, these conditions have become widely accepted.

Prior to the introduction of Rogers's conditions, Rosenzweig (1936) challenged the idea that specific interventions were responsible for therapeutic efficacy. He was the first to surmise that the efficacy of any given therapeutic intervention relies on factors that are commonly used. He advocated that most psychotherapeutic interventions share change elements that are not specific to any given model. Over the following three quarters of a century that position has been proven to be relatively accurate.

Ahn and Wampold (2001) said, "The research evidence supports the notion that the benefits of counseling and psychotherapy are derived from the common factors" (p. 255). To be clear, the question that is trying to be answered here is that, when evaluating a therapist, what specific inquiries can answer the question of efficacy? Grencavage and Norcross (1990) suggested there might be nearly 90 different common factors at play in therapy. Of those 90 common factors, not all apply to the therapist because therapist characteristics constitute only one of the five broad categories.

As previously noted, there are certain factors included in the common factors matrix that are beyond the control of the therapist (e.g., extra therapeutic factors, those life events that happen to the client outside of counseling). The components within the therapeutic environment that the therapist has direct control over are legitimately the only matters that therapists should be held accountable for in an evaluation. Grencavage and Norcross (1990) listed six broad categories that are attributable to the therapist, and they will be discussed herein. Some of these categories align nicely with Rogers's commentary of therapeutic conditions, others, not so much.

1. General positive descriptors
2. Cultivates hope/enhances expectancies
3. Warmth/positive regard
4. Empathic understanding
5. Socially sanctioned healer
6. Acceptance

Remember that the purpose of this section is to point out some areas that might prove valuable in the evaluation of the therapeutic efficacy of a therapist. Any component used in the evaluation of a therapist should offer SMART qualities in order to be useful. As one glances at the components, some of the categories obviously need more clarification to be useful in the SMART sense. The authors of the works from which this list was derived did not have the idea of using them for evaluation in mind when compiling the list. Therefore, it falls to an evaluator to redefine these components in such a way as to make them useful, and SMART compliant.

General Positive Descriptors

This component is meant to encompass the beneficial therapist qualities that clients generally find helpful. Since Rogers and Rosenzweig helped turn the focus of psychotherapy from techniques to interpersonal elements, the research on various components seems nearly endless and unclear. In reviewing research regarding the efficacy of the various elements that a counselor either has (personal characteristics) or does (personal skills), there seems to be no clear or consistent finding that can be declared unambiguous. There is no doubt that some counselors are more effective than others, but to clarify why is as of yet an unanswered question.

This author's experience has led him to the conclusion that most clients come to counseling with some understanding that a counselor is supposed to listen without judging. Clients articulate that they want a counselor to whom they can express themselves without judgment. Good listening skills are thus a commodity by which a good counselor can be evaluated. Yet, what constitutes good listening skills can be as individual as the client's perception.

So, then, how can an evaluator make sense of "general positive descriptors"? It may be as simple as choosing to allow the client to indicate responses to several broad categories. It may not pass empirical scrutiny, but clients can clearly identify on a scale of 1 to 10 how they perceived the counselor's ability to listen to them, attend to their stories, and discern details that are of importance. Did the counselor remain nonjudgmental, did the counselor listen, and did the counselor ask important questions?

Regardless of the specific variable that they may be responding to, the greater preponderance of clients can give a clear indication of how they "feel" about their therapists, whether positively or negatively. Probably the most specific indicator they can give about the nature of the relationship with their therapists is the number of times they return for services. Good managers can gather that information and aggregate the data to compare the therapists working for them. Clients vote with their feet—if they continue to come, they are finding something of value in their sessions. The first and foremost indicator, then, may be that clients simply continue to return for services.

Cultivates Hope/Enhances Expectancies

As Frank (2004) suggested: "Therapy consists of the application of special techniques to combat maladaptive patterns and encourage more appropriate ones" (p. 11). In this statement, Frank both describes and acknowledges that some techniques set psychotherapy apart from other forms of helping (e.g., coaches, pastor, and friends). He goes on to say:

> Patients seek psychotherapy not for symptoms alone, but for symptoms coupled with demoralization, a state of mind characterized by one or more of the following: subjective incompetence, loss of self-esteem, alienation, hopelessness (feeling that no one can help), or helplessness (feeling that other people could help but will not). (p. 16)

It is important that counselors recognize that some clients are ready for effective work and others are not. The promulgation of stages of change by Norcross, Krebs, and Prochaska (2011) is well known to most counselors. A good counselor should be able to detect the client's willingness to engage in change-oriented work. Clients who are unwilling can be provided sound reasons to engage in change. That is the very essence of a counselor who cultivates hope and creates expectancy.

The best way to evaluate a counselor on this characteristic is to compile self-reports from the clients. Tools for measuring client expectations exist in a variety of forms. It is interesting to see the before-and-after results of these instruments. Some counselors are very good at creating hope for their clients, and that can be identified when comparing results after as little as three sessions. The chosen measure given during the intake process and again after the third session will reflect the capacity of a therapist to instill hope in the client. The capacity to cultivate hope and create expectancy in a client is generally indicative of favorable results.

Warmth/Positive Regard

Rogers wrote of these two characteristics as if they constituted one entity. This author sees them as very distinct entities. Warmth seems to be a personality characteristic, whereas unconditional positive regard seems to be a mental construct. However, from the client's perspective, a counselor who has unconditional positive regard for that client is more likely to be perceived as demonstrating warmth. In reality, a counselor may perceive a client through the lens of unconditional positive regard but the counselor's personality may be such that warmth does not necessarily flow from that positive regard. Rogers (1951) recognized that it is virtually impossible for the therapist to stay in the unconditional positive regard mode, and said, "unconditional positive regard exists as a matter of degree in any relationship" (p. 101).

In the end, it is fair to measure a therapist based on unconditional positive regard as long as the measurement instrument is used consistently across the board. To some extent, the available instruments capture to a greater or lesser degree the concept as Rogers intended. The measurement of a counselor's ability to deliver positive regard to clients is important, because, as Farber and Doolin (2011) concluded from their meta-analysis on the subject, "The psychotherapist's ability to provide positive regard is significantly associated with therapeutic success" (p. 62). Moreover, in the end, therapeutic success is the desired product.

Empathic Understanding

What is meant by empathic understanding? It implies that the counselor is capable of understanding why someone in similar conditions might do or feel what the client is describing. In some cases, it might call for the suspension of judgment and the dismissal of current cultural biases in order to reach that state, but, at a minimum, it makes the telling of their stories easier for clients. This in and of itself is worth the price, as more comfort felt in telling their stories likely results in more details and less resistance to follow-up questions, thus enhancing the potential for the counselor to explore meaning in the client's story.

However, as a tool for clinical evaluation of a counselor's performance, the concept lacks definition and clarity. There are available instruments that potentially may provide some useful information on this conceptual parameter, but the lack of a common definition makes this difficult to measure. This concept is difficult to place in a SMART context, and that makes this component problematic for use as an evaluation tool.

Socially Sanctioned Healer

Socially sanctioned can mean many things to an individual. Is it preferable to have a counselor who has been recommended by others? Is it preferable to have a counselor who has been licensed by the state? In general, then, what this comes down to is the client's perception, and, for the most part, it is assumed that clients prefer to have a therapist who possesses the highest possible qualifications. Nevertheless, it appears that most clients do not spend a great deal of time dwelling on the qualifications of the therapist. Rather, they want to know whether the therapist can help them with their specific problems. Beyond the perception of being qualified, social sanctions do not have much connection to the therapist's actual ability to help clients achieve their goals.

However, we are addressing the prospect of using "socially sanctioned healer" in the evaluation process. This component is relatively straightforward. One has the licensure or not, one has the education or not, one has the specialized training or not. This one is simply a determination of what sanctions are important and then checking the block. At a minimum, this requires educational preparation and licensure to be meaningful in an evaluation.

Acceptance

Acceptance is, again, one of those components that depend on the client's perspective. There are a number of ways to assess the client's perspective of the therapist's acceptance. It is imperative that a good working alliance is formed between the client and the therapist if they are going to generate positive outcomes. When evaluating therapists, it seems that efforts to evaluate each of these components separately might be a significant undertaking that in the end may not be as useful as desired. It might be more useful to measure therapeutic alliance. Instead of trying to parse particular elements from the client, it would seem to be more useful to gain the larger perspective that is not reliant on subtle nuances. The benefit of using one of the global measures of therapeutic alliance is the ability to compare one therapist's body of work against another with some degree of empiricism.

EVALUATION OF THE CLIENT'S EXPERIENCE

This section will be shorter than the previous section, in part due to the dearth of information available on research in the social sciences regarding client satisfaction and experience within the counseling context. As noted in the previous section, there is a volume of material about the experience of counseling as it relates to the interpersonal experience, but there is little written on other factors that lead to a satisfied customer. This type of material is available in business and marketing literature, but it is not entirely well suited to clients involved in counseling due to the intimate and interpersonal nature of the process.

Often the social sciences focus on therapeutic outcome. Outcome can only truly be measured when a client stays engaged long enough to have therapy run its course, which (even when considering brief therapy modalities) is roughly eight sessions or more. However, global satisfaction measures outside of actual therapeutic factors may impede the client's engagement. Global satisfaction is determined by considering a multiplicity of factors. However, determining the factors to be measured can be problematic because there are few variables that are applicable across the board, and to all clients. In addition, as Hsieh (2009, 2012) has commented, how to weight each element in the measurement of the global satisfaction is often challenging. Nonetheless, this section will endeavor to discuss some of the possible elements considered as global measures influencing client engagement in therapy.

One caveat is that the use of the phrase "client satisfaction" as an evaluation measure is difficult to clarify. Client satisfaction and therapy outcome have little in common with each other. One does nothing to indicate the degree to which the other is satisfied. Defining client satisfaction is a challenging process, and the product of such an effort can only be arbitrary. Therefore, any attempt to measure client satisfaction will be met with a multitude of challenges, not the least of which is an effort to justify the variables used to determine the outcome.

As stated earlier in this section, there seems to be a very limited number of attempts to research client satisfaction with counseling that consider issues not directly related to the therapeutic interactions. In an attempt to verify the statement made in the previous sentence, this author spent an entire afternoon and evening looking through various databases with a host of keyword combinations, trying to find peer-reviewed materials (including dissertations and theses) that might shed light on client satisfaction issues. The search proved to be frustrating and only a few pieces spoke to the issue at hand, with no concurrence on the variables. However, as Royse, Thyer, and Padgett (2010) declare, "Client satisfaction alone is not sufficient as a measure of quality, but it is universally accepted as one of several necessary measures" (p. 176). Few evaluators can overlook the subject without jeopardizing their credibility.

After completing the aforementioned search, and considering business and marketing materials tangentially related to the matter, this author arrived at three broad areas that may affect the client in ways sufficient to cause the client to prematurely end his or her appeal for therapeutic help: (a) the physical environment, (b) staffing-related issues, and (c) communications between the agency and the client. One caveat needs to be offered here, and that is that one client may have an adverse reaction to exactly the same thing that appeals to another. It is difficult know what the definitive solution is in every situation.

Physical Environment

The physical environment can intimidate clients long before they ever walk into a facility. Counseling is a personal and intimate endeavor. Clients tend to be self-conscious, and the facility can be appealing and welcoming but client reactions can vary considerably. This author is aware of a client who chose the facility and time of appointment because, at the time, she was homeless (living in her car) and the facility offered her a place to park in a relatively safe and uninterrupted parking lot. She chose to be the last client of the day, which allowed her to sleep in the parking lot without being challenged by security personnel. That client was, one hopes, a rare case, but counseling facilities that offer security without exposing clients to public disclosure are in general more comfortable for clients. A counseling office that identifies itself as such with large signs, located across the street from a popular restaurant, might want to consider offering its clients an entrance that avoids exposure to the high traffic generated by the restaurant.

Quiet, concealed, secure, and clean are all features highly valued by clients. Most clients seeking mental health counseling are in some sort of distress. An environment that is high traffic, noisy, and lacks personal security is going to alienate a client dealing with high anxiety. Privacy, accessibility, and the lack of congestion can help clients keep stress at bearable levels. One client described the approach to one therapist's office as causing her distress in the same way that she might experience a 6-year-old endlessly and noisily crinkling an aluminized potato chip bag in her face. She refused to return to the office simply because of the traffic.

Once inside the building there can be a multitude of things that clients encounter that may cause them distress. A client with obsessive-compulsive disorder (OCD) might be repulsed at the disorder and noise caused by a group of children playing in the waiting area. One client noted that a Thomas Kincaid painting hanging in a public space in the hall of her therapist's facility was offensive to her, because she had been repressing her own suicidal ideations and personally thought that Kincaid had committed suicide. The sentiment in the picture was the opposite of the hopelessness she was experiencing, but her perception was all that mattered to her at the time.

The waiting room is where many different things can go wrong. It is not always possible to change what a facility provides. For instance, in an agency that works with a full spectrum of clients, it would be nice to have two waiting rooms—one for parents and children, the other for those who are not comfortable around chaos induced by many children. Nevertheless, the facilities may not provide enough space to allow for that sort of luxury.

It seems as though the size of the therapy rooms is a matter that is never quite resolved to everyone's satisfaction. In one case that the author is familiar with, a therapist was treating clients with posttraumatic stress disorder (PTSD) in a small office at the conjunction of two hallways that formed a T intersection just outside his door. Some of the clients who were dealing with extreme hypervigilance were upset by the traffic and talking that always seemed to occur at the intersection. There was no choice in the matter, however; the facility was just too small and restricted to change that situation.

At this point, you probably have some sense of how an office environment can affect the client. The environs both inside and outside the agency or offices can have adverse effects that tend to create discomfort for clients. Even seating, lighting, and wall colors can have pleasant or unpleasant effects on clients. The problem is that one client may like the color, lighting, and seating, whereas the next does not. However, another consideration should be raised here, which is that some of these same conditions affect the staff even more so than the clients, and the staff must deal with it day in and day out. This, then, turns our consideration to the next concern, staffing-related issues.

Staffing-Related Issues

The welfare of the staff should be a prime concern for management. A cranky staff will readily affect the welfare of the client. In general, the staff is a direct reflection of the management. If the staff is well prepared to interface with clients and meet clients' needs, there is reason to believe that the management of the agency considers the staff to be a worthy investment in the total presentation that management wants to accomplish. It starts with the hiring of new staff and requires a uniform and standardized approach by management to train and equip the staff. The more time management invests in monitoring and shaping the performance of the staff, the more likely it is that the global goal of enhancing the client experience is achieved.

This is not intended to be a treatise on the fine art of customer service. However, it is clear that clients have probably tried a number of ways to either avoid or cure themselves before they walk in for services. Rarely do clients seek out counseling services without having attempted some other way to take care of their concerns. In explaining that most therapeutic methods share common components, Frank (2004) notes that clients have at least one thing in common:

> Demoralization occurs when, because of lack of certain skills or confusion of goals, an individual becomes persistently unable to master situations which both the individual and others expect him or her to handle or when the individual experiences continued distress which he or she cannot adequately explain or alleviate. Demoralization may be summed up as a feeling of subjective incompetence, coupled with distress. (p. 15)

Clients can be helped by therapy first and foremost through the restoration of a sense of capacity—the belief that they have the capacity to overcome, and that by seeking treatment they are on the path to mastery of the sought-after goal. Almost 60 years ago Rosenthal and Frank (1956) discussed the usefulness of faith in therapeutic outcome as that "produced by the patients' faith in the efficacy of the therapist and his technique—'the placebo effect.' This effect may be thought of as a nonspecific form of psychotherapy and it may be quite powerful in that it may produce end-organ changes and relief from distress of considerable duration" (p. 300). An enthusiastic and helpful staff that is prepared to answer all of a client's questions in a manner that encourages belief and hope is the most significant way to help a client begin that journey to recovery. Conversely, a grumpy and ill-mannered staff can sour a client's mood and create more work for the therapist.

Keeping a staff satisfied and prepared to deal with a client has limits. One of the most powerful ways to keep a staff happy is to hire happy people. Due diligence in the hiring process can have long-term effects for any agency. There are a variety of means to measure the goodness-of-fit of any potential employee. That is not the purpose of this work. However, to raise the point that generally happy and satisfied people transmit satisfaction and happiness to clients is a point worth keeping in mind as management puts together its staff. Another point to be made is that in many cases it does not take a significant investment to ensure that staff members are taken care of and that the working environment is pleasant. But, it does require a conscious effort.

The components used to measure the staff members' preparedness and their influence on a client can be taken from a variety of sources. Some areas that can be measured include the following: (1) timeliness (how quickly the client is acknowledged and greeted), (2) greeting (appropriateness of greeting; clients in a counseling environment need to be treated with discretion, making privacy a high priority), (3) attention to client needs (which requires listening to the client, knowing the business, and using good communication skills), (4) courtesy and mutual respect in spite of the presentation (some clients are difficult; avoid taking their behavior personally), and, finally, (5) provision of a means for clients to give feedback (intentionally seek out client input and respond to it so they know they have been heard). In the example mentioned earlier, it would be appropriate to remove the Kincaid painting if it seemed offensive to the client.

Communications

A final concern that can be useful in evaluating the client's experience in counseling is how well the communication between the client and agency meets the client's need. From the very first contact with the client, the style and content of the communication are important. Every manner in which a client may interface with the agency should be a matter of concern. Convenience and ease are of primary importance.

In this technological age, there are many ways to communicate with a client. However, there must be an omnipresent concern for securing protected health information (PHI). There are static (e.g., webpages that only provide information with no means of collecting data) and dynamic (e.g., an e-mail that contains PHI) means of communicating. Only dynamic means of communication must be concerned about the potential for the disclosure of information protected by the Health Insurance Portability and Accountability Act (HIPAA) in their use. Some communications can be used for both static and dynamic communications. A webpage can be used to provide a link that allows a client to simply download an intake information form. Nevertheless, a very similar page could be constructed that collects the intake information and loads it into the agency's database. The collection page is infinitely more user-friendly and provides more convenience, but if there are no means to secure the data, the page should never be created.

By far, the most common means of communicating with a client is the telephone. Although useful, a system that uses a menu for the client to navigate will always have its limitations. Clients seeking counseling may be put off by complicated menus, and the opportunity to serve them may be lost if they become frustrated with the menu. Always ensure that clients have a means of talking to a human (from any point in the menu) if they cannot get what they want from the menu. In addition, they should receive instructions regarding what to do if they are in a state of emergency.

In the end, all forms of communication with a client should be well thought out in order to achieve the desired goals. Ease of use and content are important, but they should never be gained at the risk of potential disclosure of PHI. Consider the goal of the communication and the cost to the staff for any manner of communication chosen. There are now cloud-based programs that will contact the client in advance of his or her next appointment. That is a significant time saver for the staff, but it should be made clear to the client what the impact of such usage would be. For instance, a client may not want a message that discloses appointment information delivered to a work number where multiple people could overhear the message.

How do you evaluate the client's experience? There are instruments that have been created specifically for collecting client satisfaction information. Most collect information about the client's satisfaction with the therapeutic relationship. A few have been created (and researched) that take into consideration global concerns, including the counseling facility, staff interactions, and more. If the proper instrument cannot be found, it may be necessary to look into the marketing and business realm to collect data outside of the therapeutic relationship. It may require a combination of instruments to collect information on all of the concerns that an evaluator may have. More than just the therapeutic relationship will affect the engagement of the client. In addition, if a client is not engaged, there can be no progress.

It should be mentioned that there is an overriding problem with the use of client satisfaction as a measure of the client experience. The problem, as reported by Ingram and Chung (1997), is that the vast majority of respondents to client satisfaction measures report being satisfied. These authors report that the average reporting of satisfied clients was 78%. Ingram and Chung state that, "This positive response set creates an obstacle for decision makers who want their plans to be based on unbiased data" (p. 43). It seems that this is true in other countries as well as the United States. Clients tend to report high satisfaction rates even when they have little choice in facility, treatment type, or provider (Lebow, 1982). Some wonder why this trend may be occurring, but the problem exists no matter the reason for it. The measure of client satisfaction seems to provide questionable results, and therefore such results should be treated with caution and perhaps even skepticism by any evaluator.

QUALITY IMPROVEMENT

Evaluations are done for one reason. That reason is to assess the state of the program and to understand how well it is meeting the goals set forth in its own mission statement and then improve on its current functioning. In the end, the assessment is going to result in a judgment. That judgment may result in the execution of a multitude of corrections. The outcome may be that a program is eliminated, maintained as it is, or changed in ways ranging from subtle to dramatic.

Many employees fear assessment for this very reason. They have settled into a pattern of behavior that is comfortable and change will disturb that pattern. Therefore, introduction of assessment results to the shareholders requires some finesse. The truth is challenging because people's pride may be injured in the presentation of the outcome results. It should be remembered that the truth being presented is only one of many truths. Evaluations rarely capture the whole truth at any given time in the development of a program or agency. Evaluations generally pick various elements to generalize about the whole, and they generally only see operations for a defined segment of time.

In order for quality improvement to result from an evaluation that has been completed and presented, three things must happen. The first thing is that the shareholders, at least those shareholders who have the capacity to make something happen, must buy into the credibility and the conclusions reached in the evaluation. The second is that there must be a consensus regarding corrective measures. The third is that those with the capacity must be resolved to take action. The evaluator has no control over these elements. Nor should the evaluator have any stake in what happens after the output of the evaluation has been presented. The evaluator should remain dispassionate throughout the process. If the evaluator becomes personally involved in the project, the objectivity that should accompany any assessment has probably been diminished if not completely lost.

In some cases evaluators may offer, or be asked, to oversee the quality improvement that follows the publication of the results. To a degree, it makes sense for an agency to have those who have made the recommendations for quality improvement also implement the changes. There are a host of reasons why that makes sense. First is that those who performed the evaluation and then made recommendations for quality improvement are in the best position to objectively implement most fully those recommendations. The stakeholders can remain detached from the implementation process and from the reactions of the employees affected by the implementation. Change does not come easily in most agencies, but to expect those who are responsible for the present state of the agency to implement and support change may defy logic.

In the end, what is most important is not who implements the changes, but rather that changes are made based on an understanding of why change is both necessary and helpful to furthering an agency's mission. In part, the evaluator sets the tone for this aspect of the evaluation during the presentation of the findings. When presenting the findings, an evaluator can facilitate implementation of recommendations by breaking the tasks into short- and long-term steps. This makes the implementation of the recommendations more digestible and manageable. The last thing that staff members who have just undergone an evaluation need is to be overwhelmed by the follow-up tasks.

AMY'S NEW CHALLENGE

Amy's agency has received funding from a federal grant for the past 8 years. The agency grew to depend on the funding but did not give the source significant attention except in the bookkeeping department. Amy was asked to attend a meeting with her boss. In the e-mail setting up the meeting, Amy saw that the attendees were people with whom she was unfamiliar.

On entering the room, Amy had the feeling that this meeting had a certain gravitas that demanded her most professional demeanor. After the cursory introductions, the boss opened the meeting by solemnly reading a document that had been sent to the agency requiring formal acknowledgment of receipt, and the need to prepare a formal response in 90 days. It came from the federal agency that provided funding. As part of the funding process, the agency was required to perform a self-evaluation every 4 years. The boss had been able to retrieve the evaluation that had been previously completed. Apparently, the previous evaluation was performed before the current management had come to work in the agency, and no one on the current staff had been aware of the evaluation requirement from the federal agency. As the boss outlined the extent of the evaluation, it became apparent that the agency had failed in keeping the required data needed for the evaluation; at the least, the agency had not recorded the data in the format required by the federal agency.

As the meeting wore on, Amy began to wonder why she had been asked to join this group of people, most of whom she had no working relationship with. She did not have to wait very long to find out why she was there. The boss was announcing Amy's promotion. The first and foremost task that Amy was going to be faced with in her new position was putting together a team to reconstruct the records of the past 4 years, complete the evaluation as required by the federal agency, and then modify agency practice to ensure that these concerns become part of the standard practices of the agency. Amy was, at the same time, happy and terrified—happy for the recognition of her efforts, her capacity, and demonstrated management potential; terrified because she had only been exposed to evaluation in the one class she had taken in college (she remembered the professor's money-back guarantee). The class was required in her human services program, but it seemed irrelevant at the time and she did not give it much effort. That class is precisely why she was given the leadership opportunity, but she had not even kept the textbook. As she slowly walked back to her office she was deep in thought; her mind was racing. Where would she start with this project? She remembered that the professor was still teaching at the school and she wrote an e-mail requesting a meeting with him as soon as humanly possible.

In the midst of her racing thoughts, she knew that she had to calm herself and began to perform some of her relaxation techniques. As she regained part of her composure, one of her friends in the agency walked in and asked whether she was all right. Amy had walked right past her in the hallway without giving any signs of recognition. As Amy began to recount the events of the meeting, her friend congratulated her on the new role. After some thought her friend asked whether Amy could use any of the materials she had generated earlier in the year when she had worked on correcting the deficiencies from the state evaluation (presented at the beginning of this chapter). Amy jumped up and hugged her friend for the suggestion. It was precisely the place she needed to start.

If you were given this challenge, what would you do to get started? How would you assemble the team?

SUMMARY

Assessment and evaluation are nothing if not practical. As suggested earlier, the evaluation of an agency or program has but one significant goal. That goal is to understand how the subject is currently functioning and then make improvements. That may sound like two goals. However, inherent in improving anything is a correct understanding of the subject as it currently exists. Hence, to meet its goal an evaluation must reach an accurate understanding of the object it is examining. Not all evaluations are tasked with making recommendations for improvement, but most do, and, in some cases, the evaluators are tasked to carry out those recommendations. Just as the evaluator should consider the SMART concept while the evaluation is being conducted, the recommendations should also meet the SMART criteria if they are to be meaningful and implementable.

When this author taught this material for a course, the opening challenge consisted of a money-back guarantee to the students. The guarantee was that if they stayed in the mental health profession for at least 20 years they would be involved in some form of evaluation more than once, and good odds exist that they would be called on to conduct an evaluation. No one has tried to collect on the bet, but the point was to bring home to the students the ever-increasing presence of evaluations in this highly regulated field. In fact, a highly qualified evaluator can make a good living at doing nothing other than evaluations. The nature of the mental health field is that, for the foreseeable future, evaluations will continue to play an important role in shaping and refining the profession.

As the American society progresses and grapples with ever-more-complex issues, the demand for evaluation will grow. The assurance of quality and cost-effectiveness lies at the heart of the evaluation process, and with the forward progress of society the need for those two qualities will ever expand. Those who can formulate and execute proper evaluations will find an ever-increasing demand for their services.

REFLECTION QUESTIONS

1. How would you structure an evaluation of your agency, program, or practice so that it is efficacious and purposeful?
2. What are your expectations about the process of evaluation?
3. What ethical codes and principles are involved in the process of evaluation?
4. What, in your opinion, is the most challenging part of an evaluation?
5. What obstacles might you face in the evaluation process?

SUGGESTED RESOURCES

American Evaluation Association (AEA): http://www.eval.org/

Centers for Disease Control and Prevention (CDC), Program Performance and Evaluation Office (PPEO): http://www.cdc.gov/eval/resources/

Fitzpatrick, J. L., Sanders, J. R., Worthen, B. R., & Worthen, B. R. (2011). *Program evaluation: Alternative approaches and practical guidelines* (4th ed.). Upper Saddle River, NJ: Pearson Education.

Mathison, S. (2005). *Encyclopedia of evaluation*. Thousand Oaks, CA: Sage.

U.S. Government Accountability Office (GAO). *Designing evaluations, 2012 revision*: Available at http://www.gao.gov/products/GAO-12-208G

REFERENCES

Ahn, H., & Wampold, B. E. (2001). Where oh where are the specific ingredients? A meta-analysis of component studies in counseling and psychotherapy. *Journal of Counseling Psychology*, *48*, 251–257. doi:10.1037/0022-0167.48.3.251

American Counseling Association. (2014). *Code of ethics*. Alexandria, VA: Author.

American Evaluation Association. (2004). *Guiding principles for evaluators*. Retrieved from http://www.eval.org/p/cm/ld/fid=51

Asay, T. P., & Lambert, M. J. (1999). The empirical case for the common factors in therapy: Quantitative findings. In M. Hubble, B. Duncan, & S. Miller (Eds.), *The heart & soul of change: What works in therapy* (pp. 35–56). Washington, DC: American Psychological Association.

Drucker, P. F. (1954). *The practice of management*. New York, NY: Harper.

Farber, B. A., & Doolin, E. M. (2011). Positive regard. *Psychotherapy*, *48*(1), 58–64. doi:10.1037/a0022141

Fitzpatrick, J. L., Sanders, J. R., & Worthen, B. R. (2011). *Program evaluation: Alternative approaches and practical guidelines* (4th ed.). Upper Saddle River, NJ: Pearson Education.

Frank, J. D. (2004). Therapeutic components shared by all psychotherapies. In A. Freeman, M. Mahoney, P. DeVito, & D. Martin (Eds.), *Cognition and psychotherapy* (2nd ed., pp. 45–78). New York, NY: Springer Publishing Company.

Freeman, H. E. (1977). The present status of evaluation research. In M. A. Guttentag & S. Saar (Eds.), *Evaluation studies review annual*. Beverly Hills, CA: Sage.

Grencavage, L. M., & Norcross, J. C. (1990). Where are the commonalities among the therapeutic common factors? *Professional Psychology: Research and Practice, 21*, 372–378. doi:10.1037/0735-7028.21.5.372

Harvey, J. (Ed.). (1998). *Evaluation cookbook*. Edinburgh, UK: Institute for Computer Based Learning, Heriot-Watt University. Retrieved from http://www.icbl.hw.ac.uk/ltdi/cookbook/

Hogan, R. L. (2010). The historical development of program evaluation: Exploring past and present. *Workforce Education and Development, 2*(4), 1–14.

Hsieh, C. M. (2009). Importance counts: The role of relative importance of service elements in client satisfaction measures. *Journal of Social Service Research, 35*(1), 23–31.

Hsieh, C. M. (2012). Perceived importance of service elements in client satisfaction measures. *Journal of Social Service Research, 38*(4), 529–540. doi:10.1080/01488376.2012.699410

Ingram, B. L., & Chung, R. S. (1997). Client satisfaction data and quality improvement in managed mental health care organizations. *Health Care Management Review, 22*(3), 40–52.

Lebow, J. (1982). Consumer satisfaction with mental health treatment. *Psychological Bulletin, 91*(2), 244–259. doi:10.1037/0033-2909.91.2.244

McNamara, C. (2006). *Basic guide to program evaluation (including outcomes evaluation)*. Retrieved from http://managementhelp.org/evaluation/program-evaluation-guide.htm#anchor184773

Morris, M., & Cohn, R. (1993). Program evaluators and ethical challenges: A national survey. *Evaluation Review, 17*(6), 621–642. doi:10.1177/0193841x9301700603

National Board for Certified Counselors. (2013). *Code of ethics*. Greensboro, NC: Author.

Norcross, J. C., Krebs, P. M., & Prochaska, J. O. (2011). Stages of change. *Journal of Clinical Psychology, 67*(2), 143–154. doi:10.1002/jclp.20758

Posavac, E. J. (2011). *Program evaluation: Methods and case studies* (8th ed.). Boston, MA: Prentice Hall.

R. R. Bowker Company & Serials Solutions. (2015). *Ulrichsweb global serials directory*. Retrieved from www.ulrichsweb.com

Rogers, C. R. (1946). Significant aspects of client-centered therapy. *American Psychologist, 1*, 415–422. doi:10.1037/h0060866

Rogers, C. R. (1951). *Client-centered therapy, its current practice, implications, and theory*. Boston, MA: Houghton Mifflin.

Rose, B. (2014). *Approaching an evaluation—Ten issues to consider.* Retrieved from http://bradroseconsulting.com/index.php/approaching-an-evaluation/

Rosenthal, D., & Frank, J. D. (1956). Psychotherapy and the placebo effect. *Psychological Bulletin, 53*(4), 294–302. doi:10.1037/h0044068

Rosenzweig, S. (1936). Some implicit common factors in diverse methods of psychotherapy. *American Journal of Orthopsychiatry, 6*, 412–415.

Royse, D. D., Thyer, B. A., & Padgett, D. (2010). *Program evaluation: An introduction* (5th ed.). Belmont, CA: Wadsworth Cengage Learning.

Scriven, M. (1967). The methodology of evaluation. In R. Tyler, R. Gagne & M. Scriven (Eds.), *Perspectives of curriculum evaluation* (pp. 39–83). Chicago, IL: Rand McNally.

Stake, R. E. (1995). *The art of case study research*. Thousand Oaks, CA: Sage.

Stufflebeam, D. L. (1983). The CIPP model for program evaluation. In G. F. Madaus, M. Scriven, & D. L. Stufflebeam (Eds.), *Evaluation models: Viewpoints on educational and human services evaluation* (pp. 117–141). Boston, MA: Kluwer.

Stufflebeam, D. L. (2001). *Evaluation models*. New York, NY: Jossey-Bass Publishers.

Treasury Board of Canada Secretariat. (2010). *Evlauation guidebook for small agencies*. Ottawa, Canada: Centre of Excellence for Evaluation.

Worthen, B. (1990). Program evaluation. In H. Walberg & G. Haertel (Eds.), *The international encyclopedia of educational evaluation* (pp. 42–47). Toronto, Canada: Pergamon Press.

S • I • X

Leadership Principles

David W. Rausch and Elizabeth K. Crawford

Amy's experiences with supervision, management, and leadership have been diverse throughout her career to this point. During her employment at the psychiatric hospital, she dealt with a broad spectrum of "bosses," who she felt spanned the range from hands-off to autocratic. Even though Amy's training and education prepared her well as a clinician, she is continuing to understand her role in the supervision, management, and leadership processes. Along with this recognition, Amy realizes that her interactions in the supervisory and management roles require her to further develop her professional identity, moving beyond being an excellent clinician to engaging in the leadership process in the agency.

Amy's early experiences in balancing the role of clinician and that of clinical supervisor have shown her that she now has to deal with a number of different people and situations—clinical staff, nonclinical staff, and other stakeholders, as well as the associated business operations and processes necessary for agency management. Amy realized early on that beyond her relationships with her own clients, her supervisory responsibilities establish the need to evolve from counselor–client relationships to also include supervisor–counselor relationships and agency–client relationships.

While Amy was attending a business class last semester, she began to understand that the practice of management is more about building and developing good processes than it is about managing people. In further discussion about this concept, Amy and her professor began to examine the differences among supervision, management, and leadership. As Amy expressed an increased interest in these conceptual distinctions, her professor recommended a leadership course that she also teaches. Amy has taken her professor's advice and enrolled in this introductory leadership course this semester.

INTRODUCTION

Although there is a scarcity of specific research on leadership principles and practices and the community/mental health/clinical counseling profession at the agency level, a number of leadership theories can be related and applied to the counseling practice. As the professional identity of "counselor" continues to be defined and developed, researchers have described this concept as the cognitive frame of reference that counselors rely on to establish and accomplish their professional roles and responsibilities (Woo, Henfield, & Choi, 2014). This professional identity, along with the Principles and Practices of Leadership Excellence (PPLE), as presented by Chi Sigma Iota (1999), is supported by the recognition and application of leadership principles and behaviors within the counseling profession.

Historically, there has been much confusion over the differences between management (and supervision) and leadership. In the examination of leadership principles as they relate to supervision and agency management, it may be helpful to identify the differences among supervision, management, and leadership. As a basic definition, *supervision* is "the action or process of watching and directing what someone does or how something is done; the action or process of supervising someone or something" (Supervision, n.d.). *Management* is "the act or skill of controlling and making decisions about a business, department, ...etc.; the people who make decisions about a business, department, ...etc.; the act or process of deciding how to use something" (Management, n.d.). This definition reflects the concept that resources, decisions, and actions are managed; however, people are not managed.

For the purposes of this chapter, *leadership* is defined as a process that is established and implemented by a group of individuals working together to achieve a common goal (Northouse, 2012). In light of this definition, leadership is not the work of a single individual; it is a collaborative endeavor among the members of the group. The essence of leadership is a reflection of the relationship, not of the leader (Rost, 1993).

LEADERSHIP THEORIES AND MODELS

What is a good leader? What makes the leader *good*? How do you know? Do all good leaders share a common set of identifiable characteristics? Researchers have been attempting to answer these questions for years; the problem is that there do not appear to be clear answers. To search for a potential answer, the following is a review of leadership theories and models.

Trait and Skill Theories

Trait and skill leadership theories are based on the premise that leadership reflects the abilities of a leader. Whether these are inborn traits (trait theory) or skills that can be acquired (skill theory), both of these theoretical approaches are established from the stance that the individual, as *leader,* possesses these characteristics, which give him or her the capacity to lead. Another way to look at this is that the personal qualities possessed by an individual are the basis for the ability to lead, to be a leader, to practice leadership.

As one of the earliest leadership theories to be researched and reviewed, trait theory was established on the foundation that leaders are born, not made. Trait leadership is seen as a combined series of distinguishing qualities of an individual, which are inherited or inborn. There is much research written about the trait theory approach, and studies have established that certain specific traits contribute to those who act as a leader (Goldberg, 1990). Over the past three quarters of a century, numerous traits and characteristics have been identified as possessed by leaders. In his early work, Stogdill (1948) examined, analyzed, and synthesized over 100 studies on leadership traits over the course of four decades, from 1904–1947. The results of these studies demonstrated that those holding positions as leaders surpassed average group members in intelligence, scholarship, dependability, and sociability. In spite of these findings based on previous studies, by 1948, Stogdill concluded that it was difficult to identify a consistent and specific set of traits that would be characteristic of all leaders in all situations (Wynn, 2012). Regardless, the trait theory approach reemerged in the 1980s and may still be appealing because of the noticeable attention given to those who are out front and leading. A recent study of leadership attributes focused on five major leadership traits: intelligence, self-confidence, determination, integrity, and sociability (Northouse, 2012).

Other recent psychological research (i.e., within the past 25 years) has revealed a number of basic personality factors known as the Big Five. They are neuroticism, extraversion, openness, agreeableness, and conscientiousness. Research by Judge, Bono, Ilies, and Gerhardt (2002) identified a strong relationship between leadership and the Big Five traits. In their study, extraversion had the strongest correlation to leadership, followed by conscientiousness, neuroticism, and openness. Agreeableness was also correlated with leadership; however, the relationship was weak (Judge et al., 2002).

Related to the trait approach is the skills theory of leadership. The primary difference between the skills approach and the trait approach is the shift from personality characteristics, which are innate and believed to be inherent, to a list of characteristics, abilities, and skills that can be acquired over time. Skills are competencies that can be learned or developed. According to Katz (1955), traits are who a leader is, whereas skills are what a leader can be. According to his conceptual framework, effective leadership is built on three primary skills: technical, human, and conceptual. Unlike the trait approach, in which a leader must be born and cannot be made, the skill approach to leadership is described in a manner that makes being a leader available to everyone who is willing and able to learn, develop, and improve these skills. However, although those researchers who promote the skills approach state that it is different from the trait approach, it is still built on the basic tenets that individual characteristics (traits) play a large role in one's ability to be or become a leader. Overall, in considering these early leadership theories, the primary limiting aspects of the skills and trait approaches are that both of these theories are focused on the characteristics and exhibited traits and skills of the individual leader, and, for the most part, they do not take the follower into account.

Behavioral, Situational, Contingency, and Leader–Member Exchange Approaches

Another perspective of leadership is concerned with the behaviors that leaders exhibit. Unlike traits, skills, and abilities, behaviors can be demonstrated and observed. These behaviors are viewed as how the leader acts toward and interacts with the follower(s). In an early theory study (Lewin, Lippitt, & White, 1939), researchers analyzed what happened when leaders used leadership styles with groups of boys. These leadership styles were identified as points on a continuum from authoritarian to laissez-faire. Based on this continuum, leaders exhibit a unique style of leadership. Some leaders behave in a very authoritarian manner; they exhibit the need to control and direct what their subordinates do. According to Northouse (2012), authoritarian leaders exert influence and control over followers and remain "in charge" of the group behavior. At the other extreme of the continuum, the laissez-faire leadership style is used by leaders who do not attempt to control, nurture, or guide their followers. Using this style, sometimes labeled as "nonleadership" (Northouse, 2012), the laissez-faire leader behaves in a hands-off manner that suggests "let the subordinates do their work."

Furthering the review of the behavior of the leader, the concept behind situational leadership models and theory, also known as contingency models, is that the leader model/style/behavior changes based on the situation at hand. These models are built on the premise that no one single method or style of leadership works in every situation. Additionally, according to Sharma and Jain (2013), the situation itself will have a bigger effect on the behavior of the leader than will his or her traits—traits may be very stable over time; however, they show little consistency across all situations. Based on this model, the leader will diagnose the situation, identify the most appropriate style, and then determine the feasibility of implementation. In these cases, four dimensions must be evaluated: subordinate, supervisor/leader/manager, task characteristics, and organizational culture (Ledlow & Coppola, 2013). This conceptual viewpoint is the foundation of the premise that leadership is more about the process than the individual leader. This concept may be very attractive to counseling and other health care professions, as these environments are dynamic and stakeholder relations are multifaceted and complex.

In review of these behavioral and situational approaches, leadership behavior is based on the performance of small groups. Both behavioral and situational approaches/models are supported by Bandura's social learning theory (Bandura & McClelland, 1977), which emphasizes the importance of observing and modeling behaviors and attitudes, based on the behaviors and emotional reactions of others, namely, the followers (Ledlow & Coppola, 2013). Although these theories and models support a more comprehensive view of the group at work, they are still focused on the behaviors of the leaders as they relate to the followers.

In recent research, Uhl-Bien, Riggio, Lowe, and Carsten (2014) have reviewed the limited study of followership as it relates to leadership. As the process viewpoint of leadership cannot exist without followership, recognizing and analyzing the behaviors of followers are critical components of understanding the leadership process. Uhl-Bien et al. (2014) reviewed a number of leadership and followership studies that echoed the findings of prior leadership behavioral theory, which focused on the behaviors of leaders as they move followers toward a goal. Many of these studies concentrate on the relationship between the leaders and the followers. These reviews are built on the recognition that relational dynamics are important to the leadership process and are dependent on the mutual influence of leaders and followers.

One prominent theory of followership as it relates to leadership is the leader–member exchange (LMX) theory. While studying this theory, researchers (Graen & Uhl-Bien, 1995) examined the ways in which leaders and followers engage one another to promote and create high-quality work relationships, which are the foundation for producing effective leadership outcomes. LMX theory operationalizes the relationship-based approach to leadership. Central to this concept is that effective leadership processes occur between leaders and followers who have developed mature relationships (partnerships). At this stage in the relationship, both leaders and followers count on each other for loyalty and support. Through mutual respect and trust, the leadership process is fully developed and results in more effective leadership outcomes (Graen & Uhl-Bien, 1995). With the increased focus on behavior, situations, and relationship, these views of leadership do include the importance of followership; however, they are still primarily focused on the leader and his or her connections to followers.

Transformational: Servant, Authentic, and Instrumental Approaches

Over the past few decades, there has been a shift in the study of leadership to review the process rather than simply the parties involved. According to Burns (1978), transformational leadership refers to the process of building a commitment to organizational objectives and empowering followers to accomplish the objective. This process of leadership is based on a stream of evolving interrelationships in which leaders are continually evoking motivational responses from followers and modifying their own behavior as they meet resistance and/or responsiveness in a ceaseless process of flow and counterflow. Bass (1999) summarizes his explanation by stating that at the macro level of analysis, transformational leadership involves shaping, expressing, and mediating conflict among groups of people in addition to motivating individuals. This process of leadership changes and transforms. The person in the leadership role engages with others and creates a connection that raises the level of motivation and morality in both the leader and the follower. Subordinates (followers) connect to the transformational leader through trust, admiration, loyalty, and respect (Ledlow & Coppola, 2013).

One aspect of transformational leadership is servant leadership, which emphasizes the importance of leaders being attentive to the needs and concerns of followers. Servant leaders put the followers first; they empower them, nurture them, and help them to develop to full capacity (Northouse, 2012). In addition, the servant leadership model is built on the premise that servant leaders are ethical and attempt to promote the greater good. Conceptually identified by Robert Greenleaf, who founded the Center for Servant Leadership, servant leadership is built on 10 characteristics of leaders (Northouse, 2012, pp. 221–223):

1. Listening
2. Empathy
3. Healing
4. Awareness
5. Persuasion
6. Conceptualization
7. Foresight
8. Stewardship
9. Commitment to the growth of people
10. Building community

Although the focus of servant leadership appears to be on the leader and leader behavior, the perceived outcomes of servant leadership include follower performance and growth, organizational performance, and societal impact.

One of the most recent areas for transformational leadership research focuses on the concept of authentic leadership. Although no single definition has been agreed on in the literature regarding authentic leadership, the focus thus far centers on the interpersonal relationship perspective and includes leaders, followers, peers, supervisors, work setting, and culture. Avolio, Walumbwa, and Weber (2009) state that authentic leadership is composed of four interrelated components:

1. Self-awareness—understanding one's own strengths, weaknesses, and sense-making
2. Internalized moral perspective—being guided by internal moral standards
3. Balanced processing—analyzing relevant data objectively prior to making a decision
4. Relational transparency—sharing information openly and presenting one's authentic self as appropriate in a situation

According to Nyberg and Sveningsson (2014), authentic leadership is assumed to provide improved organizational culture, work performance, engagement in organizational citizenship, and trust in leadership. One of the purported strengths of authentic leadership is that this principle fulfills an expressed and recognized societal need for trustworthy leadership (Northouse, 2012). Similar to transformational leadership, researchers identify the need for authentic leaders to work with followers in order to foster positive self-development.

A number of researchers, including Antonakis and House (2014), consider an additional aspect of transformational leadership to be instrumental leadership. In this model, the leader applies his or her expert knowledge to monitor the environment and performance, including the implementation of strategic and tactical solutions. Those who are in leadership positions deal with challenges that arise from dynamic environments, and the instrumental leader helps to align human efforts toward strategic and operational goals. Antonakis and House (2014) identify four factors of instrumental leadership:

1. Environmental monitoring
2. Strategy formulation and implementation
3. Path–goal facilitation
4. Outcome monitoring

Environmental monitoring is the first of the four factors of strategic instrumental leadership and is concerned with knowing organizational strengths and weaknesses, and identifying opportunities by scanning both the internal and the external organizational environments. Leadership actions that focus on developing policies, goals, and objectives to support mission and vision are identified as *strategy formulation and implementation*. By setting attainable levels, leadership can increase the likelihood of organizational goal achievement. The *path–goal facilitation* factor addresses leader behavior as it relates to facilitating goal achievement through support, resources, removal of obstacles, and clarification of the goal and direction to be taken. By providing performance-enhancing feedback in a positive manner, the leadership observes the ongoing follower performance and provides constructive feedback, or *outcome monitoring*. Through examination of these factors, the instrumental leadership model adds a critical aspect of the transformational leadership perspective.

As Amy continues to learn more about leadership and leadership theory, as well as to work closely with the three prelicensure counselors she supervises, she decides that she needs to put these transformational leadership processes into practice. Amy seeks to build on her initial decision to include the counselors' perceptions as they relate to the working relationships with herself, the counselors she supervises, and the agency. During her next supervisory session, she shares with the group her understanding of the philosophy of leadership as it relates to how they conduct their practice, and she and her team begin to work on developing a shared vision of how as a group they can define and refine their client service processes.

LEADERSHIP AS A PROCESS

Supervision, Management, and Leadership

The study of leadership has moved from the early examination of traits and skills, gradually shifting to the viewpoint that the behavior and actions of leaders are dependent or contingent on the behaviors and actions of followers (as well as to the situation and the environment), and finally to an understanding that leadership is a process separate from supervision and management (Figure 6.1). This does not mean that employees or staff should be treated with a laissez-faire approach and simply be left alone to do as they will without guidance or direction. In addition, resources and processes will need to be managed and organized for the leadership process to begin. Similar to the definition stated earlier in the chapter, *leadership* is defined as: *the process results that occur when a group of individuals work together, through shared relationships and communication, to achieve a common goal or vision*. This concept has been emphasized by a number of the theories reviewed, beginning with the followership studies and supported by the transformational leadership theories.

FIGURE 6.1 • Leadership as a process.

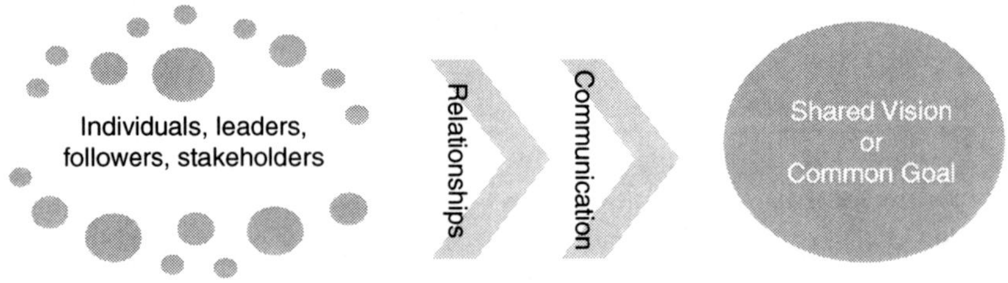

Copyright © 2014 by D. W. Rausch and E. K. Crawford.

We, Not You or I

Leadership is not about the leader or the follower specifically, but is grounded in the process of working together for a common organizational goal. The conceptual framework is built on the premise that the process of leadership is not about *you or I*; it is about *we*. Through the development of relationships and trust, coupled with communication and clearly identified processes, we all work together to achieve a common goal. Kouzes and Posner (2006) believe that the road to a great leadership process includes the following five key components: (1) challenge an existing process that needs to be improved; (2) inspire a shared vision with followers; (3) enable others to act by sharing the tools and methods for solution; (4) model the way by doing and showing, not telling; and (5) encourage the heart of the group by sharing the glory.

Uhl-Bien et al. (2014) provide an even clearer understanding of the concept of *we, not you or I*, in their statement that leadership as a process does not make assumptions that leading and following are in any way equated with positions within the organization. In any process, those in leadership positions may follow, and those with subordinate roles may lead toward the shared vision. This approach is built on the assumption that the leadership process can only occur through combined acts of leading and following. Conversely, if a person within the organization attempts to influence others, yet does not achieve any followership behavior, then there is no leadership process. By thinking about leadership and followership as behaviors and processes, instead of titles and positions, Uhl-Bien et al. (2014) believe that we can begin to see and define leadership in more meaningful ways.

LEADERSHIP IN A MENTAL HEALTH WORLD: ESTABLISHING AND STRIVING FOR A SHARED VISION

In light of these theories and the professional practice of counselors and others in the mental health field, how can the concept of leadership as a process be applied in a mental health world? Counselor leadership has been defined as:

> Leadership is defined to be those actions by individuals in professional counseling that contribute to the realization of our individual and collective capacity to serve others competently, ethically, and justly as helping professionals. This leadership

> can be found in all settings and at all levels from local through international service to others needing and desiring our assistance. (Sweeney, 2011, p. 5)

Sweeney further suggests that in all counselor settings and specialties, there are stories of advocacy and leadership. Along with Lewis (2011), who states that counselors are by nature leaders across professional roles and activities, he reiterates the need for individuals who are committed and passionate about achieving the vision of meeting the counseling needs of society to be well versed in the practice of leadership. Because of the gap in formal literature and guidelines for leadership in the counseling profession, the Chi Sigma Iota (CSI) Principles and Practices of Leadership Excellence were developed (Fulton & Shannonhouse, 2014). These 10 PPLEs were created to provide a framework for best practices and leadership ethics, in order to inform counselor decisions and actions.

In review of the CSI PPLEs (Wahesh & Myers, 2014), many of the principles reflect and align with the leadership process model. For example:

- Principle 1, recognition of service, is supported by the servant leadership model.
- Principle 2, commitment to mission, aligns with the process of working together to achieve a shared mission (or vision).
- Principles 7 through 10—respect for membership, mentoring, recognition of others, and feedback and self-reflection—all echo the underlying viewpoints of transformational, servant, and other process leadership theories.

Specific application of one or more of these principles may be seen in a number of aspects of counselors' professional practice. As mental health professionals learn and develop their professional identity, characteristics—such as caring and respect for the needs of others—have been found to be important for effective counseling leadership (Lewis, 2011). In their article about counselor community engagement (CCE), Fulton and Shannonhouse (2014) highlight the connection of servant leadership with community-based service. CCE is seen as a collaboration between professional counselors and the community in an effort to promote well-being and human dignity. As such, the principles of servant leadership—such as attending to the needs of others—can and should be applied. As professional counselors are enmeshed in the process of social influence and the social learning process, they are likely to see themselves as being in relationships with a number of stakeholders, including clients, agency professionals, community members, and more. This viewpoint aligns with the concept of leadership as a process whereby a group of individuals work together to achieve a common goal. This practice of leadership with organizational members, community members/stakeholders, and other mental health professionals working toward a common goal of serving others *competently, ethically, and justly as helping professionals* is the basis of a shared vision for the profession. In building the professional identity of the practicing counselor, an understanding and appreciation of the premise of leadership as a process may help to foster a continuous effort to work together in any setting toward a shared vision or common goal—whereby professional counselors can contribute to and support leadership as a process.

SUMMARY

Leadership is a process, not a person, position, or title. The process of leadership is exhibited in the behaviors of leaders and followers, who may not be identifiable by their official roles within the organization or situation. Although historically the literature has focused on the given traits (inborn) or skills (learned) of a leader, current research and review of professional practice reveal that leadership should be viewed as a process of individuals working together to achieve a common goal or shared vision. Despite a lack of specific literature on the subject of leadership in the mental health professions, review of the professional practice overlaid with the conceptual framework of leadership as a process reveals that the theoretical basis aligns clearly within the counseling profession; specifically, the practice of servant leadership is clearly evident. In a special edition of the *Chi Sigma Iota Exemplar* on exemplary leadership, Gibson (2013) noted that in the counseling profession, leadership begins with the individual and then is continued with service to and for others. This clearly echoes the view that the professional counselor is a part of the leadership process.

The concept of leadership as a process is difficult to grasp when the world around us, through media, movies, books, and more, continually highlights the traits and abilities of what are perceived to be great leaders. As we view counseling practice through the lens of leadership as a process, the concepts of the profession align well with the theoretical constructs. The nature of the mental health field is one of multiple constituencies working together to promote the well-being and mental health of individuals and communities, and the process of leadership is a natural fit for implementation in professional practice.

REFLECTION QUESTIONS

1. Reflect and describe the role of leadership as a process as it relates to your professional practice (current or future).
2. Reflect and describe the impact of leadership on a counseling organization or agency.
3. In small groups, identify and describe a situation in which the application of leadership as a process could/should be used to achieve a common goal (shared vision).
4. Reflect and describe on a situation in which you experienced different leaders demonstrating negative or positive behaviors and the impact that had on the group.

SUGGESTED RESOURCES

Bennis, W. G. (1959). Leadership theory and administrative behavior: The problem of authority. *Administrative Science Quarterly*, 259–301.

Darling, J. R., & Nurmi, R. W. (2009). Key contemporary paradigms of management and leadership: A linguistic exploration and case for managerial leadership. *European Business Review*, *21*(3), 201–214.

Nienaber, H. (2010). Conceptualisation of management and leadership. *Management Decision, 48*(5), 661–675.

REFERENCES

Antonakis, J., & House, R. J. (2014). Instrumental leadership: Measurement and extension of transformational–transactional leadership theory. *Leadership Quarterly, 25*(4), 746–771.

Avolio, B. J., Walumbwa, F. O., & Weber, T. J. (2009). Leadership: Current theories, research, and future directions. *Annual Review of Psychology, 60*, 421–449.

Bandura, A., & McClelland, D. C. (1977). *Social learning theory*. Oxford, UK: Prentice Hall.

Bass, B. M. (1999). Two decades of research and development in transformational leadership. *European Journal of Work and Organizational Psychology, 8*(1), 9–32.

Burns, J. M. (1978). *Leadership*. New York, NY: Harper & Row.

Chi Sigma Iota. (1999). *Principles and practices of leadership excellence*. Retrieved from https://www.csi-net.org/?page=Leadership_Practices

Fulton, C. L., & Shannonhouse, L. (2014). Developing servant leadership through counselor community engagement: A case example. *Journal of Counselor Leadership and Advocacy, 1*(1), 98–111.

Gibson, D. (2013). Editorial—Special edition: Exemplary leadership. *Chi Sigma Iota Exemplar, 28*(2), 1, 12.

Goldberg, L. R. (1990). An alternative "description of personality": The big-five factor structure. *Journal of Personality and Social Psychology, 59*(6), 1216–1229.

Graen, G. B., & Uhl-Bien, M. (1995). Relationship-based approach to leadership: Development of leader-member exchange (LMX) theory of leadership over 25 years: Applying a multi-level multi-domain perspective. *Leadership Quarterly, 6*(2), 219–247.

Judge, T. A., Bono, J. E., Ilies, R., & Gerhardt, M. W. (2002). Personality and leadership: A qualitative and quantitative review. *Journal of Applied Psychology, 87*(4), 765–780.

Katz, R. L. (1955). Skills of an effective administrator. *Harvard Business Review, 33*(1), A33–A42.

Kouzes, J. M., & Posner, B. Z. (2003). *The leadership challenge* (Vol. 3). San Francisco, CA: Jossey-Bass.

Ledlow, G. J. R., & Coppola, M. N. (2013). *Leadership for health professionals* (2nd ed.). Burlington, MA: Jones & Bartlett.

Lewin, K., Lippitt, R., & White, R. K. (1939). Patterns of aggressive behavior in experimentally created "social climates." *Journal of Social Psychology, 10*(2), 269–299.

Lewis, T. F. (2011). Foundations of leadership: Theory, philosophy, and research. In C. Y. Chang, A. L. Dixon, & C. A. B. Minton (Eds.), *Professional counseling excellence through leadership and advocacy* (pp. 21–40). New York, NY: Routledge.

Management. (n.d.). In *Merriam-Webster's online dictionary*. Retrieved from http://www.merriam-webster.com/dictionary/management

Northouse, P. G. (2012). *Leadership: Theory and practice* (6th ed.). Thousand Oaks, CA: Sage.

Nyberg, D., & Sveningsson, S. (2014). Paradoxes of authentic leadership: Leader identity struggles. *Leadership, 10*(4), 437–455. doi:10.1177/1742715013504425

Rost, J. C. (1993). Leadership development in the new millennium. *Journal of Leadership & Organizational Studies, 1*(1), 91–110.

Sharma, M. K., & Jain, M. S. (2013). Leadership management: Principles, models and theories. *Global Journal of Management and Business Studies, 3*(3), 309–318.

Stogdill, R. M. (1948). Personal factors associated with leadership: A survey of the literature. *Journal of Psychology, 25*(1), 35–71.

Supervision. (n.d.). In *Merriam-Webster's online dictionary*. Retrieved from http://www.merriam-webster.com/dictionary/supervision

Sweeney, T. J. (2011). Leadership for the counseling profession. In C. Y. Chang, A. L. Dixon, & C. A. B. Minton (Eds.), *Professional counseling excellence through leadership and advocacy* (pp. 3–20). New York, NY: Routledge.

Uhl-Bien, M., Riggio, R. E., Lowe, K. B., & Carsten, M. K. (2014). Followership theory: A review and research agenda. *Leadership Quarterly, 25*(1), 83–104.

Wahesh, E., & Myers, J. E. (2014). Principles and practices of leadership excellence: CSI chapter presidents' experience, perceived competence, and rankings of importance. *Journal of Counselor Leadership and Advocacy, 1*(1), 83–97.

Woo, H., Henfield, M. S., & Choi, N. (2014). Developing a unified professional identity in counseling: A review of the literature. *Journal of Counselor Leadership and Advocacy, 1*(1), 1–15.

Wynn, S. R. (2012). Trait theory. In *Encyclopedia of educational leadership and administration*. Retrieved from http://www.sagepub.com/northouse6e/study/ materials/reference/reference2.1.pdf

S • E • V • E • N

Budgeting and Fiscal Management for Counselors

Dana Lee Baker, Allison Louise Smith, and Deanna L. Sharpe

By the time that Amy was hired at the community mental health agency, her clinical experience spanned a variety of behavioral health settings. Amy is committed to providing counseling services to the community, but she also wishes to acquire the leadership skills necessary to assume more responsibility within the agency and advance her career. As Amy develops as a clinician, she might consider also working outside a mental health agency, but she will need to learn about fiscal management in the context of running a practice. Amy has likely found that at the community agency treatment has been funded by grants, public insurance, and occasionally self-pay or private insurance. Practice outside of a community agency cannot rely on grant payments and therefore practitioners must develop fiscal-management tools. Learning to use these tools will allow Amy to run a successful small business.

INTRODUCTION

Helping professions tend toward an ethic of self-sacrifice. Coming to terms with budgeting and financial management can be at best an afterthought and, at worst, anathema to the professional counselor. All too often the process of becoming a professional counselor involves coping with reminders from parents, life partners, friends, and society at large that choosing this profession implies deciding against a variety of potentially more lucrative careers. One defense against this criticism is to cite a higher calling beyond the simple desire to collect a paycheck. As a result, finding oneself thinking about budgeting and financial management from (generally) the dawn of one's professional career until (ideally) the day of one's retirement party can be a source of frustration for the professional counselor.

Sustaining an ability to help others requires meeting one's own basic needs. In the absence of independent wealth, failure to develop sound budgeting and financial management skills leads to stress, uncertainty, and, in the worst-case scenario, insolvency. In their book, *How Psychotherapists Develop*, Orlinsky and Ronnestad (2013) define *psychotherapy* as "therapeutic work [that] is a skilled service performed as gainful employment, an activity through which one earns one's living" (p. 11). Being a professional counselor implies being professional in all senses of the word. This does not mean that every counselor needs to gain an understanding of financial management and budgeting at the level expected of a certified accountant or financial analyst. It does, however, mean that a solid understanding of a few key basics of financial management and budgeting is fundamental to good clinical practice. In this chapter, we first discuss three key elements of sound fiscal management: (1) claiming an untapped or at least unsaturated part of the mental health market, (2) creating a business plan that articulates how you will serve the selected slice of the mental health market with fiscal responsibility, and (3) designing a strategy for day-to-day fiscal operations that attends to both income and expenses and accounts for predictable cash flow challenges while still allowing the counselor to work with a deliberately chosen level of diversity of payment sources (and, therefore, in all likelihood, diversity of individual circumstances). Toward the end of the chapter, we explore the longer term, less certain, aspects of budgeting and financial management for counselors.

YOUR PIECE OF THE PIE

Many individuals enter counseling, therapy, or social work programs intending to someday provide individual or family counseling in an individual or group practice. They receive clinical training both in the classroom and through internships and become increasingly committed to developing their skills in the service of best helping their clients. Few aspiring counselors, however, have opportunities to identify and develop the skills that are necessary for the financial management of a psychotherapy practice. As a result, it can be difficult for novice counselors to discern whether or not these types of work settings would constitute a good professional match for them.

Even so, by the time many counselors obtain their degrees, they have discovered which aspects of mental health counseling and therapy most capture their interest. Some are captivated by working with children; others thrive working with families. Often students and beginning practitioners already have a sense of what kinds of treatment modalities best fit their own working styles. Counselors and therapists (hereinafter referred to as counselors) can benefit from determining the areas within mental health counseling in which they would like to specialize, and then deciding which type of organizational structure would have the best chance of supporting the type of counseling work to which they are drawn.

A number of factors can influence specialization, including early clinical opportunities to work with specific populations or personal commitment to alleviating certain kinds of human distress. Specialization can be influenced by other factors as well, including postgraduate training and available mentorship or supervision opportunities. Among the relevant factors, continuing training and supervision can considerably affect the development of a specialization. For example, counselors who join an agency or group practice might find themselves working with children and families. Ideally, they will receive supervision at their workplace or they might pursue it independently. Their developing competencies will shape specialization.

Other practical matters can influence choice of specialization as well. The number of potential clients and referral sources can direct the type of clients with whom a clinician gains professional experience and could then build a caseload that would provide sufficient revenue. Paying attention to the iterative relationship between the particular type of work that sparks the counselor's interest and the needs of the community as demonstrated by the quantity of available clients facilitates identification of a target market.

Competition is not often acknowledged among counselors, most of whom value collaboration and connection with others. Competition exists, however, in obtaining and retaining paying clients. One of the most significant aspects of competition is the number of other counselors in the immediate area who offer the same therapeutic services to similar clients. Often counselors distinguish themselves by employing particular modalities of therapeutic work. Some work from a psychodynamic perspective, others from a family systems point of view. Still other professionals focus on structured cognitive behavioral therapy (CBT) or dialectical behavioral therapy (DBT) treatments in individual or group settings. In a sense, counselors compete to the degree to which their theoretical commitments are considered desirable by potential clients. Of course, offering only a particular modality could also diminish the number of potential clients. Within communities of like-minded practitioners, basic competition is inevitable.

In the real world of clinical work, however, competition coexists with cooperation. Competition takes place in a connected and ultimately, largely collaborative network. Counselors network with each other for professional support, as well as to identify professionals with specific competences to whom to refer clients when necessary. Counselors join consultation groups both to develop their understanding of clinical processes and to offer support to and obtain support from colleagues. From the perspective of fiscal management, distinguishing one's work and becoming known among other professionals as a skilled and committed clinician is a key aspect of both competition and collaboration. Remember, the reality is that relationships with other providers will vary across time, geographic locations, and disciplinary perspectives. Maintaining professional and largely positive relationships with other practitioners is vital. Taking good, but subtle, note of practitioners who violate the principles of fair collaboration is also good practice. It is important to remember to check on one's perspective and the potential for other points of view. However, it is a good idea to take notice of practitioners who are less supportive of their colleagues and engage in professional gossip. In addition, it can be useful to make note of practitioners who do not carefully consider the conflict of interest in accepting a new patient currently seeing another therapist, as the client may benefit from returning to the other therapist.

PUTTING YOUR BUSINESS ON PAPER

Once a target market has been identified, successfully establishing a practice involves creating a business plan. A business plan helps a provider move from being focused on good intentions to being focused on results (Dart, 2004). This process may be overwhelming at first. However, it is better to be in a position of defining results through the careful articulation of a business plan than one defined by external stakeholders or considered too risky an enterprise with which to partner. As explained by Rebecca Clay, "every private practitioner should have one if they want to monitor their practice's health, move into a new niche or seek outside funding for expanding their practices" (Clay, 2000, p. 48). To be considered viable in the medium term, counselors, as well as other entities, benefit from the existence of a solid business plan that can be consulted as a guide in times of stress, confusion, growth, or change.

Determining business goals typically involves some compromise that nevertheless supports the ideals of the provider. A business plan is necessary even if the entity is not, strictly speaking, a business. The directive that a public or nonprofit organization should be run like a business is often heard and almost always appealing to the general public. What this means to the general public is inconsistent and not necessarily rooted in the realities of public service (Dart, 2004). However, to the extent that business is used as a proxy for being professional and efficient, the maxim makes sense. Goals and plans for attaining them must be identified with as much specificity as possible in any professional endeavor. It is important to note that private practices are often for profit, even if focused on enhancing the lives of others. Although profit might not be the first on the list of goals of a for-profit provider, overt shaming of those who list profit among their primary goals detracts from the overall collegiality of the profession. Finally, not all counselors are in private practice or serving in a management capacity in a larger organization. However, understanding the basics of business plan development can help all counselors better understand organizational decision making, which affects their jobs on a daily basis and, in the long term, their careers.

A business plan is a document specifying the services (or product), market, financial position, and anticipated avenues for growth of an organization. A crucial intended audience of a business plan is generally the practitioner. If working with a partner or team, the business plan can also help identify differences in experiential reality that, if left untended, could lead to mission creep or dissonance in the day-to-day operations of the practice. As Kasewurm (2008) put it, "a business plan describes the who, what, when, where, why, and how of a good adventure story" (p. 259). A well-composed business plan helps ensure all primary actors seek to enact the same story. Business plans are also sometimes called *feasibility studies* (De Thomas & Derammelaere, 2008); however, this language can be confusing and can erroneously be taken to mean that the document is no longer necessary once a business is up and running. Determining business goals and direction through the creation of a formal but compelling document is fundamental to creating a successful practice over the long term.

Other audiences for a business plan include such stakeholders as potential investors, grant-giving organizations, and, of course, clients. Authoring a business plan forces the professional into thinking about client perspectives, including reasons for seeking out help. A business plan must be designed to make a good first impression. As Brian Finch put it, "the story of you, your business and what you propose to do with it is a fascinating story: tell it that way. . . . It is an exciting story of good ideas and hard work leading to success" (Finch, 2013, p. 6). Ultimately, a business plan is a rational expression of a dream.

The composition of business plans will vary according to factors such as the size of the practice, the complexity and saturation of the market, and the diversity of the target client base. There is no mandated length or table of contents. However, the generally recommended length for most counseling contexts is under 10 pages. In the electronic age, using consulting templates developed by other practitioners and professional groups is both possible and advisable. For example, business plan templates are available online from the Small Business Development Center at www.sbdcnet.org. Sample business plans (both real and created examples) can also be located through an online search using standard search engines. Working with advice and examples provides an opportunity to get a good feel for the nature of these documents. Even so, it is important to be judicious about the degree to which one relies on these sources in the creation of one's own business plan. Business plans must retain a degree of originality tied to the unique character and intent of the particular practice. Balance between situating and differentiating your practice in creation of the business plan for your practice.

Information included in a business plan must be accurate, persuasive, and presented in an easy-to-follow, logical format. Typically recommended components of a business plan include:

1. A well-designed cover sheet (with appropriate graphic design, logo, and/or pictures—all items that can be used later in business cards, advertisements, and presentations)
2. Table of contents
3. An executive summary (one to two pages at most)
4. Vision and mission statements
5. Description of the practice and services
6. Market analysis (including a description of competition, as appropriate)
7. Articulation of management structure and operations
8. Strategic implementation plan (including projections for growth over the next 3 to 5 years)
9. Financial statements

A business plan should be as long as it needs to be (and no longer!). The content must be optimistic, but never overstated. Infusing empirical facts accessibly throughout the document makes the document and the story it tells more compelling and believable. In incorporating measurable facts, it is crucial to keep in mind that business plans are not made for once and for all. If multiple versions of a business plan are created to target different audiences, it is important that any differences be limited to style rather than content (Finch, 2013). One way to achieve this result is to vary the amount and level of detail (but never the message!) of the data presented.

Financial documents should include estimates of cash flow. Remember that being profitable and having good cash flow are related, but not identical. A practice might be profitable and still become seriously compromised if cash flow does not cover costs when they come due. Costs are generally divided into three standard categories: fixed costs, step-fixed costs, and variable costs. Fixed costs are costs that remain the same no matter how many client sessions are conducted. Typical examples include rent for office space and phone service. Step-fixed costs are costs that increase each time a threshold of service is reached. In other words, step-fixed costs might remain steady between 0 and 20 sessions a week, then increase to another steady rate for 21 to 40 sessions, and so on. Variable costs depend more closely on the number of sessions provided to clients. Understanding the differences among these categories is crucial to accurate presentation of potential cash flow in a business plan. Additional help in understanding and applying these concepts can be found at the federal Small Business Administration website (www.sbs.gov). Also, local universities and community colleges may offer free one-on-one consultations as part of an outreach program in entrepreneurship development.

Financial documents present in a business plan should also include a break-even analysis. A break-even analysis involves a calculation of exactly how much revenue must be secured in order to keep a business viable in the short term. Break-even analysis should include differentiation of the types of costs. It should also explicitly consider the level of risk assumed when calculating the estimate presented in the business plan. Eliminating risk for business operations is, of course, impossible. For the counselor, an ever-present risk is failure to pay on the part of the client and/or unanticipated separation from services. Degree of acceptable risk is a personal decision. Discussing the preferred level of risk in the context of the break-even analysis helps readers of a business plan better understand the assumptions present in the operations of the practice, especially as articulated in the strategic implementation plan.

As a final note, attend closely to standard formatting, quality of paper for printed copies, and presentation style in business plans. It *should* be true that good ideas will be recognized regardless of the form in which they are presented. However, good ideas and potential partnerships too often go unnoticed when packaged without appeal or, worse, with an appearance of sloppiness. As Kasewurm (2008) put it, "the primary purpose of writing a business plan is to gain a deep understanding of the opportunity the entrepreneur is presenting" (p. 260). Clarity counts. Professionalism counts. A business plan that includes both good ideas and excellent presentation will generate excitement on the part of potential stakeholders and serve the practice in the long run. A business plan missing either of these elements will hurt the practice pervasively and, generally, in ways that will be next to impossible to detect.

ON THE UP AND UP: ADVISORY SUPPORT

Advisory support can be an excellent source of feedback on a business plan. Generally speaking, advisors should not be directly involved in the initial drafting of a business plan. Rather, selected advisors should be asked to comment on a draft once composed. Some recommend that authors of business plans keep careful records of all copies of business plan drafts. This suggestion involves assigning a separate number to each (paper) copy of the business plan and logging the person to whom the copy of the plan was given and on what date. Two issues stand in the way of such cautionary practices, however. First, in the electronic age, advisors might prefer an electronic copy of a document and would encounter few technological barriers to creating a copy of a numbered document. Use of "track changes" in Microsoft Word (or the equivalent in other software) provides some level of protection against this concern, as it allows for the keeping of a reasonably accurate record of comments, commentators, and the timing of feedback embedded in the document with a time stamp (assuming all who work with the document use the tool proactively). Second, selection of advisors should be done with a level of care and caution, which includes the provision that individuals selected to serve in this capacity be trustworthy enough to support access to confidential and sensitive information without a need for such external assurances of honesty. It is, nevertheless, a good idea to keep track of all distributed copies of a business plan in order to assure that feedback has been requested and obtained from those who have been asked to provide advisory support.

Formal advisory boards remain somewhat rare in private practice. Professional counselors typically work with two types of advisory support: informal/quid pro quo and professional. Informal advisory support involves drawing insight from professionals or knowledgeable individuals who are asked to provide advice on a periodic basis on general elements of the practice. Under most circumstances, it is also important to secure paid, professional support from individuals with particular skills fundamental to legal and effective practice. Whereas it is almost always tempting to do without such support in the form of lawyers, accountants, and payroll specialists, working without these specialists almost always increases the risk incurred by the practice and creates a great deal of extra work to be completed by the writer of the business plan.

KEEPING THINGS IN BALANCE

Counselors are typically helpers and facilitators, drawn to the counseling profession because they want to encourage the positive development of others. To provide that service in a private practice, however, counselors must also be business minded. To build a financially sound practice, careful attention must be given to start-up expenses, short- and long-term financial plans, the operating budget, business cash flow, and tax planning. After all, the positive development of others will be short lived if the practice cannot sustain itself!

Start-Up Expenses

Numerous expenses are associated with starting a counseling practice. Some of these initial expenses occur only once, whereas others are required for business start-up and remain ongoing. The specific type and amount of start-up expenses will depend, to some extent, on decisions made as the business plan develops. For example, as part of early business planning, a target market for potential clients should be identified based on a counselor's area of expertise and a thorough market analysis. Location of this target market information influences choice of the business site and consequently affects location-related expenses.

Of course, market information always captures a less-than-complete picture of reasons a counselor selects a particular location. Choosing a business site involves trade-offs. Therapists often, but not always, prefer to establish offices in areas where other therapists practice. There may also be a perception that there are more potential clients in these areas. However, this may mean higher rent. Leases can also vary by location. Offices in professional districts may require a 2-, 3-, or 5-year commitment. Offices in less desirable areas may offer more favorable terms. Some therapists choose to establish offices where fewer practitioners are located and rents are generally lower, but at the risk of attracting fewer clients and feeling isolated from other therapists. Difficult choices abound. For example, a child's school or parent's adult care facility might be less close than would be ideal to the best location from the perspective of a market analysis. Deciding carefully involves considering the full spectrum of factors affecting the quality of a particular location for a particular therapist at the individual and generally quite personal level.

Before the practice can accept clients, several fees and expenses must be paid. The counselor will need to secure a professional license. If insurance money is to be collected as a form of payment, state laws that impose restrictions must be recognized. For instance, some state insurance boards mandate that counselors cannot perform a formal assessment without including a psychologist, a rule that can limit scope of practice. Securing approval from insurance boards can be a very time-consuming process, involving weeks or even months. Consequently, a reasonable time frame for securing all of the licenses and approvals for practice is a useful addition to the business plan. Local, county, and state governments may assess a fee or require purchase of a business license for business operation. Legal and accounting fees might be incurred in establishing the business structure. A location must be secured. Rented office space will typically require a security deposit along with first and last month's rent. Purchase of an office would require funds upfront for a down payment and closing costs. Carving out office space in one's home may require some structural modifications. Signage needs to be designed and posted. Utilities must be paid.

Office furnishings are needed to foster client comfort as well as to provide an appropriate work space for processing and storing business records. Basic office equipment for a counseling practice would include a computer, printer, copier, fax machine, locking file cabinets, and a phone. Software needed to complete client assessments, documentation, accounting, and billing must also be acquired. To protect client confidentiality, digital storage of client data and records will require purchase and use of encryption software programs. Rental of off-site digital or physical storage space to hold backup copies of business records can be a consideration. Office supplies, such as paper, pens, paper clips, staples, envelopes, and stamps, must be obtained.

Some type of marketing or advertising will be needed to let potential clients know about the services a counselor offers. Outreach to potential clients can take several forms. Associated costs can range from low to moderate to high, depending on the methods used. Some form of grand-opening event will be needed to announce the start of the business to the surrounding community. Will ads be placed in traditional media, such as newspaper, radio, or television, or will forms of social media be used? A website or newsletter for client or professional communities can be developed. Connections can be made with the public and professional colleagues through giving presentations and classes, or establishing a referral system.

Business structure is another critical initial decision that has important financial and tax implications. The counseling practice of one individual can be structured as a sole proprietorship or a limited liability corporation (LLC). If two or more individuals are involved in the practice, it can be structured as a partnership or public liability corporation (PLC). An important similarity for each of these four forms of business ownership is that business income and losses pass through the business to the individual owner or to the partners in their proportionate share. Taxes on net business income are then paid by the individual owner or each partner. A key difference among these forms of business ownership deals with business liabilities. In a limited liability corporation or a public liability corporation, the business owner or partners are not *personally* liable for business debts. If the business incurs a debt that cannot be repaid or if a judgment is levied against the business, creditors can only seize business assets, not the assets of the owner or partners. This legal barrier does not exist if the business is structured as a sole proprietorship or partnership.

Financial plans make explicit the actions and resources needed to achieve desired business objectives. In effect, financial plans serve as the road map of the business, specifying the goals, guidelines, and benchmarks that must be met to keep the business viable, strong, and growing. Development of financial plans forces careful evaluation of the size and source of potential business income and expenses. Financial plans can be classified by the time frame considered (immediate or future) or by function (planning or tracking actual cash flow).

Short-term financial plans focus on business revenue and expenses month to month or over a year. Long-term financial plans look ahead 3, 5, or 10 years. Long-term financial plans are typically broader in scope than short-term plans, looking beyond the day-to-day business operations to include such things as future expansion or retirement funding plans. As a practical matter, use of a spreadsheet program facilitates recording and evaluating the data related to business financial planning. Use of a spreadsheet program also makes it easier to evaluate various potential outcomes when considering several "what if" scenarios.

Of necessity, short- and long-term financial plans are based on estimates and assumptions. Although the future cannot be known for sure, it is important to base projections on the best information available. When developing plans, note the assumptions made. Base estimates on historical trends, your own experience, or the experience of professional colleagues. Pay close attention to any emerging trends that might affect the number or needs of clients. Financial plans are flexible. Adjustments can be made as one gains more information or experience.

Whether short term or long term in focus, sound financial plans fulfill several critical functions (Hill, 2014) as they:

- Guide daily business decisions
- Prioritize expenditures
- Evaluate reasonableness of assumptions through comparison of estimated income and expenses against actual figures
- Indicate size of reserve fund needed as a cushion against variation in income and expenses

- Highlight potential opportunities and challenges in business operation and growth
- Encourage a long-range perspective of business operations
- Measure progress
- Provide a systematic method to continually improve business performance

FEES AND THEIR FOIBLES

Counselors must extensively consider how to set the full fee for services rendered. It can be a challenge initially to establish the amount of money one's professional skills and time are worth. Counselors generally consult their colleagues with similar credentials to estimate the average professional rate for treatment in a given area. Clinicians can also review listings in online counselor directories to determine what other counselors in a city or town charge.

After setting a full fee, counselors who are considering joining insurance panels often assess the reimbursement rates of various health insurance plans. Insurance companies will send fee schedules to potential applicants, but this information is generally not publically available. Sometimes the fee schedules are provided with the provision that the counselor not distribute the information. However, knowing what different insurance companies consider a usual and customary reimbursement for the area matters because the amount can vary as much as 100% or more. The viability of a practice may depend on setting limits on the minimum acceptable reimbursement given the costs of operating a practice.

Deciding whether or how to offer sliding-scale services to clients is another challenge faced by counselors early in their careers. Both practical and altruistic concerns can contribute to a counselor's decision to reduce the fee for individual patients without insurance coverage. Sliding-scale policies allow clinicians to work with clients who would otherwise not be able to afford treatment, and many counselors believe that reduced-fee services are part of a larger commitment to social justice and the helping professions generally.

Counselors must balance such considerations with the practical concerns of fiscal management, however. The fee charged per hour is not an hourly wage. The costs of rent, insurance, licensure, continuing education, utilities, and supplies must be paid out of each clinical hour, and the smaller the caseload, the larger the percentage of the fee that will go to overhead. In addition, cancellations, bad debt, and delayed payments are a reality of a therapy practice for beginning and master counselors alike. By valuing their time and their clinical skills, by expecting reimbursement as a professional, counselors model appropriate boundaries and self-care with clients. Clinicians who accept clients with significantly reduced fees must also be alert to the possibility of conflicting feelings toward the clients and their treatments. Accepting fees that do not allow the counselor to earn a reasonable income and provide resources for self-care almost inevitably creates resentment in the counselor. Many more experienced counselors are happy to discuss issues related to establishment of professional rates of reimbursement and sliding-scale policies because of their own experiences in struggling to set and expect a reasonable income.

In establishing a private practice and building a caseload, many beginning counselors find themselves wondering how to describe the work they do. Often clinicians have a predominate orientation, such as CBT or trauma theories of practice, and can identify themselves as counselors who work within those frameworks. Beginning counselors find that the interest in their services is partly determined by clients' preference for certain types of therapy. Some clinicians find that they can obtain more referrals when practicing within one framework than others, and counselors have to consider how willing they are to provide services according to perceived demand. For example, some clinicians work exclusively from a psychodynamic or cognitive behavioral perspective, whereas others are comfortable with a more eclectic approach or one that is targeted to each individual client. For some counselors, offering a specific type of treatment that potentially is less readily available, such as dialectical behavioral group therapy, offers the opportunity to build a successful practice. The degree to which clinicians are influenced by fiscal management in the orientation of their clinical practice varies, but can be an important consideration for beginning counselors as they establish a practice.

Whatever the clinical orientation from which counselors practice, they must understand the impact of the psychopharmacological orientation of the mental health field generally, and the insurance industry in particular. Although counselors do not prescribe medication, clients can seek treatment believing medication will be offered. Clients require education about the role and licensure of counselors and their difference from psychiatrists and nurse practitioners, who can prescribe psychotropic medications. Counselors, in effect, offer an alternative to psychopharmacology and may consider medication itself as a kind of cultural competitor in building their practice. Counselors should be aware of the current role of medication in behavioral health treatment provision so that they better understand how what they offer differs and can educate clients accordingly. Although counselors do not prescribe medication, as individuals they inevitably have biases and assumptions regarding medication about which they must be aware so that they don't allow those beliefs to affect treatment. Clients are entitled to make their own best decisions regarding which type of treatment to pursue, and clinicians, as helping professionals, are bound to respect those decisions.

TIME, TREASURE, AND TAXATION

For a business to remain viable, careful attention must be paid to finances. A budget tracks expected and actual flow of business revenue and expenses. Thus, a budget is an essential tool to be sure the business does not spend more than its revenue can support. Two types of budgets are useful in a counseling business: the operating budget and the cash-flow budget. Each type of budget has a specific purpose. The operating budget estimates the cost to achieve the stated goals of the business. It tells the counselor, if I want to do X, I will need $Y to do it. The cash-flow budget, on the other hand, is focused on the day-to-day income/expenses of the practice. This is the budget used to know whether there will be enough income to pay the rent and light bill this month. Although similar in content, these two types of budgets differ somewhat in focus and scope and should be kept separate for good financial planning. Of the two, the cash-flow budget is obviously the most critical.

An operating budget is broader in scope than a cash-flow budget. The operating budget considers all of the potential costs involved in generating revenue over the next year. This budget places a dollar amount on what is needed to achieve the objectives set in the short- and long-term business plans. Estimates for spending over the next year would include such things as marketing or professional development along with routine expenses such as rent, utilities, and tax liabilities.

The cash-flow budget is used to track actual day-to-day business cash flow and to compare that actual cash flow against short-term projected income and expenses. This budget is the key tool for monitoring business activity, and the most critical of the two types of budgets. Results of the comparison of actual versus projected income and expenses can alert the business owner of potential revenue shortfalls, identify specific aspects of the business that may need adjustment, and temper expectations of future business net revenue.

Income

In a counseling practice, income would typically come from the fees charged for providing counseling services. The dollar amount of fees would need to be sufficient to cover expenses, but also be competitive in the local market. Also, the form of payment accepted affects the timing and amount of income received. One option is to only accept private-pay patients, collecting payment before providing services and deciding whether or not to use a sliding scale. Clients would pay out-of-pocket or file receipts with their health insurer for reimbursement. This choice avoids the administrative complexity of dealing with insurance companies or government payers, but could limit the pool of potential clients.

Another option would be to join an insurance panel, becoming a provider for local health insurers, or to accept clients with Medicaid or Medicare coverage. This choice would expand the number of potential clients, but not without cost. The time required to navigate complex insurance and government guidelines and rules may reduce the time available to provide client services. But, if billing is contracted out, part of client fees will go to pay for administrative services. In either instance, claims filed with private or public insurance take time to process, and the amount paid by these insurers may be lower than fees otherwise charged. As a result of these complications, many practitioners choose not to work with insurance (Cunningham, 2013; Lieber 2012), creating enhanced opportunities for those willing to access clients relying on insurance.

Another important consideration is whether there are potential sources of income other than payment for meeting face to face with a client. For example, most states provide that professionals required to testify in a court case have the right to charge for their time away from their primary practice. A counselor will need to decide whether to bill this time based on door-to-door travel or only on the time spent in the courtroom. As another example, speaking engagements or seminars might provide an additional source of income.

A reliable income flow will take time to establish. Even after a client base has been established, income flow might still be quite variable. For these reasons, it is wise to set aside an amount equal to 3 to 6 months of necessary expenditures as a cushion against a drop in income or to pay an unexpected expense.

Expenses

As indicated earlier, business expenses may be fixed, step fixed, or variable. Expenses differ according to the location, target population, and practice preferences of the professional counselor. Categories of possible expenses include the following:

Professional Expenses

- Fees for professional license
- Dues for professional associations
- Professional journal and newsletter subscriptions
- Professional conferences and other forms of continuing education units (CEUs)

Hourly Fees for Professional Assistance

- Attorney
- Accountant
- Billing specialist

Insurance

- Malpractice and liability insurance
- Insurance on office contents

Office Operations

- Rent or mortgage payments
- Utilities
- Internet access
- Rental of off-site data storage
- Office supplies

Advertising

- Signage
- Business cards and stationery
- Website
- Advertisements placed in various media (e.g., newspaper, radio)

Payroll

- Salary (own and others)
- Quarterly estimated income-tax payments

Tax Considerations

It can be easy to overlook or underestimate the effect of taxes on business operations. Employees are accustomed to having both income tax and payroll tax withheld for them when receiving a paycheck. Business owners, however, are responsible for estimating their federal and state income-tax liability for the year and doing their own tax withholding. Income-tax payments based on expected annual income must be submitted quarterly. The Internal Revenue Service (IRS) imposes fines if these quarterly payments are underpaid or are not made in a timely manner.

The IRS considers a sole proprietorship, a partnership, or a limited liability company to be a "flow-through entity." In practical terms, this means the business and business owner are treated as one and the same for tax purposes. Business income "flows through" the business to the hands of the business owner(s), where it is taxed as personal income. In addition to any forms needed to file for personal income tax (which typically include Form 1040 and, if one itemizes deductions, Schedule A, or has interest income to report, Schedule B), business owners must use Schedule C, a supplement to Form 1040, to report a detailed listing of the business income and expenses for the past year. The purpose of the form is to calculate net business profit. Also, Schedule SE must be used to calculate the amount of Social Security and Medicare tax payments to submit. In other words, there are several specific tax forms that business owners operating as a sole proprietor, partnership, or limited liability company must file every year with the IRS.

Business owners have the option of using their own Social Security number or applying to the IRS for an Employer Identification Number (EIN). An EIN is a tax identification number associated with the business. In a counseling practice, either the business owner's Social Security number or EIN must be used when providing patients with a statement of services or filing an insurance claim to receive payment for services. An EIN offers the important advantages of privacy and protection from potential identity theft. Use of an EIN is also helpful in keeping personal finances separate from business transactions.

There are a number of tax rules specifically for business owners. The IRS describes these rules in several publications: *Business Expenses* (IRS Publication 535, 2014a), *Tax Guide for Small Business* (IRS Publication 334, 2014e), and *Small Business Tax Workshop Workbook* (IRS Publication 1066, 2014d). These publications are available on the IRS website (www.irs.gov).

Although consulting with a certified public accountant (CPA) may seem an unnecessary expense for a small business, use of professional tax services can help ensure that costly errors or omissions do not occur. Tax law is complex and rules often change. Effective tax planning can reduce the business tax bill. Many common business expenses generate tax deductions. For example, office equipment can be depreciated; work-related travel is a deductible business expense. Obtaining sound advice regarding which expenditures can be deducted and keeping accurate and detailed records of all business expenses are critical activities, not only for running a business efficiently, but also for providing evidence in the event of an audit.

When business cash flow exceeds expenses, contribution to a retirement plan should become a part of routine business expenses. In addition to helping a business owner accumulate retirement plan assets, retirement plan contributions offer current and future tax advantages. Choice of a specific retirement plan will depend on business characteristics and the preferences and resources of the business owner as well as tax law. The IRS offers several resources to help small-business owners select an appropriate retirement plan. A comprehensive list of resources related to retirement planning is available at www.irs.gov/Retirement-Plans/Plan-Sponsor/Small-Business-Retirement-Plan-Resources. In addition, the IRS offers *Choosing a Retirement Plan for Your Small Business* (IRS Publication 3998, 2014b) and *Retirement Plans for Small Business* (IRS Publication 560, 2014c).

As the business grows, it may become necessary to hire assistance. A decision will need to be made regarding whether to bring the additional help into the business as a part- or full-time employee or to hire someone outside of the business as an independent contractor. An employee would create responsibility for withholding of payroll tax and possible inclusion into business health and retirement plans, depending on part- or full-time status. Hiring an independent contractor would avoid these costs, but it is important to remember that independent contractors will also have control over when, where, and how they will complete any work given to them.

THE LONG ROAD AHEAD

The future for mental health services offers opportunity and challenge. Mental health is an important public health issue across all age groups. A study conducted by the World Health Organization (WHO) found that mental health issues, including depression, bipolar illness, schizophrenia, and substance abuse, accounted for 45% of all disabilities experienced by young people aged 10 to 24 (Harding, 2011). Data from the Centers for Disease Control and Prevention indicate that nearly one in four adults in the United States reported having a mental illness in the prior year (Reeves et al., 2011). Currently, one in nine of those aged 65 and older have Alzheimer's disease. The number of cases of this disease is expected to triple by 2050 (Warshaw & Bragg, 2014).

In the past, mental health has often been a neglected aspect of health services. Those struggling with mental health issues have faced misunderstanding and discrimination (WHO, 2013). Health insurance policies did not give the attention to mental health that was given to physical health. As a result, coverage for mental health care was quite limited and often insufficient. Although negative perceptions of mental health have not been completely eradicated, in recent years, there has been a growing awareness that behavioral health issues are as important as physical health issues in overall wellness, and the means of providing adequate and appropriate treatment for mental illness need to be developed.

In the United States, several recent changes in public policy have begun to influence access to and payment for mental health services. The Mental Health Parity Act of 1996 (MHP; P.L. 104-204) prohibited large employer-sponsored group health plans from placing higher annual or lifetime limits on mental health benefits than those applied to medical or surgical benefits. The law applied only to group health plans that offered mental health benefits; it did not force insurers to include coverage for mental health. The law had several shortcomings, however. With a focus only on the group plans of firms with 50 or more employees, it was not comprehensive in scope. Group plans could obtain a waiver from key provisions of the law if compliance would result in cost increases of 1% or more. Important aspects of coverage, including treatment limits, cost sharing, and treatment facilities covered, were not addressed in the law.

The Paul Wellstone and Pete Domenici Mental Health Parity and Addiction Equity Act of 2008 (MHPAEA) attempted to address some of the main limitations of the 1996 MHP. Under the MHPAEA, group health plan and health insurance providers are required to make the financial requirements and treatment limitations for mental health or substance use disorder no more restrictive than those for medical or surgical benefits. As a result, insurance providers must have the same treatment limits, cost sharing, and in- and out-of-network coverage for mental health treatment as for medical and surgical. The MHPAEA also applies to treatment for substance abuse disorders, which the 1996 MHP had not included. Like the 1996 MHP, the MHPAEA applies to large-group health plans and contains an option for a waiver due to cost.

The 2010 Patient Protection and Affordable Care Act (commonly called the Affordable Care Act or ACA; Public Law 111-148) defines mental health and substance use treatment as one of 10 essential health benefits. The ACA applies the MHPAEA to a broad array of health insurance providers, including issuers in the individual market and qualified health plans offered through an exchange or marketplace. Unlike prior law, the ACA mandates coverage for mental health instead of simply demanding parity if coverage is provided (Goodell, 2014).

These three pieces of legislation have helped to bring coverage for mental health on par with that for physical health, greatly expanding the number of people with health insurance coverage for mental health (Clay, 2011). Nevertheless, challenges remain. Mental health professionals foresee several future trends. Mandated integration of mental health as an explicit part of health care should enable the public to receive earlier and better screening for mental health issues. To the extent this happens, the overall health of the public would improve. But, there is a shortage of care providers. Costs to deliver all types of health care are expected to continue to rise (Clay, 2011; Thomson-Deveaux, 2014). Further, cost sharing of health insurance premiums among the federal government, state Medicaid programs, employers, and potential clients under the ACA is still in flux. Consequently, mental health treatment is not likely to be equally accessible or affordable, despite the changes in health care coverage (Thomson-Deveaux, 2014). Parity between mental health and medical care policies also subjects mental health to the same thorough reviews that medical and surgical benefits undergo, with the need for care and cost of care closely scrutinized. To manage health care costs, some professionals expect that adoption of electronic medical records will become increasingly important. Others envision growth in consolidated practices in which mental, medical, and surgical services are offered under one provider (Clay, 2011). There is also expectation that, under the ACA, delivery of mental health services will become outcome focused, shifting away from a maintenance model centered on management of symptoms to a model of long-term recovery.

While continuing to develop as a clinician, Amy hopes to acquire the further skills she will need to advance her career at the community mental health agency and beyond. Amy would like to consider practicing outside of a community agency, but she is aware that her current position may not offer her the opportunity to learn the necessary fiscal-management skills that would allow her to run a successful small business. Amy decides to enroll in small-business accounting classes at a nearby community college and joins a peer consultation group for professional support and mentorship.

SUMMARY

Counselors often pursue therapeutic work because they find it intrinsically meaningful and personally and intellectually challenging. Often, however, they do not consciously pursue the necessary skills to operate a financially sound psychotherapy practice while in training. Career development—whether in private practice or through agency promotion—depends on a basic understanding of budgeting and financial management. Maximizing true freedom to practice in accordance with the difference an individual counselor hopes to manifest in the world depends on openness to lifelong learning about and/or mastery of financial management.

Much of the resistance to learning about budgeting and financial management is rooted in two kinds of fear—the fear of irrecoverable failure made (supposedly) indisputable as a result of a financially insolvent practice and the fear of mathematics. Both concerns are best addressed head on and regularly as an expected part of a counselor's professional life. It is important to remember that counseling is far from a saturated market. Over 90 million Americans reside in locations described by the Health Resources and Services Administration as areas experiencing mental health care shortages (Cunningham, 2013). Specialists willing to work with children and youth are especially sparse (Stiffman et al., 2009). With careful thought, a proactive plan, judicious use of professionals, and an informed and attentive approach to the management of financial resources, successful practices can be created, nurtured, and progressively enhanced in keeping with the professional dreams of almost any counselor.

REFLECTION QUESTIONS

1. What motivates you to pursue private practice?
2. What concerns you about pursing private practice?
3. What is your piece of the pie?

4. How much financial risk are you willing to incur to pursue a dream of private practice?
5. How prepared do you feel to take on the financial management and budgeting responsibilities associated with private practice? What else do you need to learn to prepare yourself?

SUGGESTED RESOURCES

Consider publications created for small businesses, such as the following: *Business Expenses* (IRS Publication 535), *Tax Guide for Small Business* (IRS Publication 334), and *Small Business Tax Workshop Workbook* (IRS Publication 1066). Also useful are publications on retirement planning, such as *Choosing a Retirement Plan for Your Small Business* (IRS Publication 3998) and *Retirement Plans for Small Business* (IRS Publication 560), as well as those available at www.irs.gov/Retirement-Plans/Plan-Sponsor/Small-Business-Retirement-Plan-Resources/ and resources for starting a small business, available at https://www.sba.gov/content/follow-these-steps-starting-business/

The following online resources are also helpful:
Internal Revenue Service: www.irs.gov
9 Terrible Reasons to Start a Small Business: www.forbes.com/sites/allbusiness/2015/01/21/9-terrible-reasons-to-start-a-small-business/
Real Psych Practice, LLC: www.realpsychpractice.com/
Small Business Administration: www.sbs.gov
Small Business Development Center: www.sbdcnet.org
Startup Nation: www.startupnation.com/
Why Your Therapy Practice Needs a Business Plan (includes training): www.zynnyme.com/blog/2014/6/12/why-your-therapy-practice-needs-a-business-plan

REFERENCES

Clay, R. A. (2000). Why every private practitioner needs a business plan. *American Psychological Association*, *31*(6), 48.

Clay, R. A. (2011). The future of behavioral health care. *Monitor on Psychology*, *42*(5), 52.

Cunningham, P. W. (2013, March). *Loophole for mental health care.* Retrieved from http://www.politico.com/story/2013/03/reform-law-expands-access-to-mental-health-care-88347.html

Dart, R. (2004). Being "business-like" in a nonprofit organization: A grounded and inductive approach. *Nonprofit and Voluntary Sector Quarterly*, *33*(2), 290–310.

De Thomas, A., & Derammelaere, S. A. (2008). *Writing a convincing business plan.* Hauppauge, NY: Baron's.

Finch, B. (2013). *How to write a business plan*. Philadelphia, PA: Kogan Press.

Goodell, S. (2014, April 3). *Health policy brief: Mental health parity*. Retrieved from http://www.healthaffairs.org/healthpolicybriefs/brief.php?brief_id=112

Harding, A. (2011). *Mental illness leading cause of disability in youth*. Retrieved from http://thechart.blogs.cnn.com/2011/06/06/mental-illness-leading-cause-of-disability-in-youth/

Hill, B. (2014). *The importance of a financial plan for a small business*. Retrieved from http://smallbusiness.chron.com/importance-financial-plan-small-business-4713.html

Internal Revenue Service. (2014a). *Business expenses* (IRS Publication 535). Retrieved from www.irs.gov

Internal Revenue Service. (2014b). *Choosing a retirement plan for your small business* (IRS Publication 3998). Retrieved from www.irs.gov

Internal Revenue Service. (2014c). *Retirement plans for small business* (IRS Publication 560). Retrieved from www.irs.gov

Internal Revenue Service. (2014d). *Small business tax workshop workbook* (IRS Publication 1066). Retrieved from www.irs.gov

Internal Revenue Service. (2014e). *Tax guide for small business* (IRS Publication 334). Retrieved from www.irs.gov

Kasewurm, G. A. (2008). Writing a business plan. In H. Hosford-Dun, R. J. Roeser, & M. Valente (Eds.), *Audiology. Practice management* (2nd ed., pp. 259–283). New York, NY: Thieme.

Lieber, R. (2012). *Walking the tightrope on mental health coverage*. Retrieved from http://www.nytimes.com/2012/12/22/your-money/walking-the-tightrope-on-mental-health-coverage.html?pagewanted=all&_r=0

Orlinsky, D. E., & Ronnestad, M. H. (2013). *How psychotherapists develop: A study of therapeutic work and professional growth*. Washington, DC: American Psychological Association.

Reeves, W. C., Strine, T. W., Pratt, L. A., Thompson, W., Ahluwalia, I., Dhingra, S. S. . . . Safran, M. A. (2011). Mental illness surveillance among adults in the United States. *Supplements, 60*(3), 1–32. Retrieved from http://www.cdc.gov/mmwr/preview/mmwrhtml/su6003a1.htm

Stiffman, A. R., Stelk, W., Horwitz, S. M., Evans, M. E., Outlaw, F. H., & Atkins, M. (2009). A public health approach to children's mental health services: Possible solutions to current to service inadequacies. *Administration and Policy in Mental Health and Mental Health Services Research, 30*(1–2), 120–124.

Thomson-Deveauz, A. (2014, February 25). *The ACA can't fix our mental health crisis*. Retrieved from http://ma.northeastbehavioral.com/the-aca-cant-fix-our-mental-health-crisis/

Warshaw, G. A., & Bragg, E. J. (2014). Preparing the health care workforce to care or adults with Alzheimer's Disease. *Health Affairs, 33*(4), 633–641.

World Health Organization. (2013). *Mental health action plan 2013–2020*. Geneva, Switzerland: Author.

E • I • G • H • T

Clinical Information Management

Michael A. Hauser

Amy has worked at her new position for about 6 months, and as she has watched the internal workings of the organization, she has come to believe that there is a great deal of inefficiency in the workflow. This inefficiency puts much pressure on the staff and management. Management needs the data to inform the various stakeholders of the results that the agency is producing and how efficiently the agency is delivering services to the community. The staff members need to produce various forms of documentation to fulfill their roles. Clinicians need to enter client notes. Office personnel create a variety of documents dealing with insurance-related matters, client records, and other administrative details.

Amy has noticed that the agency uses a variety of software solutions that seem to lack integration and were designed for specific purposes without any capacity to exchange data among the various programs. Therefore, it is hard for management to get a unified and complete picture of the operational details of the agency when required. Amy has had experience working with other employers, and based on that exposure has come to think that there may be better ways to both generate and maintain records in the agency. These innovations could provide a more efficient workflow, integrate the composite data, and, of greatest concern to Amy, comply with requirements of the Health Insurance Portability and Accountability Act of 1996 (HIPAA).

In order to show her supervisor that she is learning leadership traits, she has decided to research various integrated software packages to determine how the agency could provide an improved workflow that enhances productivity, ensures greater compliance with HIPAA, and provides a more concise picture of agency operational features to management. By introducing such a tool into the agency she would expect to increase productivity, which in turn would reduce employee stress at all levels of the workforce.

INTRODUCTION

Right up front, it should be made clear that this chapter is not for everyone. However, please read, at least, the first two paragraphs of this chapter before making the decision not to read any further. This chapter is primarily about office automation and, more specifically, about systems that are useful in the mental health field, along with principles to be aware of when considering the use or purchase of such systems. Therefore, this chapter may have limited significance for some working in the mental health field.

However, most employees should be aware of the legal and ethical concerns that will be laid out in this chapter. With the introduction of the Health Insurance Portability and Accountability Act (1996; HIPAA Administrative Simplification, 2013) and other laws (Confidential Nature of Claims, 2010; Confidentiality of Certain Medical Records, 2011; Confidentiality of Medical Quality-Assurance Records, 1980; Freedom of Information Act, 2013; HIPAA Omnibus Final Rule, 2013; HITECH [Health Information Technology for Economic and Clinical Health] Act, 2009; HITECH Extension for Behavioral Health Services Act, 2010; Privacy Act, 1974), no employee in any facility dealing with sensitive personal information (as defined by HIPAA and other laws) is without excuse when it comes to violation of the laws and is subject to penalties appropriate for violations of those laws. Hence, you may want to browse this chapter to ensure that the work that you are performing does not render you subject to any penalties for inadvertent violations.

It is entirely possible at this point in time that a mental health facility could be run without or with very little use of paper. With that being said, this chapter is focused, unapologetically so, on software,[1] because that is the future of the profession. *Software*, as the term is being used in this chapter, refers to any bit of digital code that allows some form of hardware, be it tablet, phone, computer, or other device, to fulfill its design. Because of the rapidly expanding nature of both disciplines, mental health and software engineering, this chapter can never hope to be completely current, nor all inclusive. Therefore, the majority of the content is written to discuss the principles that fall in the area where the two concerns, mental health and software, overlap.

As Lloyd, King, Deane, and Gournay (2009) inform us, few people in management of mental health facilities have specific training for their positions. Far fewer are trained in clinical information management. To emphasize that point, it is difficult to find peer-reviewed materials covering this specific topic, which indicates the lack of true experts in this field. In preparation for writing this chapter, the author spoke to a consultant who is a Fellow of the American College of Healthcare Executives (FACHE), and asked him if he could point out one individual who was capable of consulting on the use of software in the mental health realm. He was completely stumped. The point is that there are few people who have any degree of expertise on the subject. Agency management at this juncture simply has few places to turn in order to find answers

[1] The term *software* and the term *system* may be used interchangeably in this chapter because of the varying conceptions about what constitutes the distinction between the two terms—for example, does a system accessed solely through the Internet constitute software? Probably not to the end user, but at some point the distinction no longer makes sense, because when you get to the bottom of it, the system can only run because someone created the code that allows you to use the system.

to these two concerns. Given this lack of information, most managers have to rely on input from outside in order to form an opinion about how to resolve complex issues. The complexity of the issue increases significantly when the current federal health care laws are incorporated into the task of choosing appropriate clinical information management software.

HIPAA COMPLIANCE AND SECURITY

Volumes could be written on the contents of HIPAA and related regulations, but that is not the purpose of this chapter. The significance of HIPAA would seem to dictate at least a brief foray into its content because it lays the foundation for virtually everything that is happening in the clinical information management (CIM) realm (another name that is used interchangeably with CIM is practice management system [PMS]). The intent of this section is to give enough information to provide a working foundation, without giving so much detail as to make it tedious. A broad overview of the HIPAA foundational body of information is intended so that the reader can begin an informed search for the most current information; anything else would result in failure.

The HIPAA of 1996, signed by President Bill Clinton, introduced a far-reaching set of rules that mandates standards for the treatment of personal health information while at the same time protecting health information by outlining practices for the confidential handling of that information. Since HIPAA came into effect, both the law and the technology available to handle health information have changed. HIPAA laws have been revised or supplemented over time to become clearer and remain current (Confidential Nature of Claims, 2010; Confidentiality of Certain Medical Records, 2011; Freedom of Information Act, 2013; HIPAA Administrative Simplification, 2013; HIPAA Omnibus Final Rule, 2013; HITECH Act, 2009; HITECH Extension for Behavioral Health Services Act, 2010; U.S. Department of Health and Human Services, 2013). Although HIPAA and related laws have significantly affected how protected health information (PHI) is dealt with, there are other laws (Confidentiality of Medical Quality-Assurance Records, 1980; Privacy Act, 1974) that should be understood when one is considering clinical information management.

These laws are not the only intellectual issue that employees must consider regarding CIM; however, they may be the most important, as the penalties for violation of these laws can be large enough (costing millions of dollars, depending on the size of the agency and the number of clients affected) to close the doors of an agency. All agencies, regardless of size, should consider having access to an attorney who is familiar with the laws governing protected health care information. Agencies would also benefit from having a designated employee to oversee security and HIPAA compliance because the regulations are increasing and are being revised, updated, or expanded to keep pace with changes in technology and practice. The Centers for Medicare & Medicaid Services (CMS) and the U.S. Department of Health and Human Services (HHS) are federal agencies that have websites (CMS.gov and HHS.gov, respectively) containing material to keep providers informed.

To some extent, the following listed entities should already be in compliance, as the implementation dates started to roll out shortly after the turn of the century (most agencies were required to be in compliance by the end of 2003). There are essentially three types of entities that must comply with HIPAA: covered health care providers, health plans, and health care clearinghouses. This book is intended for use by those who are in the first category, health care providers, and will only address their needs. HIPAA generally refers to health care providers as "covered entities." The CMS has the following two-step decision process to determine whether one is a covered entity: Does the person, business, or agency furnish, bill, or receive payment for health care in the normal course of business? Does the person, business, or agency transmit (send) any covered transactions electronically? If the answer to either is "yes," then you are a covered entity subject to comply fully with HIPAA. These criteria have no bearing on how small or large the provider is; single-person private practices must comply just as readily as large regional facilities.

Nestled among the various rules of HIPAA are the "privacy rule" and "security rule." The privacy rule defines *who* should have access to PHI, and the security rule sets forth standards that set *limits* on who should have access to PHI. When discussing PHI it is often helpful to think of PHI as sets of data, data that can further be categorized as "data in motion" and "data at rest." The distinction is helpful because there are different standards of practice for each category. The term *data at rest*[2] refers to PHI stored in a single location, such as a computer hard drive. The term *data in motion* refers to PHI that is subject to movement in some form of network, such as a client record stored in a server-based database that can be accessed from multiple locations. Note that both forms of data are in a digital format; this chapter is about CIM, and therefore discussion of HIPAA compliance matters will be confined to information in digital format. It is safe to say that when the Health Information Technology for Economic and Clinical Health Acts (HITECH Act, 2009; HITECH Extension for Behavioral Health Services Act, 2010) were completed, data encryption of digital records became the de facto standard for compliance. Any PHI that is not encrypted should be considered unsecured and is therefore subject to greater scrutiny and tougher penalties under HIPAA.

Not all data-encryption methods are sufficient to meet mandated standards, which is why the standards mentioned in the preceding paragraph (see footnote attached to previous paragraph) were introduced. Few counselors are able to make sense of the very technical encryption standards; however, there are huge incentives for ensuring that the provider complies with those standards. Those who comply with the encryption standards are provided a safe haven when it comes to dealing with the "breach notification requirements" contained in the HITECH Act. The breach notification rules mandate an onerous set of behaviors if a provider is involved in the disclosure of PHI. In general, the safe haven policy holds blameless those providers who comply with the encryption policies. As an aside, any provider using digital records should now include breach notification information in the provider's patient

[2]Either form of data must be encrypted to comply with HIPAA standards. Data in motion must be encrypted according to Federal Information Processing Standards (FIPS) 140–2 (National Institute of Standards and Technology, 2002). Any product used by covered entities for this purpose must be FIPS140-2 validated, which should not be confused with FIPS140-2 certified. Data at rest must meet the encryption standard of Advanced Encryption Standard (AES; Barker, Barker, Burr, Polk, & Smid, 2012; National Institute of Standards and Technology, 2002).

rights statement. (It is important to understand that individual states have specific statutes governing breach notifications. The National Conference of State Legislatures maintains a list of State Security Breach Notification Laws with hyperlinks to the text of each law for reference.)

The HITECH Act (2009) constituted the largest change in the HIPAA law since its introduction. The law is in excess of 400 pages and covers a vast terrain. Although there is much more in the Act that may be of concern, the three following elements deserve the most attention and are covered in some detail in the following sections of this chapter. These main points are business associate agreements (BAAs), breach notification, and notices of privacy practices (NPPs), along with related privacy and security matters. It bears mentioning that all of these rules are available in the public domain. The HHS website appears to do a good job of breaking the HIPAA regulations into manageable components, and provides links to other resources.

Business Associate Agreements and Breach Notification

At the time this chapter was written, the HHS had a webpage solely dedicated to the topic of BAAs (www.hhs.gov/ocr/privacy/hipaa/understanding/coveredentities/contractprov.html). There can be subtle nuances in the definition of a business associate (BA), but for the sake of simplicity, a BA may be anyone who has access to PHI during business interactions with the covered entity, but is not an employee of the covered entity. That is a greatly abridged definition, but allow it to suffice for this chapter. Anyone with whom the provider has a working relationship who comes into contact with PHI generated by the provider is subject to the rules covering BAAs. For all intents and purposes, that could include parties such as a cleaning crew that operates in the office when PHI is being handled or a software vendor who repairs computers for the provider. Another example may include the bookkeeper or accountant—most counselors in private practice hire these folks even if they cannot afford a cleaning crew. Therefore, practitioners should give much consideration regarding how to limit the impact of these mandates on the operation of the practice. Most assuredly, the definition includes those who are involved in the architecture of the CIM system, whether that system is cloud based, confined to a local area network (LAN), or constituted by a shared external hard drive or wireless network.

BAs are now subject to the same rules and penalties as the covered entity. Therefore, the BAA serves as a binding obligation between the parties as to how they will work together in order to ensure that PHI is properly handled and secured. It should also serve to identify the legally binding roles of each party should legal resolution be sought at some point. BAs often have working arrangements with other covered entities requiring some form of firewall between similar types of information. For instance, it is common for software providers to have multiple covered entities using the same storage venue. The entity providing the storage must be able to ensure that the PHI remains distinct and separate. BAs may have subcontractors, and their work should be covered in any contractual agreement because the rules specify that the BA is responsible for the conduct of its subcontractors.

Without going into a great deal of legal jargon, the Final Rule (U.S. Department of Health and Human Services, 2013) mandated that in the case of a breach involving PHI, all of the parties involved in the handling of that material have to conduct a risk assessment to determine the potential damage that may have been caused by the breach. From the day of discovery of the breach, all parties have a limited time period in which to inform affected individuals in writing. The covered entity must also contact the Secretary of Health and Human Services, and, in some cases, must inform prominent media outlets.

Breach notifications, using plain language, must contain a minimal amount of information to comply with the rules. The phrase "to the extent possible" is used, indicating that full compliance may not be possible in some instances. The notification must provide a description of what happened and when, a description of what elements of the protected health information were disclosed (e.g., Social Security numbers, account numbers, diagnosis, etc.), suggestions for measures that individuals can take to protect themselves from harm by the breach, a description of what the covered entity is doing to investigate, steps it is taking to reduce the potential for harm, steps it is implementing to avoid future breaches, and a means to facilitate contact for individuals who want additional information (www.hhs.gov/ocr/privacy/hipaa/administrative/breachnotificationrule/).

The point of all this is to suggest that anybody working with PHI should consider who they are working with and take care to ensure that proper BAAs have been put into place. Because of the complexity of BAAs and the potential for harm, this area is best dealt with by an attorney who has a background in HIPAA compliance. At this juncture, HIPAA compliance is a growing industry that provides a variety of solutions for covered entities. A covered entity who works with BAs would be well advised to have a breach notification plan because they will not have enough time to satisfy federal regulations if BAAs are attempted after a breach occurs. The cost of failing to meet federal mandates can be enormous, even more so if BAAs are nonexistent or ill conceived. The American Counseling Association (ACA) and other professional organizations have at least one full-time individual whom members can consult with concerning these types of matters.

Notice of Privacy Practices

With few exceptions, providers are required to distribute a notice providing clear explanations of the client's privacy rights and the entity's practices regarding the protections and limitations of the client's privacy rights (notice need only be given in English; however, for the benefit of your clients you may consider having it translated). The notice can serve as a good introduction to discussing privacy concerns with clients and to ensure that they are properly informed.

Individuals must have access to a personal copy of the notice of privacy practices (NPP). According to the regulations, the content of the NPP is required to be in plain language. HIPAA laws also dictate the minimum content that must be included in notices. Content must include a clear and comprehensible notification of how the covered entity might use the individual's protected health information. In addition, the rules stipulate that an individual should be informed regarding how the PHI may be disclosed to other entities during the normal practice of business. For instance, it is quite common for one covered entity to provide PHI to another entity during the referral process. However, this can be done only when the client agrees to it, and signs a release of information that directs exactly what elements of the records are going to be provided to another covered entity. It may also be wise to discuss potential risks to the client's PHI as a means of protecting the covered entity in the case of accidental disclosure—for example, a secure web portal is hacked and the information is destroyed or stolen.

The following are five additional elements that all notices must contain:

1. A statement outlining individuals' rights regarding their protected health information
2. How they may exercise those rights and initiate a complaint to the covered entity
3. The legal duties of a covered entity in handling the PHI as they are specified by law
4. A specific point of contact that an individual with questions may contact for more information
5. An explicit effective date for implementation of the policy

When any of the practices are changed, the covered entity is under mandate to disseminate promptly the changes made to its privacy practices.

There are specific rules that cover how the notices will be provided to the public. Copies of the NPP must be made available on request. If a covered entity maintains a website that is used for customer service and the provision of benefit information, it must make its privacy practices available on that site in some conspicuous manner such that clients do not have to do a lot of digging to get at the information (i.e., within one or two clicks of the mouse). If during the enrollment of a client, the client agrees to have the notice delivered electronically via e-mail, the practice may do so. For the agency's own protection, the practice should have all clients initial that they have read and understood that they have granted permission for e-mail delivery of the NPP.

Direct treatment providers have additional rules with which they must comply. As most counselors, regardless of setting, could qualify under this definition, a few of the rules will be listed herein. Direct treatment providers must provide the required notice no later than the first date on which the client receives services from the provider. The provider is also required to make a "good faith effort" to get the client's acknowledgment of receipt indicating that the client has been given a copy of the provider's privacy notification rules. If the client's signature cannot be obtained, for whatever reason, the provider must document all efforts to obtain the signature of the client. This author is aware of one instance in which a client, during the first visit and as the privacy notice was being discussed, started to pass a kidney stone and was evacuated to a hospital because the source of the client's excruciating pain was unknown at the time. In such a case, it would be understandable that the client did not sign the receipt form; however, on return of the client for the second visit, the matter was immediately rectified.

When changes occur in the privacy information, direct treatment providers must make the revised copy available to clients as soon as possible and make every effort to ensure that the client is aware that the information contained therein has changed. If the client is receiving services remotely in any way (e.g., via e-mail, Internet, etc.), the provider must ensure that the notice is provided at the commencement of services. The provider must also confirm that the client has received the notice, perhaps through an electronic signature or some other means, such as a recorded digital statement, that is inserted in the client's records.

Direct treatment providers may or may not work for an organization. Organizations have some options under current rules that may not be available to those working outside of an organizational umbrella. For instance, a covered entity that is formed as an organization has the option of making a variety of different privacy notices that cover specific organizational functions. This can be a significant benefit to the entity because, as most mental health professionals know, the provision of group and individual therapy can be very different, and the benefit of having specific notices for each type of therapy should be evident to most practitioners. As an example, the assurance of privacy can be quite different in a group setting as opposed to an individual counseling session.

This section has endeavored to provide a brief overview of some of the specific elements of HIPAA and related regulations in an effort to establish a foundation for discussing client information management. Anyone who exercise influences over the choice of CIM providers should be aware of the aforementioned HIPAA rules to ensure that the system they work with or within is compliant. This is a pressing concern in CIM, as HIPAA compliance failures can be a game changer for therapy providers of any size.

The remainder of this chapter addresses specific issues that anyone involved with CIM might need to understand or consider. In order to do the topics justice, let's take a moment to consider the following assumptions:

1. All CIM, regardless of the size of the agency or practice, will be moving to a digitized format, in part or in whole.
2. Data need to be secured, whether in storage or in transmission.
3. Any personal health information generated by a practice will generally belong, ultimately, to the client.

There is always going to be a need to secure the PHI, yet at the same time it must be readily available for counselors, the client, a supervisor, or others who may need to be given access.

Because of the potential for misuse of PHI, there will and should be a collective effort to manage and regulate the use of PHI. This can place significant requirements on practitioners to keep abreast of, and in compliance with, all of the rules and regulations. An entire industry has grown up around the need to secure PHI, and providers can engage advisors and consultants to ensure compliance. Yet without some knowledge on the part of the end user of the CIM system, there can be no way to ensure that any system is able to meet regulatory demands and at the same time meet the specific needs of the practitioners. There is no cookie-cutter solution that can fit the need of every practitioner. The expression "to be forewarned is to be forearmed" seems to be an appropriate warning here. In the section that follows, consider Amy's dilemma in terms of HIPAA compliance and CIM systems.

AMY FACES A DILEMMA

Amy made a bank deposit for the agency. She has done this before but today the events surprised her. She was greeted by a friendly teller who has dealt with Amy and others from the agency. Today the teller, while preparing the deposit, casually asked Amy whether Mr. Heathrow was a customer of the agency. Being security minded, Amy is bewildered by the question and ponders the HIPAA implications of her response. Finally, Amy asked the teller, "Why would you ask that?" Again in a casual tone, the teller responds to Amy with, "Oh, when I was preparing the last deposit for your agency I saw two checks he had made out to your agency. He's my neighbor so it stuck out in my mind. I really like him and didn't know that he was having troubles." Amy is confused about her responsibility to protect Mr. Heathrow's status. She thinks about this all the way through her lunch, and when she gets back to the office she asks her boss whether the agency needs to have a business associate agreement with the bank.

What do you think? See the answer at the end of the chapter.

CLOUD-BASED OR LOCAL SOLUTIONS

In the last 5 years, there has been a large migration of digital data. Many companies are now storing their data in the cloud,[3] and many more are contemplating the move from storing their data onsite to storing it in the cloud. There are strong points in favor of each type of operation. The benefits and problems are discussed here.

Cloud-Based Solutions

Cloud-based computing is often referred to as software as a solution (SaaS), or variably as software as a service (SaaS). Cloud-based solutions or services can take many forms. For the purpose of this discussion, the term *service* refers to the provision of storage (backup and secure storage services via the Internet by third-party providers that allow the user to upload and store any type of digital information) or online software.

Although cloud-based solutions have the advantage of low upfront expenditures, in the long run they can be just as expensive as localized solutions. Google is perhaps the largest and most well known of these types of services. Google provides free storage space for anyone signing up for its services; more storage can be gained by paying for it. As an example, when the author signs in to his Google e-mail account, he gets the following message, "You are currently using 0.07 GB (0%) of your 15 GB." Google provides the author 15 gigabytes of free storage. A lot of documents, music, videos, and pictures can be stored in 15 GBs (a gigabyte can be thought of as the equivalent of all the print content of a 30-foot row of books, or over 200, 5-minute-long songs). At the time of writing, if the author needed more storage from Google, he could purchase 100 GBs for less than $5.00 a month.

However, Google does not provide just free storage; it also provides a multitude of programs that can be used without requiring the program to

[3] *Cloud*, as it is used here, can be a metaphor for the Internet.

reside on the user's computer (thus saving storage space). Google has many such offerings, an example of which includes a full office suite. The suite is perhaps not as sophisticated as other productivity suites, but is has its strong points. The author created a number of interactive surveys, and by simply sending the active link to recipients, they were able to click on the link and start the survey. The data generated by the survey could be imported into other software programs to produce state-of-the art statistical analysis. Google is but one of many providers of cloud-based computing.

Among other benefits, SaaS offers an agency[4] lower upfront costs, shorter periods between making the decision to use the cloud and the actual implementation, less implementation risk, and reduced need for technical resources, and offers the flexibility needed to size the service to meet agency needs. SaaS is also effective at reducing resource demands. One of the significant advantages of SaaS is that every time it is used, the user is accessing the most current version of the software. This means that, unlike traditional computer-based software, there will never be fees for upgrading or updating the software. In some ways, SaaS can serve as an insurance buffer in that material is stored offsite and generally in multiple locations so a local or large-scale disaster does not destroy the information. This also facilitates the restoration or use of services in remote locations and at multiple sites if or when desired.

Perhaps the largest concern with cloud-based solutions is the security of the data. It seems to be a regular occurrence to hear that hackers have stolen information from a cloud-based provider. According to a software firm specializing in cyber security, "an upper limit of the cost of cyber espionage and crime is somewhere between 0.5% and 1% of national income—for the US, this would be about $70 billion to $140 billion" in 2013 (Lewis & Baker, 2013, p. 16).

Another downside to the use of cloud-based products can be the loss of productivity when access to the information is lost. When the loss of information is made public it can be a blow to a firm's reputation. In 2006, an employee of the Veterans Administration (VA) suffered the theft of a laptop from his home. That laptop contained unencrypted data on as many as 26.5 million people. That sort of incident has immeasurable costs to the agency and the people affected.

Localized Solutions

Localized solutions are defined as software or digital information either stored on one user's computer solely for the use of that individual or stored on a server located at the location in which it is being used. A server may serve multiple users in the same location, but to be considered localized it must operate independently, purportedly secure from external access. One of the most significant benefits of localized solutions is the lack of need for BAAs. Because software and data reside on a local computer, it is free from the need for BAAs.

It is also, more or less, free from the prescribed encryption requirements mentioned earlier in this chapter. The phrase "more or less" is used because

[4] The term *agency* is used herein to simplify the discourse, but may also refer to other types of users, such as the sole proprietor of a private practice.

it still benefits the agency to pursue the highest order of encryption that it can afford. Compliance with the higher requirements of encryption may be a benefit if faced with any legal burdens regarding data storage breaches. At a minimum, agency-generated PHI information should be stored on encrypted external drives and locked up (behind two locks) after use.

In a related concern, local solutions should be less vulnerable to security failures and/or intentional breaches of security by hackers. They are more susceptible to physical losses caused by theft or disasters such as fire or flooding. In spite of this susceptibility, good practices (the same security measures used for hard-copy documents) used on a regular basis can prevent significant losses of this sort. However, from the author's personal observations, good practices (for all contingencies) are rarely planned with any degree of thoroughness, uniformly taught to all employees, or enforced across the board.

Localized solutions also free the user from loss of service when there is some form of network problem such as a disruption of service (for whatever reason). Loss of power, loss of transmission sources, system failures, and system maintenance can all deny the end users access to their information and/or solutions. Local solutions can also be interrupted by power failures or system failures; however, they have fewer critical links and theoretically should be less susceptible to this type of inconvenience.

One aspect of localized solutions that should be considered is how to review and store all accumulated forms of data. Data that are stored locally have more options that may be more beneficial to the agency. For instance, depending on the volume of the data and details collected by the agency, an agency may desire to make archival copies on a quarterly or semiannually basis and edit that data for such purposes as tax preparation. That is certainly far more easily executed if all the material can be collected from a local platform.

The author asked a cloud-based provider whether the provider had the capacity to combine all of the data generated by the author's practice, and then provide it in a "zipped" version for semiannual storage. The answer was categorically "no." The impetus for the question was that the author was thinking about switching to a different provider and the desire was to either download and store the historical information or download the information and integrate it with the new system, neither of which appeared to be an easy task—in fact, it looked like it would be a significant challenge. The takeaway here is that if an agency decides to switch providers, for whatever reason, the data that the agency has generated may not be easily translated for use in a different system. For many reasons, an agency may need to reexamine information generated at some point in the past, and ready access to that information is a must. Nevertheless, there is no surety that the old information will always be translatable to different applications, or even newer versions of old software. It is probable that cloud-based solution providers will store your information for long periods after you switch to another user, but consumers should ask themselves what costs may be associated with the need to gain access to the stored data.

Although the aforementioned is not an exhaustive list of benefits of each data-storage format, it does give a brief overview. In addition, although only two formats are discussed, there are increasing numbers of options, including hybrid options that make use of both types of solutions. It is a challenge to find the solution that best meets the needs of any given agency, but it appears that the trend is toward cloud-based solutions. As time goes on more of the disadvantages of cloud-based solutions will be addressed, although some capabilities will always be of concern. For instance, security and access may always be of concern regardless of the solution chosen.

This chapter is primarily about CIM, and a host of concerns must be considered to maximize operations. Those concerns are not primarily dependent on whether a system is cloud based or local. It is more likely that agencies will need to consider whether the different aspects they consider important to their operation are available through any given software solution, at what cost, and how well integrated the software is. To exemplify the nature of this problem, consider that most agencies need to accomplish several distinct processes: take demographic information of any client, create different types of therapy notes, and bill the customer or insurance providers. In some cases, an agency can buy totally separate packages to facilitate these processes. The question, then, concerns how much information can be shared among the packages and what difficulties are involved in moving information among them. Other packages may have separate modules that, when combined, do everything that is needed, but the various components can be added separately as the agency grows and expands. Some packages simply try to meet all operational needs with one integrated solution that cannot be broken into component parts. It should be apparent that no one package has all of the answers for all agencies, and in fact most require compromises. One package may offer a very good accounting system, meeting all of the needs of the office manager, while at the same time be weak in meeting the need for creating notes.

Unfortunately, most agencies do not discover the limitations inherent in their systems until after making a sizeable investment or signing a long-term contract. The following sections are provided to help agencies look at their specific needs and ask helpful questions of the provider before committing to a purchase or contract. The caveat here is that in any case, no matter what level of scrutiny is given, no package will be without compromise. It is hoped that by asking the tough questions upfront, agencies can minimize their transition effort and maximize their effectiveness when choosing CIM software.

CREATING CLIENT FOLDERS

As discussed earlier in the chapter, there is not much of a need to keep client records in hard copy. However, is it possible to go to a completely paperless office environment? Is it even desirable? Existentialism aside, this author believes that it is not only possible but it is also highly desirable to have a completely paperless office. Logistically, the paperless office can be transported on a couple of external hard drives or stored in the cloud—no more rooms full of locked filing cabinets and rings full of keys. Physical security can be less cumbersome and access could be gained from virtually anywhere. But, for offices that already have a large investment in the storage and security of hard-copy documents, does it make sense to go fully digital?

There are no easy answers to some of these questions. Perhaps it is just easier to hire a consultant when trying to answer these questions, but for many smaller practices, the budget does not allow for consulting. In given cases agencies can make a decision to phase in digital services while maintaining the current system until such time as the records can be converted to a digital format, or perhaps keep them in hard copy until such time as they are no longer required. At any rate, it is advisable to take a deliberative approach toward the implementation of a digital system. Taking the wrong steps in implementing a digital system can create a dead end from which it may be hard to recover, handcuffing administrator and counselor alike.

The content of a client folder at best is an eclectic choice. Some content is a matter of common sense (e.g., names, contact information, insurance data), but other material may not be. In deciding what to put in a client folder, it is helpful to know the limitations of the system that is being used. Some systems limit you to what they decide should be in a folder, others are more generous and allow you to add custom fields, and others are even more wide open and allow you to import and attach any type of document you believe is necessary. For instance, if you do formal assessments, do you want to keep just the report that is returned, or would you also like to have access to the raw data as well? Can the publisher's test report be downloaded and attached, or will you have to print it out and then scan it into a common file format, such as a pdf, in order to place it in the client's file? Those types of questions will help you understand what you need to do in order to keep the types of folders that you want to have.

As an example, say you run an office in which you use the Personality Assessment Inventory (PAI). After you collect the raw data an assistant enters the data into the computer and you get the results almost immediately. If the software system that you use allows you to attach files you may be able to save the PAI output file directly to the system, but if you want a copy of the raw data you may need to scan it. Scanning it into the system requires a scanner as well as someone in the office who knows how to do the work. If the system does not allow you to attach such files, you may need to keep your own database for each client, and thus you will have at least two different digital locations that are not integrated. The more places in which information is stored, the more complicated it becomes to keep current and manage all of the data. Add in hard copies and it becomes an even more challenging environment.

SYSTEMS FOR COUNSELING AGENCY MANAGEMENT

Each agency has its own unique needs. Therefore, when attempting to create a new system it is useful to create a "snapshot" of current business practices so that the agency can analyze those practices and make informed decisions regarding how distinct processes and management systems could be integrated or redesigned to achieve maximum efficacy. One of the most common problems encountered in this phase of any transition is the inability to visualize new processes. That can be facilitated by the use of interrogative questions, the five Ws and an H (who, what, where, when, why, and how). Purchasing a new CIM system presents a great opportunity to openly and honestly rethink what is being done and why. It is easy to purchase more features than one truly needs. One way to avoid that is to consider whom and what will be involved in feeding the beast after it is created.

A variety of software solutions may be needed in any given office. What is needed and what is nice to have can be two separate and unrelated concerns, especially when it comes to the purchase price or fees. It is always nice to get steak for the price of a hamburger, but rarely does that happen with software. The range of features, level of integration, and sheer usability of any system generally become better as the price increases. The level of sophistication integrated into software may serve to increase the learning curve and time involved in the transition process. However, if the product is ultimately more user-friendly it can provide significant return on the investment. In short, if the whole process is thought through from beginning to end, the cost of any given package may look considerably different once all of the factors are considered. Small things that may seem inconsequential at first can tend to be magnified as time passes. For example, as discussed earlier in the chapter, consider whether you chose to save only the output of a specific test in the client's file and the parents of a child challenge the assessment results. If you had the raw data, the challenge may be more easily determined. However, by the time you realize that you would like to have, and may need, that kind of information, you may have lost a lot of the raw data, and may be stuck with software that doesn't allow you to recover the raw data.

According to research done by Spira and Feintuch (2005), diversions from the workflow can cost the average-knowledge worker to lose more than 2 hours of work in any given 8-hour day (estimated total loss to U.S. corporations is in excess of $588 billion annually). Diversions can come from dropping one stream of work to begin work on another. The diversions are often measured in seconds and occur when a worker leaves one process and has to mentally reorient him- or herself to the work engaged in previously. Alternatively, when one worker is interrupted by a phone call, responds to an e-mail, or is summoned to the boss's office, the worker must then try to pick up where he or she left off before the interruption. The less time an employee spends working around system deficits, the more efficient an office can be, and that impact may become significant over the course of time.

So what types of software are useful in a mental health facility? Truthfully, there is no good answer to that question. One of the best ways to decide what is needed is to look at what is currently being done in that office. The author suggests prioritizing tasks using two separate criteria. The first criterion is that the processes that are most important, for instance, the creation of client progress notes and treatment plans, should have the highest priority. The second criterion for prioritization is based on the amount of time allocated to any given task. Those tasks that are mundane and repetitive but consume a lot of time would have a higher impact on office efficiency and merit more consideration than others. Looking at office workflow can be profitable for clarifying what is needed and what is desired, serving to identify that which is needed from something that might be nice to have.

The author was recently involved with an office where it was discovered that the system provider had incorporated a new feature that would allow the agency to remind clients of upcoming appointments. Prior to this feature becoming available, the office had never considered how much time employees spent in completing this work. The system provider also included a record of attempts and methods (e-mail, telephone, etc.) used to contact clients, which proved useful when clients complained that they had not received the expected notification.

The point of this anecdote is to show that the provider had no idea that the staff was spending upward of 2 hours per day making calls or sending e-mails and that employees did not take very good notes of their attempts. They could have used a variety of tools to provide this service, but the fact that it was integrated into the client demographics and the scheduling tools of the system that they already possessed further reduced the workload involved in accomplishing this essential task. Had the agency done a workflow analysis prior to purchasing the software, the agency may have considered the feature to be critical when comparing the available packages.

Keep in mind that there is no way to avoid every misstep in the process, but performing a good analysis and creating a statement of needs can go a long way toward avoiding the majority of missteps. It may be helpful when system providers are able to respond to individual agency needs, but it is not always possible or even desirable for a provider to deliver custom solutions. It cannot be said forcefully enough that planning and forethought are very helpful. However, when a staff is too small or busy to afford a thorough analysis of needs it may be helpful to compare and contrast features of the available CIM offerings. The comparison between various features often provides valuable insights that illuminate how well those features meet the needs of the agency. If the aforementioned efforts prove insufficient to get the agency moving in the right direction, there are various sources on the Internet that have done some of the heavy lifting by providing comparisons of various systems.

If all efforts thus far mentioned fail to yield sufficient information, a consultant may be needed. The last thing most agencies can afford is to make a significant error on the CIM system. It is hard to recover if the wrong software is chosen, especially if significant time and money have been spent on the transition (if the new system requires the conversion of data for compatibility reasons, the effort to recover may be even more dramatic). Keep in mind that there is no perfect system and that some systems may require you to learn and implement new ways of doing business. Nevertheless, as suggested previously, the expended energies and learning curve can be kept to a minimum with sufficient planning and preparation. Take time to know what you need and you will be forearmed!

Note: The material that follows is not a comparison of different systems, but more of a listing of specific features that you may want to consider when looking for a CIM system.

Scheduling Clients and Client Information

When a practice first lands a client, workers must input various pieces of information that can be retained for future use. For instance, HIPAA requires certain pieces of demographic information, but agencies are free to use whatever additional information they need to fulfill their professional duties, with an emphasis that the information that is collected must serve a useful purpose. Collection of information that is nice to have but currently fulfills no useful purpose probably has legal and ethical implications. One example might be the collection of client credit card information for storage, just in case there is a future need. Most clients will have a negative reaction to the storage of their credit card data, plus a breach of information may have legal implications.

Data required by the software might also be worthy of consideration here. Does the system require completion of various fields before the counselor moves on to other pages? It is helpful when the system is flexible enough to have the practice determine what it considers to be mandatory information. When a system comes prepackaged with required fields, it may restrict or encumber what any given practice is trying to accomplish. Flexibility in this area can save management lots of problems. There are plenty of reasons why required fields may be helpful; one example is accruing information mandated by different insurance companies, which may levy different requirements for authorizing payment.

Let us consider a new client approaching a practice for the first time. Insurance providers can give clients differing benefits that would be helpful for a provider to disseminate throughout the practice. Some insurers limit the number of sessions that a client may receive. One program may be limited to six visits, whereas the same insurer may give a different insured client in another program a greater number of sessions. Systems that disseminate and track that information are helpful in that everyone working with that client, including the counselor, can provide more appropriate care and avoid providing services that are not reimbursable.

Maintaining data from new clients in a paperless office can be demanding, especially if insurers require that the practice be able to produce a hard copy on demand. Essentially the only way that this can remain a paperless office in light of the need to produce such a document is if state laws allow for electronic signatures. The creation of an electronic signature can be done in a variety of ways, but it would be wise to inquire about the particular state laws governing electronic signatures in your area. Many systems facilitate the collection of electronic signatures. Some even permit the client to complete intake documents online. The client's signature can then be collected on an input device at the provider's office, or, in some states, it can be given over the web with proper certification.

A good system will provide alternative functionality but should also reduce data-entry requirements. After working with a client, a treatment plan should be created and then it should be the driver of future sessions. With that in mind, a good system will have the treatment plan prepopulated into other types of documents created thereafter. For instance, when a counselor is writing a new progress note, the treatment plan can be presented in some fashion so that the counselor sees parts of the treatment plan without having to leave the current page. That facilitates maintaining fidelity with the original goals set forth in the treatment plan. This type of integration reduces data entry and shortens the time it takes to create a good note by reducing the need to switch pages within the system. It also helps the counselor maintain a goal orientation. Other considerations that may affect client information collection are as follows:

- HIPAA requires that client information be kept separate, while also ensuring that it is locked and signed. Once a counselor creates a progress note it should be a separate document and must carry the counselor's signature. These requirements can make accessing client information cumbersome in some systems, but others have simplified access to client data, never more than a few clicks away from whatever information is needed.
- Most clients have multiple methods and points of contact and emergency contacts. This information should be maintained in the client records. Records should clearly indicate primary points of contact and emergency contact numbers. Leaving messages or e-mails at listed contacts can be a matter of privacy, and some clients will be put off if their privacy concerns are violated. Therefore, systems should allow input of multiple contact points and be able to record whether the client is comfortable with having messages left or e-mails delivered at those points.
- When dealing with children, contact information can be much more problematic and potentially contentious, especially when the family is divided or blended. Who has access to the child's information is often spelled out in court orders. It is helpful if the system will allow for the importation and storage of such documents. Perhaps more important, those relationships should be available to everyone in the practice, accessible with little effort, and clearly articulated so that a child's privacy is not compromised.
- Insurance information and preauthorization authority should be readily accessible to the client and the practice before treatment is initiated. Systems can make this more or less onerous for the practice. Various procedures, such as assessments, may be considered optional by insurers, and the client should be informed and given the opportunity to make an informed decision if it is going to result in an out-of-pocket expense.
- Likewise, systems can make the billing process more or less difficult by the way in which billing is integrated into the client information process. Copays and other features should not be a surprise to clients. Unfortunately, this process can often be a separate procedure or add-on module for some systems. If billing is not integrated into the CIM, there may be a time lag between receipt of services and the billing, because it is a time-consuming process. This time lag can be a point of contention when clients receive charges after the fact.
- It has been suggested in this chapter that systems should provide both the means and the storage space to attach important documents to any client folder. The amount of storage that is provided may turn out to be far more limited than is needed to fulfill the needs of the practice.
- The client section of a CIM should offer a way to create reports. One of the features of any database is the ability to create reports on any combination of fields. Most systems have some pregenerated reports that are in common use, but they are not likely to generate all of the reports that a practice may wish to have. The programmers can always create a custom report, but more useful is the ability of a system to give the end users the ability to run queries on any of the data that they have collected. A query allows the

user to search for, sort, and isolate any bits of data that he or she desires. For instance, a practice may wish to list all of the sources that have referred clients to them in the previous 12-month period, in order to express their gratitude and enhance professional ties with the sources. That ability may not come prepackaged, but should be available on demand. The complexity required to generate such reports should be considered when selecting a system.

Scheduling clients is a core function for any practice. It is never easy, but it can be less painful, especially when the CIM system is well integrated and interactive. It is probably safe to say that most agencies collect more data than they need, either because they expect that data to be useful at some point, or because the system came preloaded with various data points and agencies just start filling in the blanks. In the scheduling process, there can be a lot of data points. Clients have a limited perspective on the scheduling process and, generally speaking, the less they have to concern themselves with the process, the better they consider themselves to be served by the practice. The practice, on the other hand, may have to consider many variables when scheduling, and the system should be able to manage all of those parts. The system should be capable of scheduling clients (including recurring appointments), counselors, facilities (e.g., group rooms, classrooms, etc.), and a variety of appointments having nothing to do with the client, such as lunches, meetings, training, supervision sessions, and other events that may affect the availability of the counselor. It should be able to display that information in a variety of ways, such as daily, weekly, or monthly, as well as offer a whole-practice overview, or by individual counselor, and there should be a seamless transition among these views. All of these should be relatively easy to switch between. Well-integrated systems allow users to switch among scheduling, billing, and other views painlessly, or in new windows that allow them to be kept side by side if there is sufficient display space available to the user.

One item that should permeate every nuance of any given system is the ability to provide administrative oversight, restrictions, and controls. At any given time, the designated person or persons given management privileges within the system should be able to assign who can use the system, what features any given user may access, and the ability to get feedback on system usage. For instance, it may be useful to know how much time users spend on specific functions; for example, a supervisor may want to know what amount of time is spent creating intakes in contrast to progress notes. The system should be able to collect that type of information for performance monitoring within the agency.

Perhaps more important, systems need to control user access. A supervisor may need to be able to access all of the notes created by several counselors for whom the supervisor is responsible. However, it would not be appropriate in most cases for counselors to access each other's notes. Perhaps one of the more essential controls in any system is the read-and-write access functions. The read-and-write access functions determine who has the ability to input, access, and alter data in the system. All systems should allow system administrators to control who can see inputted data (the read function) and, perhaps more important, who can actually enter or alter data (the write function).

The ability to control read-and-write access can become a major HIPAA compliance concern. Counselors will need to input and access their own notes but, once entered, changes to those notes should not be allowed. Changes should come in the form of editing the contents or adding to the contents (usually in the form of an addendum to the original). Deletion of any given note should only be done at the supervisory level with proper justification and notation (e.g., "progress note was deleted because it was entered under the wrong client name, and new note under correct name was created"). No system should allow all users the same degree of access. There are exceptions—for instance, in a private practice with only one counselor the practitioner would have to exercise the role of system administrator and therapist. Imagine what it might be like if any employee could access all information, make whatever changes he or she wants, delete whatever he or she wants, or, at an even more problematic level, change the structure or form of the system components.

Billing and Third-Party Reimbursement

Few providers can afford to work for free. Providers must communicate the precise cost of the services they are billing for to the appropriate payer, regardless of who that payer is. Billing is difficult at best, but a functional system makes the process manageable. Systems need to support change in billing processes. In 2013, the change in the Current Procedural Terminology (CPT) codes caused some degree of distress for providers. The newest version of the *Diagnostic and Statistical Manual of Mental Disorders* (*DSM*; American Psychiatric Association, 2013), the *DSM-5*, and the 10th revision of the *International Statistical Classification of Diseases and Related Health Problems* (*ICD-10*; World Health Organization, 2014) are expected to be mandated by HIPAA in the very near future. This makes clear that change tends to be a constant in health care, and systems need to be flexible in order to continue to be useful.

A warning is in order when it comes to the consideration of the financial capabilities of integrated solutions for providers. Although most systems are adept at keeping track of invoicing and payments, they may not be sufficient to do all of the accounting an agency may require. They can be more appropriately thought of as an adjunctive component of this responsibility. This often leads to a conversation about compatibility of the data. Can the data generated by the CIM be imported or used in a standalone accounting package? The use of application programming interfaces (APIs) can allow software systems designed to use different data formats to interface. It is certainly an important consideration but one that lies beyond the scope of this chapter.

This can become a complicated matter with major consequences for an agency. For example, consider the following scenario. The system that an agency uses to bill customers and to interface with insurance companies may generate one form of data sufficient for those purposes. The program itself may not be capable of compliance with all of the complex state and federal corporate taxation laws. It is common for agencies to have accountants for this exact purpose. However, the accounting firm may need the data in a different format. Is the agency's chosen system capable of separating the financial aspects of the agency's operation from the customers' PHI and personally identifiable information (PII)? The extracted information required by the accountant may need to be converted to a different format, and be void of all information that could violate HIPAA rules. Imagine the challenges involved in finding out at the end of a year of operation that the collected data cannot be used by the chosen accounting firm.

Integration is an often-repeated concern in this chapter. For the purposes of this discussion, the author defines the term *integration* to mean that various components of the system work easily together and that disparate pieces of information can be gleaned without a lot of clicking and scrolling. For instance, can someone writing a progress note get that same client's most current bill with no more than two or three clicks of the mouse?

The following is a list of some abbreviated billing-related questions and issues that may be of concern when reviewing viable CIM systems for purchase:

- What types of charges can be entered in the system? Can the system be set up to handle custom fields that may be specific to the practice and that reoccur? Some practices have specific fees for things such as charges related to a counselor's participation in a hearing or trial or charges related to testing and assessments.
- Can the various therapists in a practice charge different rates (according to the current CPT codes) easily? A multidisciplinary team may have licensed professional counselors (LPCs), psychiatrists, psychologists, and a host of others who charge different rates for different purposes (e.g., intakes may be billed at a higher rate than a regular session).
- A well-structured system will allow for the generation of a variety of reports based on different criteria. Aging, billing, and payments for both the clients and insurance providers may all fit into different categories within the system, but it should not require a lot of workarounds to put the various elements into one meaningful report.
- One of the subjects that is closely related to this topic is the generation of insurance claims. For most office managers the creation and tracking of insurance claims tends to become the bane of their workday. Insurance billing is a time-consuming responsibility for most practices and merits a significant look when pursuing the purchase of a CIM. Some systems try to incorporate insurance billing forms (the term "try" was used here to indicate that some systems are more successful than others), whereas others make no attempt to do so. What should be considered if the system does not incorporate a billing module is the ease of interface between the two systems (CIM and billing). If it is easy to swap information back and forth, life gets just that much easier for the office manager (OM). In my experience, making the OM happy is a mutually beneficial endeavor.

WEBSITE MANAGEMENT AND COMMUNICATION

Not all practices will want to create and maintain a presence on the Internet, which is why this topic was saved for the end of the chapter. Although most would consider a presence on the Internet a wise marketing and business investment, there can be downsides, and a web presence may cost more than it actually returns in profit. This is especially true if the site is done poorly or haphazardly.

This author is aware of one situation wherein the proprietor of the practice tried to generate his own webpage and gave the content little forethought before going "live" with the site. The first week of live operation of the website caused the office manager to spend an inordinate amount of time trying to answer questions and give supplementary instructions to confused customers, so eventually the site was taken offline and revised. It consumed a lot of energy and time to fix. There is an old caveat when it comes to website management that may bear repeating here, "It is often easier to create the beast than it is to feed it!" This caveat recognizes that it is often much easier to do a good job with the original programming of a website than it is to correct or maintain a poorly designed website.

One example that might clarify this is the addition of a calendar of events to a practice website. Although this can be very meaningful to some practices, consider what it takes for an organization to keep the calendar current and to have someone on staff who is capable of turning calendar events into website content and keeping it updated (particularly demanding if it is subject to change often). It may not be worth the effort to keep feeding that beast if particular items on the calendar engender questions from the public, because responding to the inquiring public may detract employees from more productive work.

The aforementioned website travails apply to the creation of a personal, standalone website. However tempting it may be to create a dedicated practice website, the options may be more beneficial and certainly worthy of at least a cursory consideration. Many practices are opting to connect their PMS to a web portal, which allows the practice to offer a direct interface to the client. With such a portal, clients can create their own accounts. After establishing an account, the client can make payments, schedule appointments, or exchange electronic messages in a secure environment.

Use of the client portal creates security concerns for both the client and the practice. One option that is helpful in the alleviation of security breaches is the enforcement of the creation and use of strong passwords. Systems can mandate that a client, in the creation of the client account, use various characteristics to ensure that the password is as secure as possible. Systems should provide a means to limit the amount of information a client can access via the web portal. Once security measures are in place, the matter of monitoring portal usage should be considered. Who will do the monitoring and for what purposes should be spelled out in the BAA so that responsibilities and limitations for the security aspects of the portal are clear to all parties. In addition, the responsibility for monitoring and responding to security concerns should be addressed before the client signs on to the portal.

Integration specifics should never be visible to the user. Systems can be integrated into your website such that when clients log in they may be directed to the servers of the system provider without knowing it. Good system integration allows the portal access to be customized so that it looks like the website theme that is in use by the practice. When clients log into this integrated system they may check their current appointment schedules, change existing appointments, schedule future appointments, or check their current outstanding bills. One of the handier components of an integrated system is the ability of a client to complete intake and new-client forms before the first appointment, allowing staff to be prepared as well as allowing the client to spend less time in the waiting area.

For the counselor, this portal can be a very useful medium of exchange with the client and make the relationship more proactive as well as productive. Counselors can read the intake information in advance of the first meeting with a client, thus giving them a sense for the issues at hand as well as allowing them to be better prepared to make a proper assessment. Formal assessments can be ordered and scheduled so that the client can deal with a host of issues quite rapidly in the first few sessions. In well-integrated offices, some clients can be assigned the completion of various assessments with sufficient time to have the results in the counselor's hand before the first session, adding to the client's perception of the counselor's competence. To facilitate the ongoing relationship the client and counselor can exchange e-mails (regular e-mails are not secure, but a portal can facilitate secure messaging between counselor and client), journal entries, and various home practice assignments to move therapeutic interventions forward.

MISCELLANEOUS COMPONENTS

This section covers various details that may not have been discussed in other sections of this chapter. Some elements just did not fit in with previous conversations; therefore, they will be addressed here. In prior sections of this chapter, an effort was made to disclose the liability and responsibilities of anyone currently using or contemplating the use of a CIM or PMS. HIPAA was, no doubt, a game changer in how providers and clients interact while conducting business. HIPAA contains nearly 50 specific safeguards that can be classified into one of three domains: administrative, technical, or physical rules. With that many rules it would be easy to get lost in the details and intricacies. However, it might be more beneficial to start with the big picture. The easiest way to take the larger perspective is to start with a definition of your needs.

The information provided in this chapter can give a backdrop by which current practices can be examined for goodness of fit with the available client information management systems. The marketplace has a way of weeding out those systems that are not strong performers. Nevertheless, agencies may find some systems more compatible with their own business practices than others. At the same time, the introduction of a new system may be the best time to establish new business practices that align with best practices. Oftentimes businesses establish practices that get entrenched and should change over time to keep current with new regulations and practices, but, for a variety of reasons, the changes never take place. The introduction of a new system may be the perfect time to both reexamine old practices and implement new behaviors. The introduction of a new system can be a tumultuous process, but this chapter can help prepare practitioners to be informed consumers, which means they can be prepared to ask the system vendors the tough questions and make sure that there is a consistent understanding of basic duties, responsibilities, and limitations during the purchase and implementation of a new system. The practice administrators can also ensure that they are getting the best fit for their needs. The information included here can provide a catalyst for agencies that are preparing to incorporate a new system or for those that are currently running some form of CIM to examine their current business practices and future needs to ensure that they can both withstand external scrutiny and enhance their own business practices.

There are hosts of informative sites that can help one understand CIM and PMS systems as well as the interface of these systems with HIPAA requirements. There are sites dedicated to understanding HIPAA, with checklists to aid a practice in compliance with all of the security rules in the HIPAA-associated laws (not listed here to avoid the appearance of endorsement, and to avoid the problems associated with the continual turnover of webpages). All of the available help, including that of consultants, does not compare with personally taking systems for a trial run for the purpose of comparing them. With some forethought and work, an agency can narrow the list of possible contenders to a few that most closely fit the agency's needs. After that, the best means for making a final decision is to take the system for a test drive. Most of the available systems have trial modes available for up to 30 days. There is nothing that will answer the questions of a potential user better than taking the system for trial run.

Further commentaries on the various components are as follows:

- Progress notes made in CIMs are repetitive and take up large chunks of a counselor's day. It is helpful if that task can be reached easily from anywhere in the program, and have prepopulated entries to make the task less onerous. The addition of the ability to customize to any dropdown list is helpful in terms of saving time.
- Oftentimes, for the benefit of insurance companies, a diagnosis is required on intake. If the diagnosis automatically populates future progress notes, along with particulars of the treatment plan, it satisfies the needs of the insurance company and helps to keep the counselor on track.
- Some agencies use the SOAP (subjective, objective, assessment, plan) format for notes, others use data assessment plan (DAP), and others use their own format. Whatever your preference, the system should facilitate either format or the creation of your own.
- The use of prescription medications is often important to track. It is imperative that clinicians be aware of current prescriptions and track any changes in medication. In a perfect world, the list would be standardized and the side effects of any given drug would be readily available to the clinician. As an example, this author had a client who started a regimen of Risperdal (risperidone). The client started to experience a host of strange physical symptoms and called the author to inquire about them and ask what to do (he was referred to his prescribing physician but called back because he could not reach the physician). After doing some research, the author came across a list of side effects for Risperdal that resembled the client's experience. The symptoms are rare, but the point is that the client was not well informed by his physician and the client specifically asked what to expect when adding this medication to his regimen. The information that the author originally referred to did not address the possibility of neuroleptic malignant syndrome (NMS).
- The more sophisticated systems take into account the client's age. As most counselors recognize, the rights of children in therapy can be much more complicated than those of adults. Systems that recognize and provide for

the different requirements of children help the practice avoid legal issues. For instance, when a child is brought in by a single mother (as the result of a divorce), is it required that the father be informed of the fact that the child is being seen for services? If that information is annotated and the divorce document is attached to the child's records, the practice may avoid a messy legal entanglement.

AN ANSWER TO AMY'S DILEMMA

The question seems to be whether Amy's agency needs a business associate agreement. There is no easy answer! According to lawyer Marcia Augsburger, "Thus unlike other entities, whether financial institutions must comply with HIPAA does not turn on their receipt, disclosure, or use of PHI. . . . However, OCR [the Office of Civil Rights] instructs that the focus is [not] on the nature of the information but on what financial institutions are doing with the information" (Augsburger, 2013, n.p.). The Office of Civil Rights issued the latest HIPAA update in 2013 (HIPAA Omnibus Final Rule). In that rule it states, "Section 1179 of HIPAA exempts certain activities of financial institutions from the HIPAA Rules, to the extent that these activities constitute authorizing, processing, clearing, settling, billing, transferring, reconciling, or collecting payments for healthcare." Activities outside of those just listed may require the institution to commit to a BAA with the agency. However, in this scenario, Amy was absolutely correct in that she did not reveal any relationship to, or knowledge of, Mr. Heathrow as a client of the agency.

SUMMARY

As you can see, there are numerous aspects of any given CIM or PMS that can have significant impacts on a practice. This chapter is far from being exhaustive but it serves to enumerate a variety of aspects that might be considered when adopting a new system. Although the discussion refers primarily to online systems (cloud-based systems), almost all of the components that have been addressed can, in some form or another, be applied to standalone systems. No one system is going to meet all of the desires of a practice, but many will meet the needs of the practice. There is no doubt that you will be forced to adapt to any new system, but perhaps that is not an altogether bad thing, as it allows for introspection and consideration of what must be done in light of HIPAA-specific requirements. Good systems can only help you become more efficient!

A few themes were developed throughout this chapter. One of the themes that has been prominent throughout is the impact of HIPAA and related laws and regulations (Confidential Nature of Claims, 2010; Confidentiality of Certain Medical Records, 2011; Confidentiality of Medical Quality-Assurance Records, 1980; Freedom of Information Act, 2013; HIPAA, 1996; HIPAA Administrative Simplification, 2013; HIPAA Omnibus Final Rule, 2013; HITECH Act, 2009; HITECH Extension for Behavioral Health Services Act, 2010; Privacy Act, 1974; U.S. Department of Health and Human Services, 2013). This has been emphasized in this chapter for two reasons.

The first is to highlight the complexity of adhering to the rules, and the second is to provide understanding when dealing with vendors of system solutions. Becoming an informed consumer is the best way to avoid costly litigation. There is no reason to believe that vendors either understand or have complied with HIPAA rules, even when they assert full compliance. It would be easy to bury the truth, but a good BAA could place the onus for compliance back in the hands of the vendor, thus ensuring that the vendor has a vested interest in the outcome.

A second theme has been the enunciation and clarification of the many aspects that an agency may need to consider when purchasing a client information management or practice management system. It is a difficult task to attain a goal if the goal itself is unclear. Defining the goal will require time and input from a multitude of people. The perspective of the office manager regarding the desired outcome could be far different from that of the counselor. As the functionality of the desired system is being outlined, there is potential to review the current business practice as well. If the system lacks some desired function, is it because the system is deficient, or is it perhaps that the practice itself is no longer appropriate in the current business environment? That is a difficult question to ask of any practice, and it presents the opportunity to invite a more objective evaluation from a consultant. If nothing else, a discussion of business practices with those employed in other, similar practices in the local area might shed some light on possibilities.

A third theme that occupied much of the chapter was the various details and aspects of a CIM system that one may or may not be aware of but could be considered when comparing systems. One of the dominant themes explored was the choice between a cloud-based system or a standalone system. A standalone system is going to cost more upfront, and updates can only be acquired on a for-fee basis. A cloud-based system may cost less upfront, and updates are generally included with cloud-based systems. However, in the end, both systems (with comparable features) probably cost roughly the same if used over an extended period. Some practices, particularly small ones, can exist with an office suite and a finance package. However, the long-term efficiency of such a setup is questionable and may hamper growth, if the practice desires future growth.

In the end, there are a lot of elements to be considered in managing client information. Moving from introduction to receipt of payment can be significantly challenging in any environment, but it pays to spend a bit of time considering how to make it as pain-free as possible.

REFLECTION QUESTIONS

1. Why is it important to look at HIPAA regulations and the ACA ethical code when deciding on an online system?
2. What obstacles and challenges might you face when operating a new system?
3. In your opinion, what are some of the pros and cons that the age of technology and online systems have brought to the mental health field?

REFERENCES

American Psychiatric Association. (2013). *Diagnostic and statistical manual of mental disorders* (5th ed.). Arlington, VA: American Psychiatric Press.

Augsburger, M. L. (2013, February 15). *The convergence of health care and banking*. Retrieved from http://www.healthcarelawmatters.com/compliance/the-convergence-of-health-care-and-banking/

Barker, E., Barker, W., Burr, W., Polk, W., & Smid, M. (2012). *Recommendation for key management—Part 1: General (Revison 3)*. Retrieved from http://www.nist.gov/customcf/get_pdf.cfm?pub_id=910342

Confidential Nature of Claims, 38 U.S.C. 5701: Title 38: Part IV: Ch 57: Subch I: § 5701—Confidential nature of claims. (2010).

Confidentiality of Certain Medical Records, 38 U.S.C. Part V, Ch 73, Subch III: Protection of Patient Rights: Title 38: Veterans' Benefits: Part V: Boards, Administrations, and Services: Ch 73: Veterans Health Administration—Organization and Functions: Subch III—Protection of Patient Rights: Sec. 7332—Confidentiality of certain medical records. (2011).

Confidentiality of Medical Quality-Assurance Records, 38 U.S.C. 5701: Title 38: Part IV: Ch 57: Subch I: § 5705—Confidentiality of medical quality-assurance records. (1980).

Freedom of Information Act, 5 U.S.C. Title 5: Government Organization and Employees Part I: The Agencies Generally Ch 5: Administrative Procedure: Subch II—Administrative Procedure Sec. 552d—Public Information; Agency Rules, Opinions, Orders, Records, and Proceedings. (2013).

Health Information Technology for Economic and Clinical Health (HITECH) Act, Title XIII of Division A and Title IV of Division B of the American Recovery and Reinvestment Act of 2009 (ARRA), Pub. L. No. 111-5, 123 Stat. 226, 42 U.S.C. §§300jj *et seq.* and §§17901 *et seq.* (2009).

Health Insurance Portability and Accountability Act of 1996, Pub. L. No. 104-191, 110 Stat. 1936, 42 U.S.C. § 300gg, 29 U.S.C § 1181 *et seq.*, 42 U.S.C. 1320d *et seq.* (1996).

HIPAA Administrative Simplification, § 45 CFR Parts 160, 162, and 164 (2013).

HIPAA Omnibus Final Rule, 78, Fed. Reg. 5566 (Jan. 25, 2013) (to be codified at 45 C.F.R. pts. 160 & 164).

H.R. 5025—HITECH Extension for Behavioral Health Services Act, 42 U.S.C. 1395w-4, 1395ww, 1395x, 1396b and 300jj. (2010).

Lewis, J., & Baker, S. (2013). *The economic impact of cybercrime and cyber espionage*. Washington, DC: Center for Strategic and International Studies.

Lloyd, C., King, R., Deane, F., & Gournay, K. (Eds.). (2009). *Clinical management in mental health services*. Ames, IA: Wiley-Blackwell.

National Institute of Standards and Technology. (2002). *Security requirements for cryptographic modules*. Retrieved from http://csrc.nist.gov/publications/fips/fips140-2/fips1402.pdf

Privacy Act of 1974, Pub. L. 93-579, 88 Stat. 1896, 5 U.S.C. § 552a.

Spira, J. B., & Feintuch, J. B. (2005). *The cost of not paying attention: How interruptions impact knowledge worker productivity*. New York, NY: Basex.

U.S. Department of Health and Human Services. (2013). *Modifications to the HIPAA privacy, security, enforcement, and breach notification rules under the Health Information Technology for Economic and Clinical Health Act and the Genetic Information Nondiscrimination Act; other modifications to the HIPAA rules*. Washington DC: Author.

World Health Organization. (2014). *International classification of diseases (ICD), version 10*. Retrieved February 10, 2014, from http://www.who.int/classifications/icd/en/

N • I • N • E

Marketing for the Professional Counselor

Lorrie B. Slater and Amiko W. McPherson

The agency Amy works for is partially funded through grants and other funding sources from local, state, and federal agencies. During her interview process, Amy was informed that she would be assuming some marketing responsibilities for the agency if she demonstrated the requisite skills for the position. Her supervisor was vague in describing what those skills might be. Amy works to ensure her clinical skills are beneficial to the community; at the same time, she is trying to acquire the marketing skills that will assist in forwarding her career. She attends night classes and seeks mentorship from sources well versed in the challenges she will face. These steps can assist Amy in agency development and, potentially, facilitate growth in her career.

Amy's educational background did not equip her with the essential marketing skills necessary to facilitate growth in a community mental health agency. Her mindset is that of a counselor, focused on the well-being and health of clients. However, one of the most important factors for success in her position is the overall health of the agency as a business. Word-of-mouth referrals can be an effective way to cultivate an agency, but they are insufficient as marketing tools. Marketing for the agency is crucial. Through her night classes and mentor, Amy learns that the challenge of marketing her agency is differentiation. Amy understands the concept of differentiation from its use in family dynamics and decides to apply the idea of separation and independence to her marketing plan. The key to differentiation in business is the development of an operational business and marketing plan.

INTRODUCTION

Most counselors are introverts who do not necessarily enjoy business, marketing, or networking (Grodzki, 2000). In the field of counseling, "marketing" usually conjures negative connotations, but marketing is not an expletive, earning a living is not criminal, and networking is not a fate worse than death. A simple business and marketing plan can help a nonprofit agency, group, or private practice grow and thrive. Even shy counselors can learn to contribute to the success of nonprofit agencies, join a large group practice, and start their own private practice, all while concentrating on their gifts as counselors and goals for the health and well-being of their current and future clients.

THE BUSINESS PLAN

When working with an agency that possesses an extremely vague business plan, it is essential to develop and clarify a plan for the success of said agency. There are key elements of a business plan that will help agencies and private practices to be successful. In order to develop an operational business and marketing plan, following these steps can lead to success:

- Market analysis
  - Competition demographics
  - Client demographics
  - Current trends
- Mission statement
- Business structure
- Key objectives
- Ongoing analysis (Grodzki, 2000; Stout & Grand, 2005)

The Market Analysis

In order to understand the marketplace it must first be analyzed. This analysis begins by researching and understanding the competition. At first glance, it may appear that there is no competition for a community mental health agency, but competition has many different forms. Beyond consideration of the client population that an agency treats, determinations must be made about which community support, grants, and other community service opportunities will help an agency gain the financial support and community awareness needed to facilitate growth. An understanding of other types of agencies that are requesting funding, volunteers, and donations will help identify areas to be targeted in order to augment what the agency needs to grow into a valuable asset for the community it seeks to serve.

It may be beneficial to define the competition by looking at how many other nonprofit businesses or private practices exist within a 5-mile radius, 10-mile radius, and the community as a whole. An understanding of what types of services are offered and at what professional level the agencies operate can be gained through this search. In other words, if there are other private practices or nonprofit agencies in the community, are the services offered similar? Do these agencies' employees hold degrees (bachelors, master's, PhD, MD, etc.)? Do they have volunteers? This investigation may continue by discovering what type of marketing these agencies are doing.

Marketing can occur through several mediums (Stout & Grand, 2005). One very common practice is listing an agency in the Yellow Pages, or creating an Internet website (Stout & Grand, 2005; Terkan, 2014). The next step is to simply search these media to see who is vying for the same clients (it is important to note here that although Yellow Pages and the Internet can be used for marketing, they are not, in themselves, sufficient to facilitate the type of growth one may hope to provide for the agency). Once the agencies have been identified, use the information to gain a better understanding of what those agencies offer to the consumer. You may want to gain an understanding of how a potential client views your competition through a more extensive exploration of the competing businesses. Investigating where the competition is located can be advantageous because it provides useful information to define the competition. Explore what type of buildings they have. Are they easily accessible? Are they in a private or very public location? Call the office with a prepared marketing survey of the area and ask questions based on hours of availability, types of clients, areas of specialization, fees for services, and local government support. You will gain an understanding of office procedures and office staff members who interact with potential clients. Remember, you're trying to discover what types of services are offered that are similar to the services offered by your agency.

Discovering the demographics of the client base is another piece of creating a business plan. The important part of understanding the demographics served by the competition comes from asking these two critical questions: What are the challenges presented by my competition? What are the areas of opportunities for our agency? Demographic information includes data about the people in the area. Such data can include information pertaining to age, income, education, occupation, marital status, gender, family size, homeowner percentage, and mean home price (Babbie, 2013). This information is found through websites, such as census.gov and city-data.com, and through local business listings, chambers of commerce, local libraries, and even real estate offices. Gaining an understanding of local demographics will ensure that word of services offered is communicated to the people who are in need of these services.

Local, state, and federal politics play an important role in understanding the demographics of the field. Becoming a member of a professional organization, such as the American Counseling Association (ACA), can help one to be aware of the lobbies available for professionals such as counselors. An ACA member can contact his or her local and state chapters of the ACA to learn of political opportunities and potential issues for future clients as well as counselors. A firm understanding of the ACA *Code of Ethics* (2014) will also assist in developing an ethical marketing plan, as well as an ethical practice (see sections C.3.a, C.3.b, C.3.c, C.3.e, C.3.f, and C.6.d).

The last piece of the market analysis is to understand current trends. Current trends worth noting include the types of families moving into the area, senior citizen population expansion, local company structures (expanding and/or downsizing), movement of transient groups (migrant workers, homeless, at-risk youth), and the impact of any recent disasters in the community. These trends can be seen by observing local news and listening to talk-radio programs; watching people at local community centers, malls, and parks; and surfing the Internet. Once an understanding of local trends is gained, the marketing analysis is complete. Observing trends and coupling this information with demographic information can provide insight into areas of need and services already in existence. One now holds an understanding of the competition, client base, and community trends and is ready to move on to the next section of the marketing plan: the mission statement.

The Mission Statement

The next step in a good marketing plan is a clear and definitive mission statement. The mission statement is primarily for the benefit of the agency to help define and focus its objectives; it can be used for marketing purposes if it proves helpful and should be included in the agency website. In private practice or other service agencies, a well-written and concise mission statement is essential. There are several important components of an effective mission statement:

1. A mission statement is consistent with the values, vision, and strengths of the agency.
2. A mission statement should cover what the agency does and to whom the agency provides services.
3. A mission statement must be brief. Long mission statements are forgotten easily and can be confusing.
4. A mission statement must be specific; a vision can be general, but a statement is a specific plan of action.
5. A mission statement must state the action planned and what the agency will do.
6. A mission statement is a clear, easily understood statement. If the statement is vague, it will fail to motivate and will not provide direction for what needs to be accomplished.
7. The mission statement must be measurable or at least point to something that can be measured.
8. A mission statement will need to answer the question, *how will we know whether our mission is being accomplished?* If the agency cannot show how it is accomplishing its mission, the mission statement is not very helpful.
9. A mission statement must be motivating. Words have the ability to inspire, and the statement should supply a compelling reason to move forward.

The Business Structure

There are many factors to consider regarding marketing. When considering going into private practice, it is important to understand business structure. The components of a spreadsheet and the concepts of accounts receivable (money the business brings in) and accounts payable (money the business sends out) are important aspects to understand when looking at business structure. Business structure also includes the cost of running an agency or private practice, such as rent, utilities (that are not included with rent), taxes, Internet and phone services, mental health care software, office supplies, cleaning supplies, insurance, office staff, and marketing expenses.

Consideration of expenses is important in setting fee structure (Hunt, 2005). Using Excel spreadsheets or financial planning systems (such as Quicken) can provide insight when setting up a fee structure. When determining fee structure, be sure to include any expenses related to your practice, the ratio of necessary appointments kept, and the costs of running your practice. Consider about 20% for bad debt (bounced checks and no-shows; Stout & Grand, 2005). The importance of understanding costs is critical to your success (Stout & Grand, 2005). Fee structure is determined by practice costs divided by billable annual hours (Stout & Grand, 2005) and should be in keeping with regional fee structures. Fees from other practitioners can be located at www.psychotherapyfinances.com and are available to American Psychological Association members (see research.apa.org/99salaries.html) (Stout & Grand, 2005).

Key Objectives

The key objectives in a marketing plan are business objectives, not objectives or goals set when making a treatment plan. However, understanding how to develop a good treatment plan helps to understand the importance of defining key objectives for a private practice or agency's business and marketing plan. Defining specific service and financial goals for an agency or private practice is crucial.

In order to better understand the service goals for an agency, an understanding of whom the agency serves is important. In other words, what audience is the agency trying to attract with its marketing? A service goal of helping those in need is too vague and must be better defined. Agencies need to clarify the type of patients they currently serve. For example, does the agency see in-home, in-patient, long-term, acute care, or crisis stabilization clients? Does the agency have a crisis intervention team? Are there support groups available? If so, what kinds of support groups are available (anxiety, depression, Alcoholics Anonymous, Narcotics Anonymous, etc.)? Are there more people or groups the agency should consider in its service goals? Clarification of this information (the niche, as it is referred to later in the chapter) is important in designing the marketing plan.

Goals are based on the cost of running an agency or private practice. A determination is made on how many clients need to be seen each week and what kind of sliding scale can be provided. If clients are unable to pay, how will the agency or private practice stay in operation? In some cases, options for raising money must be considered, such as fund-raisers, community support, and grants. These ideas can be further developed when implementing a marketing plan. The final step of establishing the key objectives for an agency is to write short- and long-term goals. Understanding the significance of goal setting and the difference between long-term and short-term goals is necessary in creating the marketing plan, and the use of goals in the marketing plan is similar to their use in treatment planning. Therefore, when writing agency goals, the process of writing treatment goals can be emulated. One concept to contemplate when writing goals is what the visions are for the agency 5 years into the future. Where do you want the agency to be and whom do you want the agency to serve? Based on these answers, develop short-term goals and small steps that will help the agency move toward the direction of the long-term goals. Just as in treatment planning, these steps need to be well defined and measurable.

Ongoing Analysis (SWOT)

SWOT is an acronym encompassing the analysis of the *strengths* of the business, the *weaknesses* of the business, *opportunities* for growth, and *threats* to the business (Grodzki, 2000; Stout & Grand, 2005). The final piece of a market analysis is to determine how often the SWOT analysis should be conducted. The first analysis should be run after the first few months of operation and then quarterly or annually. When running a SWOT analysis, consider these questions on the strength of the agency: What am I or the agency doing right professionally (as a counselor[s] and as a business)? Where are the marketing resources returning the highest yield on my/our investment? Evaluate areas of weakness by asking: Where can we/I improve professionally (as counselor[s] and as a business)? Where are the marketing resources returning little to no results? Once an evaluation of strengths and weaknesses is conducted, look toward opportunities for professional growth. For example, evaluate whether more licensed clinicians are needed, whether sending the staff to conferences could be a way to facilitate better treatment, or whether it would be worthwhile for the agency to expand its business space or marketing efforts. Once an analysis is run on the return of marketing energy and dollars, a shift can be made to minimize energy and money being spent in bad endeavors and shifted toward areas that see more growth. For example, if an agency's billboard advertisement in one location is bringing in many new clients, but a billboard advertisement in another location is never referenced in the "where did you learn of us" section on the intake form, cease paying for the impractical billboard. Finally, look at the threats to the private practice or agency's professionalism (e.g., liabilities, termite infestation, loss of grant money, etc.) and marketing (e.g., bad press, graffiti-filled billboards, lack of engagement, etc.). The SWOT analysis provides an evaluative tool to ensure continued growth for the agency.

SWOT Analysis

Strengths: What makes the agency (or practice) effective and unique? *[List four or five]*
Weaknesses: Where are there opportunities for improvement? *[List four or five]*
Opportunities: How can the agency (or practice) be enhanced and (existing or new) goals be attained? *[List four or five]*
Threats: What threatens the success of the agency (or practice)? (These threats are different than the weaknesses of the agency [or practice]). *[List four or five]*

THE MARKETING PLAN

Once a better comprehension of the client profile and agency setting is achieved, defining ways to set an agency or private practice apart can be accomplished. There are two basic ways to market an agency: promotion and actions (Collins, 2002; Grodzki, 2000; Hunt, 2005; Stout & Grand, 2005). In each, the goal is to reach the greatest number of people. An excessive expenditure of money is not necessary to maximize the population reached.

Promotions

The Website

The creation of a website is crucial to the success of an agency, and a website can reach an unlimited number of people. A huge benefit of an agency website is that it doesn't have to be expensive. A website designer is relatively inexpensive and can provide direction for website design and the inclusion of important information. If the agency is unable to afford a website designer, there are low-cost and free website design services available on the Internet. In fact, a tech-savvy counselor can create a website with absolute control over content and format with a minimal investment of time and resources. At the very least, the website should include the agency mission statement, treatment goals, and available services. An anonymous testimonial page can have a great impact, but can also be a challenge to ethical codes. If testimonials are to be included, they should be directed toward the agency and not individual counselors (see the ACA *Code of Ethics* [2014, c.3.b and c.3.c]). Each counselor should be represented on the website page with a profile picture and professional information that includes education, credentialing, specializations, memberships, and a personal statement of counseling theory and practice. A link for contact information and directions should also be provided. However, a word of caution is necessary: There can be legal issues with counseling websites, so refer to Chapter 8 of this text as a starting point.

Social Media

Social media can be a very powerful marketing tool. Facebook, Twitter, Instagram, and e-mail chains provide free advertisement and a means with which to reach a large number of people from numerous areas. Although patient information and treatment plans are not appropriate for social media, a thought for the day, mindfulness exercises, or other suggestions (such as "fake it 'til you make it") can maintain a presence on social media for the agency and keep the agency name in the thoughts of participants.

Advertising

Advertising is expensive, and the amount of advertising obtained is often dependent on budgetary constraints. Television and radio ads, newspaper ads, billboards, and ads in local magazines can be quite expensive. However, there are ways to obtain free advertising. Local talk radio and television stations often invite volunteers from local agencies to speak about their services and community interests as well. Pertinent issues of community, such as how to cope with seasonal affective depression in the fall, how to relax when the kids are home all day during the summer, or other community issues can be discussed in these advertisement time slots. Advertising brings awareness to the community about the services offered at the mental health agency or private practice and lets businesses know about the services offered. There may also be occasions when agency work can be offered as a public service notification (e.g., a spouse support group or Alcoholics Anonymous meetings open to the public may be listed in public service notifications). Also, whenever an employee of the agency can represent the agency in a professional capacity, the agency receives free advertising.

Although free advertising is not always available, there are inexpensive, efficient ways to advertise, such as promotional objects (e.g., pens, sticky notes, key chains, magnets, etc.), pamphlets, and business cards. Tentoni (1997) found that promotional objects that display contact and service information increase both the number of clients seen and the number of appointments made. Business cards are easy to distribute and can assist with networking, and pamphlets can be distributed to local business offices, public facilities, and physicians' offices.

Special Events

Special events provide a relatively inexpensive way to get the name of the agency out to the community. Health fairs, fun-runs, and community events provide an inexpensive way to increase community awareness of the agency. A booth with agency information, populations served, and services offered can be set up at local health fairs, hospital fairs, and even at local job fairs. Agency employees can participate in fun-runs and other community events wearing agency t-shirts. Special events are crucial in the nonprofit world. An agency may sponsor a fun-run, a walk, a concert, or a similar event. Be sure to be present at each event, handing out pamphlets, meeting people (clients and potential community connections), and educating the community about the services provided by the agency.

Actions

Word of Mouth

Word of mouth is vital to agency success (Collins, 2002; Grodzki, 2000; Hunt, 2005; Stout & Grand, 2005). Clients should be encouraged to suggest services to others who may be in need. Supporting agencies can be asked for recommendations and introduction to other philanthropic businesses that may offer helping services as well. A certain number of referral sources should be contacted weekly to maintain a good rapport. Referral sources might include primary care physicians, pediatricians, gynecologists, corporations, churches, schools, learning centers, and others who come in contact with those who may need the services the agency provides as well as those who may be willing to donate to the ongoing expenses of the mental health agency.

When networking for referral sources it may also be beneficial to use what Dasenbrook and Walsh (2005) call "cross-pollination." This concept expresses that when seeing a new client (always with permission from that client), the counselor contacts the client's primary care physician for a conversation regarding the coordination of treatment. By doing this, a connection has been made and a good rapport has been established with that physician. This is a simple way to market oneself and to create new referral sources in a brief time period.

Have an "elevator speech" prepared. An elevator speech is an approximately 2- to 3-minute presentation on what the agency has to offer clients and how this can benefit the person with whom the information is shared (Collins, 2002). For example, when speaking with a primary care physician, stress that his or her patients will be given the best possible care and counseled in a manner that keeps the goals the physician has set for the patient in mind. When speaking with a business owner who may offer financial support, stress the services the agency provides to the community (e.g., the agency serves the community by providing a service that would otherwise not be available). With each referral, a release of information should be obtained and a written thank-you note for the referral should be sent. With each financial endorsement, a written thank-you note should be sent.

Speaking Engagements

Speaking engagements help establish the agency as a resource to the community and the counselor as an expert in the field. This is an opportunity to use the elevator speech to exhibit expertise and to highlight the benefits the agency provides to the community. This can be done by visiting churches, schools, physician groups, and local television and radio stations, and by volunteering to speak at events. Accept invitations to speak about relevant mental health issues in the community. Educate the community on important issues and begin to be seen as an expert in the field. Radio and local television shows maximize the population reached in the community.

When choosing a topic for discussion, consider relevant social and personal situations happening in the community (acts of nature such as fires and tornados, community tragedies such as public shootings, and local divorce/marriage rates). This is an opportunity for investigative work. View the news as a window into the community and an opportunity for a need to be met. For example, discussions can change seasonally. In the fall, discuss how to get your child ready to go back to school, how to rekindle the romance for empty nesters, and coping mechanisms for life stress. Winter is a great time to discuss seasonal depression. In the spring, discuss anxiety (due to final exams, graduation, and other life transitions associated with marriage and/or divorce). Summer can be a good time to discuss the benefits of exercise for depression. Look for community needs and ways in which a competent mental health care provider is uniquely qualified to help meet those needs.

Outreach Programs

Outreach programs raise awareness of the services agencies and private practices offer. One excellent way of doing this is through public service announcements (PSAs) through local radio stations. If an agency has a 501(c) tax status, it qualifies for free PSAs. Because a PSA cannot technically be an advertisement, be careful to avoid any mention of fund-raising or solicitations for money. If needed, seek the help of the marketing department and the radio station communication directors to develop messages that educate the community about the services provided and the need for a greater focus on the mental health of the community. Counselors can contact local newspapers to ask for a public interest story on the programs available at their community mental health agency. Volunteering to do a lunchtime presentation to the employees of local corporations, who may be faced with finding services provided by the agency, can be beneficial.

Grant Writing

Grant writing is a unique way that an agency can obtain needed funds to facilitate financial stability. Although grant writing may feel overwhelming, in some circumstances, it is a fundamental tool that is lacking in agencies. In some instances, referring to previous demographic studies will reveal local foundations that offer grants to locally based agencies that serve the needs of the community. There are two major areas to research for grants: (1) foundations and corporations, and (2) federal, state, and local government agencies. A foundation is a nonprofit organization whose sole purpose is to give money away to charitable organizations (Grantspace.org). Once the names of potential foundations that may support an agency's mission have been learned, the free *Foundation Directory Online* (*FDO;* https://fconline.foundationcenter.org/) can be used to find the website, contact information, and a brief description of each foundation. Search engines, such as GuideStar, which is a directory of nonprofit organizations, and the National Center for Charitable Statistics, which provides the national repository of information on nonprofits in the United States, are valuable instruments. Corporate-giving programs are different from foundations in that they are not separate organizations from the business that funds them and they are required to make contributions to nonprofits (Grantspace.org). The Funding Information Network Partners directory is a search tool for locating local grant-giving corporations. Being meticulous in the disclosure of an agency and requests for funding can be beneficial in securing funds. Foundations are required by law to give a percentage of their holdings away each year.

Evaluation

Evaluation can be obtained with each new client, or each new donation. During intake, each client can be asked, "How did you hear about our services?" Each new financial donor may be asked, "How did you learn of our services? What motivated you to give?" Track the effectiveness of each marketing effort and eliminate those with inadequate return and expand those that are successful. There are many avenues through which an intake form can be created (Wiger, 2005).

After 3 years of working for the nonprofit community mental health agency, Amy decides it is time for a change. Amy begins to explore the possibility of joining a counseling group. Amy has developed her professional identity within the community and she is quickly offered a space in a large counseling group.

She is offered a 70/30 split for each client she sees (this is fairly typical—see www.psychotherapyfinances.com). Amy is surprised by this split and wonders whether it is a fair split for her. Amy speaks with the business manager and learns what the 30% taken from her fee does for the office (helps pay for rent, utilities, office staff, taxes, office supplies, and cleaning). Amy is still responsible for her own liability insurance, licensure fees, and membership dues. The group has a marketing manager, and Amy quickly makes an appointment to meet with her and begins her journey into a group private practice.

The marketing director explains to Amy that effective marketing requires that she choose a niche. Amy tells the marketing director that her niche is "children and adolescents," to which the director replies, "That's your specialization, not your niche."

MARKETING FOR INDIVIDUALS IN A GROUP PRACTICE

The Niche

A niche answers the question, *to whom do you provide services* (Clark, 2011; Collins, 2002; Dasenbrook, & Walsh, 2005; Grodzki, 2000)? A specialization focuses on what you do, not whom you serve. Specializations focus on the what—credentialing, skills, abilities—and are generally based on a broad population, such as children and adolescents. Marketing based on specializations focuses on the provider's qualifications and abilities, but it does not reach out to a client and shout, "Hey, I'm here to help you." Marketing based on a niche, on the other hand, targets specific people who can benefit from your services. Identifying a niche is necessary to creating a marketing plan that will reach a target population. An example of a niche would be working primarily with girls (elementary age through high school) who live in a single-mother home and have been abandoned or rejected by their fathers.

Once a niche has been identified, effective ways to market to individuals in this niche must be discovered. *Who* they are is understood, but now *where* they are needs identification. In the previous example, relevant referrals might include school counselors, pediatricians, and attorneys who work primarily with family law. Appointments can be made to establish these relationships. Using previously discussed techniques (e.g., pamphlets that provide details about specialization and niche, personal business cards, elevator speech) can be used in these referral appointments. Sending hand-written thank-you notes to these potential referral connections can create an excellent impression. Volunteering to speak on talk radio and appearing on local television shows can be beneficial techniques to advertise one's niche to the community.

When moving into a new office space within the group, decorate with a niche in mind. With the example niche of adolescent females, office decoration might include popular colors and furniture and accessories relevant to that population. Use care to avoid fads and popular culture (pop stars, specific cartoon characters, and specific sports affiliations—no one specific school team or professional team) when decorating. Considering a niche when decorating can help to avoid client triggers and help to align the counselor with each client's individual needs. Therapeutic books, wall art, tools (art supplies, toys, pillows, etc.) and blankets can assist in providing a safe and welcoming environment for clients and assist clients in self-expression.

Amy finds she is able to relax her marketing because the group practice generates its own referrals and she has become the "go-to" counselor for several local schools and pediatricians. After 5 years of group practice, Amy begins to wonder whether she could make it without the group. She misses the days of marketing and engaging in the business side of a busy counseling practice. Amy begins to network again and plans for a journey into private practice. She remains at the group for another year and begins saving to establish a private practice.

Amy has been a good steward of her money and has saved enough to consider purchasing office space, rather than leasing it. Amy wishes to establish her practice in Billings, Montana. She has done her demographic research and knows that the Billings area is growing and has a larger-than-national-average married population. She has also learned that there are only two other counselors specializing in couples counseling serving this large population. Amy loved working with the children of divorce, but has decided she would like to do marriage counseling and see whether she can prevent some divorces, thus helping children avoid counseling altogether. Amy's continuing education has consisted of marriage and family counseling courses and she can ethically market herself as a marriage counselor (specialization).

MARKETING FOR INDIVIDUALS IN PRIVATE PRACTICE

Establishing a private practice requires a business plan. This will include research to determine the demographics of competition, client base, and current trends in the area in which the practice will be. Sites like census.gov and city-data.com can be useful in planning where to draw clients in regard to practice location. It is necessary to identify a niche in private practice (*whom* will you serve) and identify the number and locations of competing practices. The following is a helpful expense checklist when creating a business plan:

Estimated expenses:

- Professional advancement
  - Books, continuing education, association dues, supervision
- Media
  - Internet, paper and postage, supplies, business cards, phone service
- Personal transportation/expenses
  - Auto, parking, travel, meals
- Licensure and insurance
  - Professional license, business license, malpractice insurance, renters' insurance
  - Medical, disability, and life insurance
- Accounting expenses
  - Computer-based accounting products versus office staff

New-practice expenses:

- Rent
  - Security deposit, first and last month's rent
- Furnishings and equipment
  - Furniture and accessories such as pictures, plants, pillows
  - Computer, copier, fax machine

- Assessments
  - Beck Depression Inventory, Beck Anxiety Inventory, Beck Scale for Suicidal Ideation
- Therapeutic tools and/or play-therapy toys

Ongoing expenses:

- Rent
- Insurance
  - Business, renters', professional
- Supplies
  - Paper, printer ink, business cards
- Advertising

Creating a mission statement (*what* will you do?) is the next step. A mission statement should be short, concise, and measurable. The mission statement of Bill Gates, "a computer on every desk running Microsoft software" (Academy of Achievement & Gates, 2010), is an excellent example of a purposeful mission statement. Clarifying a mission statement can be done through an easy three-step exercise. First, identify the vision; next, clarify the purpose; and, finally, declare a mission.

1. Vision: What is the vision I have for my future practice?
2. Purpose: What are the changes that must be made to fulfill the vision?
3. Mission: What are the specific, measurable steps I will take to make my vision a reality?

A good mission statement describes with whom you will work, the service being provided, and the measurable steps taken to accomplish the mission. "To offer hope and healing solutions to broken and hurting families through effective family counseling and useful written material" is an example of a good mission statement. A decision must be made about whether the *vision* for a new practice is a small, intimate, private practice with one or two other counselors, in a quiet location, seeing a specified number of clients weekly; a larger practice with multiple counselors seeing any type of client; or some variation of the two.

The next step after creating a vision is to locate an office space. Begin by asking these questions: Should I buy, lease, or rent space? If purchased, what does financing look like? Will space be rented/shared or will I be a sole practitioner? What will the overhead costs be? How many clients must be seen in order to cover overhead and provide enough income with which to live? Overhead includes rent (or mortgage payments), utilities, phone and Internet services, taxes, liability and property insurance, office supplies, mental health care software, cleaning supplies, and possibly office staff. A spreadsheet can be helpful for identifying and keeping track of expenses. Many effective spreadsheets can be found on the Internet. Spreadsheets can be personalized and provide a valuable marketing tool by helping you stay on target financially.

One thing to consider with private practice is whether to have an office staff. Waiting to hire office staff until the growth of a practice can financially support the addition of an office manager can be beneficial. Using mental health care software that provides support for compliance with the Health Insurance Portability and Accountability Act (HIPAA) can be a useful alternative. These programs can assist with managing office needs such as making appointments, confirming appointments, billing, filing insurance forms, marketing, and paying bills.

It is important to determine how many clients will need to be seen each week and at what fee structure in order to cover overhead expenses and earn an income. Consult with insurance companies in order to understand paneling requirements and reimbursements. Insurance paneling and reimbursements are always changing, and thus a knowledgeable contact in the insurance company will provide a valuable networking resource. Referral sources will also be important in maintaining a private practice. Set short-term goals for these necessities, such as "see 15 full-pay clients per week and make contact with at least five new referral sources per week." Long-term goals for the practice must also be set, such as "become the preferred provider of counseling services for local primary care physicians, gynecologists, and attorneys." When the key objectives have been set, move on to the next stage of creating a business plan.

Ongoing SWOT analysis helps one to identify strengths and weaknesses in a business, as well as opportunities and threats for the growth of a practice. After several months in practice, a SWOT analysis can tell what's being done right and what could be done better. The SWOT also helps identify obstacles that have been encountered and whether there is something else that could be done to avoid these obstacles and improve the business.

Once the client profile and practice setting have been set, begin developing a marketing plan. Create a professional website for the practice. To assist with marketing yourself, ask friends on social media (Facebook, Twitter, and Instagram) to "like" the website. Tweeting inspirational messages or posting pictures on Instagram about one's niche can be valuable. As mentioned, billboard and television advertising may be too expensive. However, putting an ad in the local newspaper announcing the opening of the practice or taking out ad space on the local news website can be inexpensive ways to advertise. Joining a professional organization, such as the American Counseling Association, where you can be listed as a licensed professional counselor (LPC) and paying to be listed as a mental health professional through *Psychology Today* are also inexpensive ways to advertise. Free advertisement might include calling the local radio and television stations and volunteering to speak about mental health and healing. Be sure to ask clients how they heard about the practice and track the results to see which marketing tactics have worked the best.

Much like the rest of life, marketing is an ongoing process that is always changing. Annual SWOT analysis, continuing education, and community involvement will keep a private practice thriving and relevant in a continually changing environment.

SUMMARY

Define your niche. The challenge to marketing your practice is differentiating yourself. Think beyond counseling (the *what*) and consider the specific population with whom you want to work. Develop a business plan. Regardless of the setting, there are key elements of a business plan that will help any type or size of business to be successful. Perform demographic research before finalizing your business plan. Market analysis includes the demographic data for your area, your client profile, and identification of the competition. The mission statement is primarily for your benefit and helps you define and focus your objectives as a counselor. The mission statement can be used for marketing purposes if you think it is something that would attract your preferred clients, and it can be included on your website. Remember that it should be short, concise, and measurable. Business structure varies by type of practice. Research the setting of the practice and weigh the costs and benefits of the business type. Key business objectives are similar to treatment plans, but with long- and short-term goals pertaining to your business practice rather than your clinical practice. The marketing plan helps you set yourself apart through *promotions* (websites, social media, advertising, and special events) and *actions* (elevator speech, speaking engagements, evaluation).

REFLECTION QUESTIONS

1. Reflect and describe the role of marketing as a process as it relates to your professional practice (current or future).
2. Take a moment to consider your niche or what you would like your niche to be. How might the marketing of this niche differ in each of the settings discussed (agency, group practice, and individual practice)? How might you market your specific niche?
3. What are the pros and cons of marketing on social media and other electronic technologies? What ethical concerns might you face?
4. What are your expectations of marketing yourself or an agency?
5. How will diversity affect the way you market yourself?

SUGGESTED RESOURCES

Dasenbrook, N. C., & Walsh, R. J. (2007). *The complete guide to private practice for licensed mental health professionals* (4th ed). Rockford, IL: Walsh & Dasenbrook Consulting.

George, B., Sims, P., McLean, A. N., & Mayer, D. (2007). Discovering your authentic leadership. *Harvard Business Review, 85*(2), 129–138. Retrieved from https://hbr.org/2007/02/discovering-your-authentic-leadership/ar/1

Marketing Mentor: http://marketing-mentor.com/pdf/hourly_rat_ worksheet_overhead.pdf

Steele, D. (2011). *From therapist to coach*. Hoboken, NJ: John Wiley & Sons.

REFERENCES

Academy of Achievement (Interviewer) & Gates, W. H. (Interviewee). (2010, March 17). *Bill Gates interview* [Interview transcript]. Retrieved from http://www.achievement.org/autodoc/page/gat0int-1

American Counseling Association. (2014). *ACA code of ethics*. Alexandria, VA: Author.

Babbie, E. (2013). *The practice of social research* (13th ed.). Wadsworth, CA: Cengage Learning.

Clark, D. (2011). Reinventing your personal brand. *Harvard Business Review, 89*(3), 78–81. Retrieved from https://hbr.org/2011/03/reinventing-your-personal-brand/ar/1

Dasenbrook, N. C., & Walsh, R. J. (2005). Marketing and advertising: Traditional and nontraditional approaches. *American Counseling Association*. Retrieved from http://www.counseling.org/docs/private-practice-pointers/marketing-and-advertising.pdf?sfvrsn=2

Grodzki, L. (2000). *Building your ideal private practice*. New York, NY: W. W. Norton.

Hunt, H. A. (2005). *Essentials of private practice: Streamlining costs, procedures, and policies for less stress*. New York, NY: W. W. Norton.

Stout, C. E., & Grand, L. C. (2005). *Getting started in private practice: The complete guide to building your mental health practice.* Hoboken, NJ: John Wiley & Sons.

Tentoni, S. C. (1997). A marketing technique to increase visibility and use of health center counseling services. *Journal of American College Health, 46*(2), 93–95. Retrieved from http://www.tandfonline.com/doi/abs/10.1080/07448489709595593#.VRF0D005C70

Terkan, R. (2014). Importance of creative advertising and marketing according to university students; perspective. *International Review of Management and Marketing, 4*(3), 239–246.

Wiger, D. E. (2005) *The clinical documentation sourcebook.* Hoboken, NJ: John Wiley & Sons.

T • E • N

Critical Incidents and Crisis Response

Sherry Todd

Unfortunately, when Amy transitioned to her new position and terminated her caseload, a client with an attachment problem became distressed. Amy's leaving became a critical incident for that client. Amy was thrilled to be moving up in her career and perceived this move as a positive change. Meanwhile, the client perceived this change as abandonment, was significantly distressed, and evidenced signs of a crisis response, including making a threat to harm herself. Because Amy was transitioning between the two jobs, she was not sure about seeking supervision and was unsure which supervisor she should approach.

Amy has worked in high-risk environments in the past, and she is aware that any suicide statement must be taken seriously. First, she assessed the situation thoroughly using the SAD PERSONS scale (Patterson, Dohn, Patterson, & Patterson, 1983). Amy determined that informing the client's parents and placing her on a risk watch in the home would suffice. Because Amy was no longer part of the treatment team at the former agency, she asked the client to sign a release of information so the supervisor of the treating agency could be informed. Experience in the psychiatric hospital gave Amy the training and skills to assess the client for intent, means, and motivation. As she was comfortable with her decision, Amy did not respond to this event as a crisis. Amy then contacted the supervisor of the agency treating the client and processed the situation.

Amy used this critical-incident experience as a "lessons learned" opportunity. To give her an edge in the position and ensure her emotional, physical, and professional safety, she will propose a comprehensive plan for addressing critical incidents in the new office. The plan will include preincident training, prevention/risk assessment, intervention, and postvention.

INTRODUCTION

Critical incident is a term that carries different meanings for various professions and even within professions. Jackson-Cherry and Erford (2014) recognize that the terms regarding crisis events are "used inconsistently, interchangeably, or without specificity" (p. 12). In light of this, a look at the definitions and meanings of the terms *critical incident* and *crisis response* seems pertinent. For example, (a) in the behavioral and social sciences, the critical-incident technique (CIT) is a research method; (b) *critical incidents* are "significant learning moments, turning points, or moments of realization that were identified by counselors-in-training as making a noteworthy contribution to their professional growth" is yet another definition (Howard, Inman, & Altman, 2006, p. 88); and (c) a critical incident may also be defined as an overwhelmingly distressing event. Critical incidents offer supervisors and supervisees real-life legal, moral, ethical, and clinical challenges (Tyson, Culbreath, & Harrington, 2008). For the purposes of this chapter we use the final meaning. More specifically, we will define a critical incident as an event that is "outside the usual range of experience and challenges one's ability to cope. The critical incident has the potential to lead to a *crisis* condition by overwhelming one's usual psychological defenses and coping mechanisms" (Everly, 2006, p. 25) and is significant enough to facilitate learning and effect change (Howard et al., 2006). The crisis is the reaction or response to the critical incident, whereas the critical incident is the event (Everly, 2006; J. Mitchell, 2006). These definitions of critical incident and crisis can apply to treatment, supervision, and agency management. Assisting supervisors, counselor educators, and agency managers to understand the nature of critical incidents and crisis response, and subsequently to develop the strategies necessary to incorporate this important concept into practice is the purpose of this chapter.

LITERATURE REVIEW

As indicated by a comprehensive search of the literature, there is virtually no research or information specifically dedicated to critical incidents and crisis response in clinical supervision or agency management (Dupre, Echterling, Meixner, Anderson, & Kielty, 2014; Hipple & Beamish, 2007). A search of Academic Search Complete, APA (American Psychological Association) PsycNET, EBSCO Online, ERIC (Education Resources Information Center), and the Psychology and Behavioral Sciences Collection evidenced a dearth of literature on counselor education and supervision and crisis response. This is true for both counseling and crisis literature (Hipple & Beamish, 2007; McGlothlin, Rainey, & Kindsvatter, 2005; Peake, Nussbaum, & Tindell, 2002). Current literature about crisis response and counseling offers an unsophisticated and naïve conceptualization of crisis events, and the focus is on the particular critical incident or event rather than the reaction to the event. Approaches that offer practical guidelines may be beneficial; however, they are based on the faulty assumption that the crisis counseling process is completely contingent on the precipitating event or critical incident (Dupre et al., 2014; Everstine & Everstine, 2006; Roberts, 2005). This is not the best practice for crisis intervention and may cause counselors to over- or under intervene (Everly, 2006). Crisis counseling should be based on the *reaction* to the event, not the event itself. In the Dupre et al. (2014) study the counselors' reports "provide powerful evidence that the portrayal of crisis in the literature does not adequately capture its complexity and dynamics" (p. 91), nor does the literature accurately conceptualize crisis intervention. This chapter offers the reader a more comprehensive understanding of how to practically manage critical incidents and crisis response.

CRITICAL INCIDENTS

For an incident or event to be considered "critical" it must deviate significantly from the ordinary events of a day or of expected outcomes (J. Mitchell, 2006). An individual's perception of an event is the controlling factor of whether an incident is *critical* or not (Everly, 2006). Our perception of an incident, then, regulates our response to the incident. Not every critical incident will result in a crisis response, nor will all individuals respond in the same manner.

A supervisee may perceive a situation as a critical incident, whereas a seasoned supervisor may not perceive it in the same way. The reverse may be true as well; a supervisee or client may perceive a situation as less than critical. Perception of an event is therefore a vital consideration in clinical supervision, especially as related to critical incidents (see Figure 10.1).

The types of events that may be classified as critical incidents are too numerous to list, and no one could predict every event that might occur. Prior to the Oklahoma City bombing and 9/11 the vast majority of the population could not imagine such horrific events. That does not negate our responsibility as counselor educators, supervisors, and managers to discuss critical incidents and crisis response as well as prepare counselors in training for such situations. Some of the critical incidents that might arise in supervision are countertransference, assaultive clients, discrimination, use or threat of weapons, mandated reporting, terrorism, nonsuicidal self-injurious behavior, domestic violence, lethality, death of a counselor in the agency, natural disasters,

FIGURE 10.1 • Event perception.

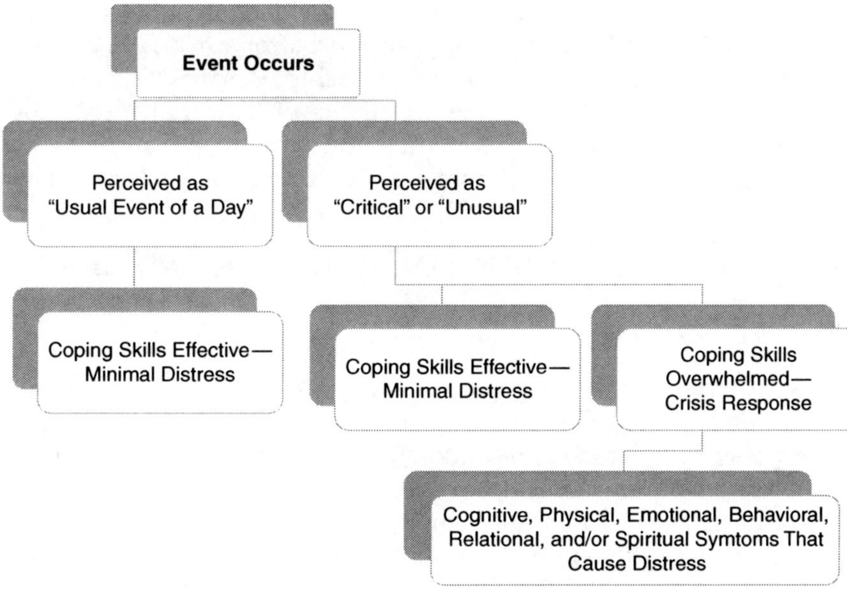

and sexual harassment, and the list could go on and on (Howard et al., 2006; Myers & Wee, 2005; Trepal, Bailie, & Leeth, 2010). Although terrorism and human-made disasters tend to cause the most psychological distress (Everly, 2006), suicidality is reported to be one of the most stressful critical incidents in counseling and supervision (Hipple & Beamish, 2007), as well as one of the most frequently occurring (McGlothlin et al., 2005).

As previously stated, critical incidents are a part of life, and our response to those critical incidents determines outcome and often policy (J. Mitchell, 2006; Ting, Sanders, Jacobson, & Power, 2006). Unfortunately, policies and procedure changes often follow the critical incident rather than preceding the event. Training a new employee is costly for any business, and critical-incident stress is a significant contributor to employee turnover.

In terms of counselor wellness and self-care, compassion fatigue and burnout are frequently identified as problems. Compassion fatigue is a contributor to employee loss, but critical-incident stress, especially workplace violence, has been shown to seriously affect employee morale, attendance, leave, productivity, and workers' compensation claims, in addition to the potentiall loss of the employee altogether and incurring the cost of advertising, hiring, and training a new employee (J. Mitchell, 2006; Ting et al., 2006). Policies addressing critical incidents and what should be done before, during, and after an event must be developed and implemented to avoid compassion fatigue, burnout, and vicarious traumatization as well as the aforementioned employee problems. Although this seems obligatory for agency management, it should be common practice to explore these issues in supervision as well.

Critical incidents in residential facilities typically include client assaults on staff and vice versa (James, 2008). The Bureau of Labor Statistics reports that health care workers, including mental health care workers, are among the most likely workers to be assaulted in the workforce today (Center for Personal Protection and Safety, 2011). It is not uncommon for the facility supervisor to blame the staff member (James, 2008), citing not using the training that was provided, when in reality the training provided was likely insufficient. This situation thus creates two critical incidents for the counselor-in-training, the initial assault and the lack of support afterward. This behavior may result in a compromised supervisory relationship, which ultimately impedes the supervision process. Despite the prevalence of critical incidents, these events are rarely addressed in counselor education, supervision, or mental health agency management until after a problem has occurred or made national news, if ever.

CRISIS RESPONSE AND COUNSELOR EDUCATION AND SUPERVISION

Counselor Education

Despite the prevalence of critical incidents and traumatic events, crisis intervention appears to have taken a back seat in the education of our mental health professionals. Morris and Minton (2012) report a serious deficit in counselor crisis response and suicide risk training. Crisis response was not a mandatory part of counselor education until the Council for Accreditation of Counseling and Related Educational Programs (CACREP) 2009 standards required programs to include crisis in the curriculum. In the Morris and Minton study (2012), student participants reported "practical coverage of crisis to be an essential component of counselor preparation" (p. 265). The study further notes that "in order to critically examine and deliver [crisis] curricula," counselor educators must also be competent in crisis response knowledge and skills (p. 266). Counselor education programs must ensure that graduates possess the fundamental knowledge, skills, and abilities necessary for crisis counseling across a variety of critical incidents. Further, there should be an emphasis on the importance of broaching and confronting critical incidents in supervision sessions.

The confusion over the vocabulary and basic precepts of critical incidents and crisis response suggests that counselors, counselor educators, and supervisors do not have a clear understanding of crisis prevention, intervention, and postvention that is congruent with other disciplines that provide crisis response. Counselors do not understand the terms, definitions (Jackson-Cherry & Erford, 2014), or concepts associated with crisis intervention with any consistency. Educators and authors frequently misuse terms such as *trauma*, *crisis*, and *stress*. As mentioned earlier, there is confusion among counselors and other mental health professionals that the crisis is the event rather than the reaction to the event or critical incident.

If crisis response and suicide were not previously being taught in counseling programs, are we as counselor educators, supervisors, and agency managers prepared to address crisis and suicide with our supervisees? A significant percentage of the counselor educators and supervisors currently providing training completed training prior to the 2009 CACREP requirement to include crisis in the curriculum. Therefore, critical incidents and crisis response are most likely not being addressed in supervision because supervisors have not been formerly trained in crisis prevention, intervention, and postvention (Morris & Minton, 2012; Vincent, Stanhope, & Taylor-Adams, 2000). Even with many state licensing boards managing supervision activities more closely, crisis response guidelines for supervision are not included in the professional standards of practice or ethics (Hipple & Beamish, 2007).

Supervision should involve education on the various aspects of crisis management. Counselors-in-training, both students and prelicensed residents, should pursue continuing education in crisis response and join an interdisciplinary emergency response team such as the Citizen Emergency Response Team (CERT), Medical Reserves Corp (MRC), Critical Incident Stress Management (CISM) teams, Green Cross, Red Cross, Disaster Medical Assistance Teams (DMATs), or the National Organization for Victim Assistance (NOVA). Understanding the effects of critical-incident and disaster stress on various populations, and understanding "crisis intervention and suicide prevention models, including the use of psychological first aid strategies," are requirements of the 2009 standards of the CACREP (Section II.G.5.g.). The Dupre et al. (2014) study emphasizes the importance of training in crisis response and emergency services throughout graduate education and training, during the counseling residency, and throughout the course of a counselor's professional career.

Crisis Response

A crisis is the response to a critical incident (Figure 10.2). This is a vital point that must be understood.

FIGURE 10.2 • Crisis response.

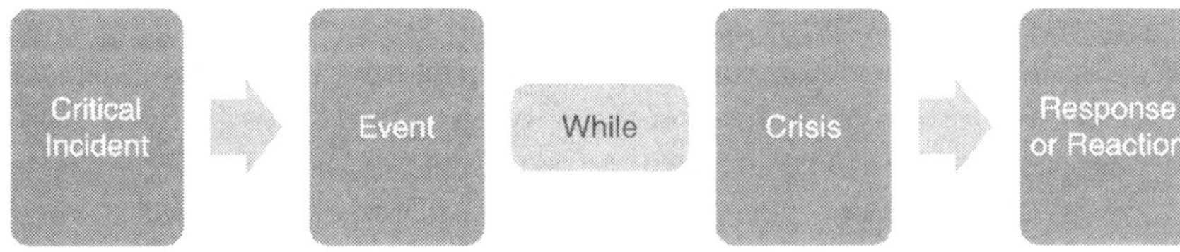

This is a commonly misunderstood detail in mental health services. A crisis is "a perception or experiencing of an event or situation [critical incident] as an intolerable difficulty that exceeds the person's current resources and coping mechanisms" (James, 2008, p. 3). Roberts (2005) reports a crisis as a defined period of psychological distress following a specific precipitating event or critical incident. "Failure to understand that the event is NOT the crisis, can easily lead to over intervention, and the potential to interfere with natural recovery mechanisms" (Everly, 2006, p. 121).

It would behoove counselors to speak the language used by the crisis community as a whole, because this provides a common language for understanding, similar to using the *Diagnostic and Statistical Manual of Mental Disorders* (*DSM*-5; American Psychiatric Association, 2013) codes. It has been this author's experience that emergency planners do not generally think of mental health in strategic planning for an event or have limited resources during an incident. However, the mental health needs exist long after the event is over, and the needs are generally identified as the event progresses. In all honesty, mental health needs are secondary to survival needs. Consider Maslow's hierarchy; basic needs, such as food, water, and shelter, must be met before a person is able to delve into how he or she has perceived an event (Jackson-Cherry & Erford, 2014; James, 2008). If the counseling and helping professions are trained to intervene and speak the language of first responders, everyone wins. This is the main intent of the deployment requirements of the Federal Emergency Management Agency (FEMA).

Operational interventions should be based on the crisis response or reaction and not the critical incident or event (Everly, 2006) because one event can evoke different responses from various individuals despite them having experienced the same event. Remember, it is the individual's perception of the critical incident as creating significant distress or experiencing the event as overwhelming his or her coping that is relevant. Crises are individual in nature (Hipple & Beamish, 2007) and rooted in many factors, such as values and beliefs (Jackson-Cherry & Erford, 2014). Experience with crises will affect how a particular situation is perceived (Hipple & Beamish, 2007), and reexperiencing the same crisis repeatedly may result in desensitization to the emotional distress caused by a critical incident. Client and supervisee reactions determine how the supervisor should intervene. For instance, if a client responds to a counselor's call to child protective services by making a written threat of violence, the supervisor may encourage the counselor-in-training to file a police report. Of course there are many factors that will contribute to the decision to file a police report on a client, and the more experienced the supervisor, the more informed the decision. Legal, ethical, moral, and safety factors must be considered, making this rough water to navigate.

Suicides

Suicidality is reported to be one of the most distressing critical incidents for both counselors and supervisors (Hipple & Beamish, 2007). Suicide rates in the United States are on the rise for certain populations, such as those in the military, those over 45 years old, and preteens (American Association of Suicidology [AAS], 2012; Clark, Thompson, & Welzant, 2007). Despite the staggering statistics on suicide, the devastation the family, friends, and colleagues experience is not described in the numbers. For every one suicide there is a minimum of six people who are intimately affected (Clark et al., 2007; Jackson-Cherry & Erford, 2014). The six people suggested to be affected most likely do not include the helping professionals. Suicide prevention, intervention, and postvention are important in counselor training. In this section, we cover suicide signs and symptoms, suicide prevention, and counselor supervision during suicide intervention and post suicide.

Prevention

Prevention efforts should include preincident training. Unfortunately, no mental health practitioner is able to predict with 100% accuracy whether a client will complete suicide. That does not negate our responsibility to conduct a thorough and comprehensive assessment of risk factors, and then to develop interventions based on immediate suicide risk factors (Juhnke & Granello, 2005). The first step is to become familiar with the signs and symptoms or risk factors associated with suicide. One method of identifying risk factors originally developed for medical students by Patterson, Dohn, Patterson, and Patterson (1983) is the SAD PERSONS scale. SAD PERSONS is a good assessment method used to gather information quickly and to determine the need for further evaluation or intervention. It is *not* a clinical evaluation; rather, it is a *risk* assessment. Juhnke adapted the Modified SAD PERSONS scale for use with children in 1996. The modified SAD PERSONS scale is as follows:

- S: Male sex = 1
- A: Age 15–25 or 59+ years = 1
- D: Depression or hopelessness = 2
- P: Previous suicidal attempts or psychiatric care = 1
- E: Excessive ethanol or drug use = 1
- R: Rational thinking loss (psychotic or organic illness) = 2
- S: Single, widowed, or divorced = 1
- O: Organized or serious prior attempt = 2
- N: No social support = 1
- S: Stated future intent (determined to repeat or ambivalent) = 2

The client is assigned points as indicated by the number following the equal sign if any of these conditions are present. Amy's client, for example, has the following characteristics: female, under 18 years old, in treatment for depression, no known previous attempts or substance use, presents as rational, has a support system, does not have an organized plan, is single, and has no illness. Thus, she would have a score of 4. The score of 4 is earned because of "A," age, as she is under 20; "S," she is single; and "D," she is in treatment for depression. Therefore, Amy's assessment and intervention to inform the parents seems appropriate.

This author would add trauma to the checklist. If a person has experienced a traumatic event the chances of suicide increase (Afifi et al., 2008; Amir, Kaplan, Efroni, & Kotler, 1999; Ferrada-Noli, Asberg, Ormstad, Lundin, & Sundbom, 1998; Kimerling, Gima, Smith, Street, & Frayne, 2007; Thompson et al., 1999; Ystgaard, Hestetun, Loeb, & Mehlum, 2004). There are no specific cut-off scores, so a rule of thumb is that a score under 2 requires follow up, a score of 3 to 4 requires closer follow up and monitoring with a consideration of inpatient treatment, a score of 5 to 6 requires a serious consideration of inpatient treatment and the client is only sent home with a safety plan that includes supervision, and a score of 7 to 10 will most likely require voluntary or involuntary inpatient treatment (Curran, 2010).

Studies have shown that the SAD PERSONS scale has little, if any, clinical value (Birnbaumer, 2013; Saunders, Brand, Lascelles, & Hawton, 2013). One criticism is that it does not assess for access to means and the viability of the plan. If a client reports having a viable plan and access to means to carry out the plan, the client is in imminent danger and the authorities should be contacted. However, the SAD PERSONS scale offers a new counselor a structure to use to begin assessing the suicide situation. Most states have a mental health authority that will determine the most appropriate placement if the counselor identifies numerous red flags. SAD PERSONS is a quick *risk* assessment that determines the likelihood of the client making an attempt. The risk assessment is to determine the next step or level of care or intervention. Supervisors must ensure that counselors are not practicing beyond the scope of their training by requiring supervisors to know the supervisee's experience with and resources for suicide.

Formal training, supervision, and field experience will assist the counselor to become more competent in suicide prevention, risk assessment, intervention, referral, and postvention. Agency managers and supervisors have the responsibility to assess and confirm competency in all aspects of suicidality for counselors-in-training and resident counselors. In addition to the aforementioned experiences, being prepared also means having comprehensive knowledge about the impact of a completed suicide on family, friends, coworkers, and treating clinicians (Ting et al., 2006). It makes sense for the supervisor to be required to possess competency in suicidality in order to provide ethical and relevant supervision relating to this significant problem.

Intervention

Training beyond graduate work is necessary for a clinician to become competent in suicide intervention. A basic overview of suicide intervention is provided here; it does not constitute comprehensive training. Comprehensive training in suicide is generally takes 2 full days at a minimum. Training should include role-play and practicing the techniques learned. After the overview, practical application of suicide intervention for counselors and supervisors follows.

Suicide intervention should begin by ensuring the environment is as safe as possible. For obvious reasons the environment is very important when providing a suicide intervention. Simple office supplies can become weapons and in general should not be accessible. Stabilization and facilitating understanding are initial steps in the process (Everly, 2006). To facilitate understanding the counselor allows the person in crisis to vent or tell his or her story. Ask, "What is the worst part?"' Crisis reactions, including suicide, are emotional in nature, and therefore being able to move the client from an affective state to a more cognitive state is beneficial (Everly, 2006). Having to think about the worst part tends to move people toward thinking or cognition. Because suicidal ideation is a crisis of problem solving (Clark et al., 2007), a starting place for the suicide intervention is facilitating problem solving around what the client identifies as the worst part of what is causing the suicidal thoughts or ideation. Some basic steps for problems solving are as follows: Identify that a problem exists, specifically name the problem, generate all the possible solutions to the problem, for each possible solution generate potential outcomes, and determine the solution with the most desirable or least objectionable outcome. Some clients are at greater risk or just intent on dying and will require a referral to the next level of care. If at any point a client is in immediate or imminent danger you must contact the proper authorities; calling 911 will generally suffice.

The guidelines for suicidal clients should be clearly spelled out in the agency policies and procedures, as well as in the supervision agreement. As clinical counselors this information is necessary to intervene with clients. As a clinical supervisor or an agency manager, it seems logical to obtain training beyond that provided in graduate programs and to ensure those we supervise are appropriately trained as well.

Postvention

The completed suicide of a client may have profound and lasting effects on a counselor at any point in his or her career. "The death of a client can be extraordinarily painful for counselors who have had the privilege of walking through aspects of their lives with them" (Juhnke & Granello, 2005, p. 217). Feelings of professional incompetence, loss, guilt, and shame, as well as fear of legal implications, may be experienced. This distress has the potential to affect both a counselor's personal and professional life. Unfortunately, the counselor who loses a client to suicide may experience professional isolation or even termination of employment (Juhnke & Granello, 2005).

Confusion, difficulty making decisions, and poor problem solving are all cognitive symptoms of critical-incident stress. This is also true for counselors who experience the loss of a client to suicide. Therefore, as previously stated, having a plan for such critical incidents is vital. Juhnke and Granello (2005) "suggest creating two, three ring, Pre-Suicide Preparation Plan binders. Each should contain an index page, and color-tabbed, clear vinyl sheet protection pages" (p. 217). Having two plans allows for one to be accessible from home, and of course one should be kept at the agency. Technology allows for copies of the plan to be accessible from a smartphone and through online storage services. Juhnke and Granello (2005) recommend including insurance carrier information, supervisor information (clinical and administrative), professional peer and nonprofessional support network contact information, and a statement about the potential for a client to complete suicide. Creating a critical-incident binder or electronic folder may prove invaluable when in crisis and should be a requirement for supervision. The most effective postvention provides prevention components (Clark et al., 2007).

Suicidality is reported to be one of the most frequently occurring (McGlothlin et al., 2005) and distressing critical incidents experienced by counselors (Hipple & Beamish, 2007). Despite this evidence, formal training about suicide in graduate programs for counselors and supervisors appears inadequate. For counselors who had experienced the completed suicide of a client, the relationship with the supervisor was identified as one of the most beneficial aspects of supervision (McAdams & Foster, 2002; McGlothlin et al., 2005). This suggests that suicide prevention, intervention, and postvention should be required components of supervisor training.

It is probable that there is a relationship between the Morris and Minton (2012) report of a serious deficit in counselor crisis response and suicide risk training and the findings of Vincent et al. (2000), which identify significant deficits in supervision during critical incidents. A cycle appears to be in place in which supervision during crisis response is lacking and counselors-in-training are not being trained in crisis response and suicidality. Because supervisors may not have been trained in crisis and suicide, they may not feel competent to provide supervision during crisis response. It is easier to critique a counselor-in-training's response after the fact. Supervision during crisis response is necessary for novice counselors to develop strong crisis-intervention skills (Myers & Wee, 2005). That may require supervisors to seek continuing education. The field of suicidology is rapidly evolving, so clinicians and supervisors must stay cognizant of current trends.

"The Cube Model of Supervision and Suicide is a tool that supervisors can use at various points in the supervisory relationship with all supervisees . . . [the model] integrates Stoltenberg et al.'s (1998) Integrated Development Model (IDM) and Bernard's (1979) Discrimination Model along with client suicide lethality" (McGlothlin et al., 2005, p. 145). Additionally, two exceptional nonprofit organizations are devoted to reducing the number of completed suicides. The American Association of Suicidology (www.suicidology.org) provides training, statistics, fact sheets, and membership (McGlothlin et al., 2005). Another organization that provides resources, education and training, statistics, and research is the American Foundation for Suicide Prevention (www.afsp.org/).

COUNSELOR IMPAIRMENT

Altruistic motives are characteristically the most common reason people enter the helping professions, and this includes "the desire to help others and to make a positive difference in the world" (Dupre et al., 2014, p. 93) and to encourage and help clients in the healing process (Juhnke & Granello, 2005), although it is not uncommon for people to enter mental health professions in a fool-hearted attempt to resolve some personal problem, to become affected by clients' distress, or to use faulty coping strategies such as substances. The counselor's characteristic aptitude for empathy and the recurring exposure to critical incidents may generate a synergy that results in a multitude of crisis reactions that may lead to counselor impairment. "Crucial categories that need to be considered when thinking about student [supervisee] deficiencies: (a) unethical behavior, (b) trainee incompetence, and (c) impairment of any kind" (Wilkerson, 2006, p. 208). Counselors are duty-bound to intervene when their colleagues display signs of impairment, as stated in the ACA *Code of Ethics* (2014). The same applies for supervisees and counselors-in-training. The earlier a problem is detected, the more time the supervisee has to satisfy remediation strategies or to allow for gatekeeping due process (Parker et al., 2014). In some cases, supervisors, counselors-in-training, or counselor educators may be called on to testify in court, and thorough documentation is essential in such situations. Supervisors should be motivated to seek peer supervision or consult a legal service when in unfamiliar territory. Dr. Kienlen, threat assessment expert, offers this simple but sage advice, "when in doubt, confer" (McGuire, 2013, p. 6).

SITUATIONAL CRITICAL INCIDENTS AND CRISIS RESPONSE

Natural Disasters

Natural disasters universally "create significant social, political, and economic upheaval that disrupts people's lives and displaces them from their homes" (Bemak & Chi-Ying Chung, 2011, p. 3). Earthquakes, fires, hurricanes, tornados, and floods create widespread destruction, leaving families without their basic needs: food, water, and shelter. Families may be separated without any means of contacting each other. During disasters, supervisors must broach countertransference while providing a safe space for supervisees to process their own disaster stress and the emotional burden of sitting with people in their anguish. Supervisors must monitor "helper fatigue" (James, 2008, p. 594) or compassion fatigue, also known as secondary traumatic stress (STS), diligently while a supervisee provides disaster mental health services (Pulido, 2012). The cumulative effect of hearing stories of devastation and loss may result in symptoms of posttraumatic stress disorder (PTSD; Cinamon & Hellman, 2006; Everly, 2006; Jackson-Cherry & Erford, 2014).

Disaster resources are frequently depleted, and those available are designated for first responders to the disaster, such as search and rescue, road crews, and chainsaw/dig teams. Cell towers are overloaded if they are working at all. Recharging technology is a challenge without electricity or a generator. Lodging is generally scarce as a result of displaced families and disaster response workers. Limited resources are the main reason *no one*—counselors, social workers, compassion animals, psychologists, well-meaning disaster junkies—*should ever self-deploy*. Despite how self-sufficient you believe you are, you will require resources of some sort and that will take away from someone who has been invited or is just trying to survive in the aftermath. Supervisors and agency managers should strongly discourage the highly inappropriate and unprofessional activity of self-deployment. Mental health professionals interested in deployment should contact Red Cross, Green Cross, or Samaritan's Purse. Additionally, the chaplains, compassion animals, and feeding units all have deployment groups.

Supervisors of counselors working in disasters must be cognizant of the nuances of disaster mental health and diversity. First and foremost, not all people who experience a disaster or a critical incident will experience long-term significant emotional distress. In fact, the majority of people will experience an immediate or short-term disequilibrium and a smaller percentage of people who experience a disaster or traumatic event will develop significant symptoms or PTSD (Everly, 2006; James, 2008; Myers & Wee, 2005). As mentioned earlier in this chapter, it is the individual's perception of the critical incident as creating significant distress or experiencing the event as overwhelming one's coping that creates the crisis. Triage, assessment, and resources are important in the initial stages of a disaster. Confidentiality and meeting space are often compromised in a disaster and should be addressed in supervision. Another factor to consider is that not all cultures value independence as much as Americans. Collective communities may treat confidentiality differently, being more open with community members. Mental health disaster responders must "always remember that they are the guests of the disaster communities or countries in which they are working" (Bemak & Chi-Ying Chung, 2011, p. 11), and supervisors must emphasize this message. Further, the nature of disaster causes separation and disconnection. Group intervention may offer a means of reconnecting survivors (Bemak & Chi-Ying Chung, 2011). The literature on crisis intervention supports group interventions with survivors (J. Mitchell, 2006), and group supervision has the same potential and benefits for counselors (Campbell, 2006). Finally, participation in post action support services to process disaster stress and assess for compassion fatigue (James, 2008; Clark et al., 2007) should be an automatic requirement for disaster responders. Supervision provides a forum to engage the counselor or counselor-in-training in post action support services.

Terrorism

Acts of terrorism are difficult for people to process. It is challenging to make sense of seemingly senseless acts of violence. Terrorism is unpredictable, uncontrollable, and unexplainable. Domestic or homegrown terrorism involves acts of violence by Americans on Americans. The Oklahoma City bombing and, more recently, the Boston Marathon bombing are examples of domestic terrorism. International terrorism is more likely to involve a group or have political or religious significance. Counselors providing services to survivors of terrorism may experience symptoms similar to those of PTSD.

Because treating survivors of terrorism is not the average day at the office, clinicians may be faced with problems beyond their training in many cases. Supervision, including guidelines for roles and responsibilities while treating victims of terrorism, may decrease the counselor's "sense of professional isolation, doubts about competence, spillover of work into the family arena, and overextension of responsibility" (Cinamon & Hellman, 2006, p. 227). In the Pulido (2012) study, in which participants treated 9/11 survivors, the "majority reported that they needed additional support and supervision during this time. One clinician was upset with her agency's stance that mental health providers should be strong enough not to need additional support" (p. 312). The identification of a counselor's level of development will enhance the usefulness of the supervision provided, especially during response to terrorism, which can produce extreme stress reactions (Cinamon & Hellman, 2006).

RESPONSIVE TREATMENT

Trauma-Sensitive Supervision

Hipple and Beamish (2007) suggest that early in supervision there should be an assessment of the supervisee's knowledge and experience with crisis response. Further, it is the supervisor's responsibility to confirm that the supervisee has a clear understanding of the emergency procedures for the agency, mandated reporting, the involuntary commitment process, and the rules and regulations governing counseling in your catchment area (Hipple & Beamish, 2007). Evaluating suicide and other clinical critical-incident skills in the initial supervisee assessment may also be beneficial. This information is helpful in determining whether, as a supervisor, to intervene immediately or wait and review the incident in the next supervision session. The degree of freedom a supervisee is allowed is typically based on supervisee level of competence, knowledge, and experience.

As in the relationship between the client and counselor, trust between the supervisor and supervisee is necessary for the supervisory relationship to be effective (Pfeifer, 2011). Robbins and Cenzo (2001) list eight skills for building trust as a supervisor: "practice openness, be fair, speak your feelings, tell the truth, show consistency, fulfill your promises, maintain confidences, and demonstrate confidence" (p. 319). Bernard and Goodyear (2014) provide an extensive description of the processes involved in creating a working alliance in supervision. At the very least, trust and a good supervisory relationship are necessary to address complicated or critical incidents.

The early establishment of clear goals and expectations for supervision is important (Bernard & Goodyear, 2014; Pfeifer, 2011; Trepal et al., 2010) to the process and will help to ensure supervision is relevant and professional growth continues during critical incidents. Counselors-in-training who regularly participate in supervision are less likely to experience the negative ramifications of critical-incident stress and crisis responses (Myers & Wee, 2005). Supervision during critical events may need to be conducted in the here and now. Crisis supervision is usually conducted at off hours and not always at the office (Hipple & Beamish, 2007). The school counselor crisis that occurs on Friday at 3 p.m. is something we are all familiar with, as crisis intervention does not usually occur at the most opportune times, and supervisors need to be prepared and plan for such events.

Counselors-in-training should experience support, self-awareness, and professional growth through supervision (Myers & Wee, 2005; Pfeifer, 2011). Students are taught to seek supervision for challenging clinical issues, crisis response included. As supervisors we must broach difficult topics, including critical incidents and crisis response, in supervision. Students may not bring certain critical incidents to supervision for various reasons, such as embarrassment, minimizing, avoidance, inexperience, and so forth (Bernard & Goodyear, 2014). The lack of knowledge and experience in crisis response on the part of the counselor-in-training may create a serious liability issue (Falvey, 2002; Hipple & Beamish, 2007), and that is rarely addressed. Supervision is generally based on self-report and reviewing written documentation, rarely involving in-the-moment supervision (Hipple & Beamish, 2007), creating a supervision loophole in some cases. A thorough assessment of a supervisee's knowledge and experience with critical incidents is important to ensure the safety of the client, the supervisee, the supervisor, and various stakeholders. The supervisor's knowledge, training, and experience with critical incidents and crisis response will come into question if liability becomes an issue. Therefore, it is imperative that counselors providing supervision are trained in crisis intervention. The lessons learned from 9/11 and Hurricanes Katrina and Rita led to significant changes in the field.

Campbell (2006) suggests combining methods and techniques to construct knowledge, skill, and personal self-awareness in crises. Supervisees are tasked to understand the laws, regulations, and ethics of crisis intervention and to read articles and current literature on critical incidents and crisis response. Supervisors and agency managers are obligated to provide written crisis plans that include detailed expectations and steps with a rationale for each action. The clinical supervisor should assist the counselor-in-training to recognize the clinical, systemic, and cultural intricacies of crisis intervention (Dupre et al., 2014). Unfortunately, Hipple and Beamish (2007) suggest that it is more common for supervisees to experience poor supervision in relation to critical incidents.

Crisis-intervention skills demonstrated by the supervisor can be very beneficial. Modeling, role-play, and practice vignettes offer skill-building opportunities. Self-awareness in crisis response is important (Campbell, 2006), as counselors must be cognizant of their emotional responses during crises. Supervisees should be aware of personal unfinished business, triggers, and hot-button issues. Counselors-in-training may benefit from self-reflection tasks such as visual journaling (Deaver, 2009). Campbell further suggests discussing thinking errors, such as counselor need to be needed and the need to be liked by our clients, which may interfere with appropriate crisis response. It is the supervisor's responsibility to assess counselor competence and preparation to provide crisis intervention before a critical incident occurs. Providing crisis intervention that is ethically based and culturally sensitive is imperative (Dupre et al., 2014).

When supervision is experienced as supportive and understanding, supervisees are more motivated to seek supervision during critical incidents. Critical incidents offer supervisees real-life teachable moments when they are open to learning. Appropriate supervision and support can aid in the assurance that counselors-in-training do not become overwhelmed by the critical incident or crisis response and that "personal needs and professional roles do not become blurred" (Myers & Wee, 2005, p. 124). Counselors may "over identify with clients, engage in misguided attempts to rescue, or assume inordinate responsibility for fixing chronic and complicated situations. Crisis supervision can help counselors to manage these difficult countertransference reactions and maintain an empathetic distance" (Dupre et al., 2014, p. 93). Clinical supervision has the potential to be a transformational process in counselor development, ultimately leading to professional maturity and competence (Pfeifer, 2011).

FRAMEWORK FOR CRISIS MANAGEMENT: A PLAN FOR SUPERVISORS AND AGENCY MANAGERS

Prevention and Risk Reduction

"Violence in the human services setting has increased exponentially in the past three decades" (James, 2008, p. 493). Risk assessments are necessary and have the potential to save lives. Numerous variables contribute to the imprecision of the science and complexities involved with assessing risk (Reeves, Wheeler, & Bowl, 2014). In our fast-paced, busy world, we want to believe that we will not experience a critical incident. I am sure that is what all those affected by school shooters and agency assaults thought prior to the critical incident they experienced. A thorough and annual check of the property, facility/agency, policy, personnel, and clientele will pay off when something does occur. "If the expectation is that risk assessment skill development primarily takes place within supervision rather than within the taught element of the course, it becomes more difficult to monitor consistencies of model or application" (Reeves et al., 2014, p. 243), and this should be a consideration of future research.

Safeguarding the work environment to protect the physical and mental health of supervisees is the legal responsibility of the supervisor (Robbins & Cenzo, 2001). Although there is quite a bit of literature on counselor mental health, physical safety is rarely addressed in the education or supervision of counselors. Dr. Kienlen, president of Minnesota Threat Assessment & Forensic Professionals, Inc., endorses the American Society for Industrial Security (ASIS) and Society for Human Resource Management (SHRM) national standard of Workplace Violence Prevention and Intervention: ASIS/SHRM WPV.1-2011. This resource offers employers a framework for constructing and applying a workplace violence prevention program (McGuire, 2013). A good place to start is by assessing the general agency vulnerability. Some very basic considerations include employee hours, employees working alone, office/agency location, employees handling cash, and clientele.

Certain mental health jobs necessitate safety as a regular theme in supervision. Consider in-home therapists, hospice counselors, and emergency service jobs that require a counselor to go into the field and possibly into someone's home. Residential facility counselors should be included in this group where safety is a theme. Quite often we operate under the idea of "don't ask, don't tell" when it comes to dangers in the home or work environment. As supervisors we should ask our supervisees if they know who lives in the home that a counselor may visit and if they are aware of weapons in the home. Do your supervisees carry their cell phones, tell people when they have appointments in the community, and have a safety plan? These questions are imperative and must be answered to ensure the safety of our supervisees and clients.

Residential facilities are notorious for assaults on staff, including counselors. Statistics indicate the probability of human service workers falling victim to violence at some point in their careers (James, 2009). The training provided in most facilities is not adequate, as the training does not always cover how to avoid situations, de-escalate events, and decrease incidents. Not only is the prevention and intervention training insufficient, the postvention interactions frequently leave the counselor feeling responsible for the assault and less than supported by the facility (James, 2008; Ting et al., 2006). Supervisors and counselor educators have the ability to empower novice counselors to seek training outside what an agency or facility provides. Assaults on staff should be documented as part of the risk assessment. Programs should be implemented to reduce the number of assaults based on the data, as this will ultimately reduce staff turnover and promote safety.

In his chapter titled "Violent Behavior in Institutions," James (2009) mentions training for staff in de-escalation as well as "critical incident stress debriefing and psychological autopsies" as a required follow-up for incidents involving violence against staff (p. 494). One program that offers the type of support James discusses for staff members who have been assaulted by patients is the Assaulted Staff Action Program. Flannery (1995) developed a "state-of-the-art comprehensive approach to employee debriefing for hospital personnel" (p. 93) that incorporates crisis intervention, family counseling, unit debriefing, and assaulted staff support groups. Flannery's approach is called the Assaulted Staff Action Program (ASAP). ASAP is adaptable to various agency types and treatment settings, such as emergency rooms, inpatient and outpatient facilities, residential facilities, corrections, homeless shelters, and more. Flannery's program provides support to "employee victims and has resulted in sharp declines in facility-wide violence as well as dollar cost savings in terms of less sick leave, less medical and legal expense, less industrial accident claims, less staff turnover, and sustained productivity" (J. Mitchell, 2006, p. 200). Flannery's approach is cost-effective and easily implemented in any type of agency.

Preincident Training

Hipple and Beamish (2007) said that "who, what, when, where, and how questions are best answered before an actual crisis occurs," which speaks to preincident training (p. 13). Consider what happens when we hear a fire alarm. As you were taught in most public schools, because it is mandated, you line up single file and calmly proceed to the nearest exit. This procedure is practiced once a month, and when the fire alarm sounds, we all know what to do. School fire drills are a great example of the efficacy of preincident training.

Establishing critical incident and crisis response protocol early in supervision will provide a structure for counselors-in-training. "Making the implicit explicit" is essential (Hipple & Beamish, 2007, p. 4). A thorough assessment of the supervisee's personal and professional experience with critical incidents, crisis response, and training will provide information for establishing procedures and guidelines related to the individual supervisee. This information will further assist in determining the specific training needs of the supervisee and agency as a whole. This assessment information should be an automatic part of the employee or supervisee file.

Based on the needs assessment of the agency or individual supervisee, preincident training may include the following: cardiopulmonary resuscitation (CPR) and first aid, psychological first aid (PFA), critical-incident stress management (CISM), FEMA training, Applied Suicide Intervention Skills Training (ASIST), QPR (question, persuade, refer), and others. Further, training in self-defense, negotiations, conflict management, and lethality may be advantageous. In planning preincident training, supervisors and agency managers should be cognizant of and include training that is specific to the population or cultural nuances of the clients.

Supervisors and agency managers should be aware that the federal government requires that anyone deploying to a national disaster take two FEMA courses: IS102—Deployment Basics for Response Partners and IS 800.b—National Response Framework: An Introduction. Both are available online and free. The rationale for taking the courses is to make sure that all responders are on the same page as far as communication and the incident command structure (James, 2009). It only makes sense for counselors to clearly understand this structure for a larger scale response, and by using it in our practices we are more likely to be prepared for large-scale events. This training and strategic planning must take place prior to any incident as part of the prevention efforts.

Intervention

The National Voluntary Organizations Active in Disaster (NVOAD) approved the following five points of consensus in 2005 (Everly, 2006):

1. Early psychological intervention (EPI) is valued.
2. EPI is a multicomponent system designed to meet the needs of those who have been affected by the disaster. Specific early psychological interventions should be included in any disaster response initiative.
3. Specialized training in EPI is necessary.
4. EPI is one point on a continuum of psychological care.
5. Cooperation, communication, coordination, and collaboration are essential to the delivery of EPI.

The points of consensus support the goals of crisis intervention: stabilization, reduction of symptoms, facilitation of adaptive coping, and return to usual functioning or referral to the next level of care (Everly, 2006). These goals of crisis intervention are applicable to individuals and groups, clients, supervisees, and agencies.

During crises, counselors must juggle numerous critical and often conflicting tasks to include: promptly developing a helpful relationship with an extremely distressed person, performing a rapid assessment of the person's mental health, formulating a strategic crisis-intervention plan, managing bystander and concerned family/friend reactions, and ensuring scene safety (Dupre et al., 2014). This juggling of tasks by the helping professional is often experienced as chaotic, and according to Everly (2006), "the antidote to chaos is structure" (p. 114). A 1989 study by Tracey, Ellickson, and Sherry found that when working with suicidality, novice to advanced supervisees unquestionably prefer more structure in supervision. Counselor participants in the Dupre et al. (2014) study unanimously reported directive and clear supervision during crises to be the most beneficial because it organizes the evaluation process, facilitates problem solving, and expedites crisis resolution. The need for structure in the supervision of critical incidents and crisis response is fundamental.

A comprehensive plan that supervisees and agency employees are very familiar with can reduce the negative impact of an event on those involved. As stated in the previous example regarding fire drills, students in the United States do not die in school fires because there is a good plan in place that everyone is familiar with and it is practiced with regularity. Boscarino, Adams, and Figley (2005) through "rigorous scientific evidence(s) suggest that post disaster crisis interventions in the workplace significantly reduced mental health disorders and symptoms up to two years after the initial interventions" (p. 9). The data indicate that supporting staff exposed to critical incidents may accelerate the recovery process (James, 2009; J. Mitchell, 2006; L. Mitchell & Resnick, 1981), and this should be true with counselors as well. Crisis intervention is a necessary skill set for counselors and may have lasting effects on participants and the provider.

Postvention

When a critical incident does happen, having a good idea of how to respond is vital to the future functioning of the client, supervisee, and agency. Unresolved critical incidents tend to linger and leave the metaphorical door open to additional incidents. Research has shown that employees who feel valued and supported before an incident happens will have more positive outcomes (Ting et al., 2006). Supervision can provide the support and genuine appreciation for the supervisee prior to an incident. Further, preincident planning provides a structure in the chaos created by a critical event. This structure empowers the counselor to intervene more competently and confidently.

Postvention activities must be part of a comprehensive system of interventions and not standalone services (Clark et al., 2007; Everly, 2006; J. Mitchell, 2006; Paterson, Leadbetter, & Bowie, 2001). Any interventions following an event will be determined by the crisis reaction, although some circumstances suggest an *automatic* response. Specific situations that compel an automatic response may include suicidality and assaults (J. Mitchell, 2006). Even in those cases, the reaction to the event determines the type of crisis intervention required, not the event itself. For instance, reactions to suicide include but are not limited to anger, guilt, shame, and denial. The intervention should be based on the reaction. The response to anger will be different than the response to shame or denial. The client may experience various reactions, as will the counselor who experiences the suicide of a client. It is the reaction, such as guilt, for example, that should be addressed. Supervisors meet the supervisee where he or she is in terms of reacting to a critical incident.

SUMMARY

The reality is that critical incidents are a part of life, and it is not an issue of *if* an incident will occur but *when* it will occur (J. Mitchell, 2006). "Brains learn best in times of real world challenge" (Pfeifer, 2011, p. 33); therefore, counselors will learn the most about critical incidents and crisis response during their clinical experience and field training—thus placing the onus of the crisis response training on clinical supervisors. A review of the literature found that articles and research on theory and application of counseling as related to supervision are abundant. However, there is a significant void in the literature on supervision or agency management as related to critical incidents and crisis response in counselor education and supervision. Bernard and Goodyear's (2014) text is frequently used to train counselor educators and supervisors, and it does not cover critical incidents, crisis response, or suicidality.

Agency managers and supervisors have an obligation to protect their supervisees, clients, and employees, especially when known risks exist (Paterson, Leadbetter, & Bowie, 2001). Taking the time to conduct thorough assessments will provide valuable information about gaps in training, counselor level of experience, clientele, and risks in the physical environment. The information gleaned through various assessments may significantly reduce the negative consequences when a critical incident occurs, further reducing liability.

Preincident training should include a variety of themes relevant to the clientele being served in addition to standard critical incident and crisis training. Standard trainings should include psychological first aid, suicidality, and basic crisis response. The data collected through the risk assessment(s) should influence the training decisions. In planning preincident training, supervisors and agency managers must be mindful of and include training that is specific to the population or cultural nuances of the clients.

Crisis intervention and postvention training are absolutely necessary. On a personal note, the best training programs that I have experienced in intervention and postvention are the International Critical Incident Stress Foundation's (ICISF) CISM trainings. CISM is designed as an "entry into the life situation of an individual or group during a period of extreme distress" (J. Mitchell, 2006, p. 183). In my work I have used these trainings with groups and individuals in correctional facilities, schools, disasters, private practice, and supervision. Ting et al. (2006) recommend developing a crisis-intervention plan to provide CISM services in agencies that experience frequent critical incidents (James, 2009). The crisis response skills that I have gained through CISM enhance the work I do with trauma, as clients working on trauma generally arrive in crisis mode and occasionally experience crisis reactions during the course of treatment.

Participants in the Dupre et al. (2014) study reported experiencing crises that were "dynamic processes during which troubling circumstances led to a cascading of consequences that posed significant and immediate risks for clients, family members, first responders, other service providers, and the counselors themselves. The data suggest that a crisis is a multifaceted, systemic, and cultural phenomenon" (p. 91). Critical incidents may have an enduring effect on the supervisee's perception of counseling, self as counselor, and the counseling profession (Howard et al., 2006; Skovholt & McCarthy, 1988). It seems prudent that counselor educators, supervisors, and agency managers should regularly check in about critical incidents and implement crisis response plans. The plan should include protocols for suicidal clients and self-care postincident (Ting et al., 2006). The plan should be a comprehensive, integrative, systematic, multicomponent approach (Everly, 2006) to crisis response that is easily accessible to all supervisors and counselors-in-training.

The findings of the Dupre et al. (2014) study related to clinical supervision appear to signify the benefits of supervision beyond that of licensure as both a "necessity and a professional right" (p. 94). Licensed professionals are able to practice independently and without supervision in the United States. Bernard and Goodyear (2014) report that other countries require mental health professionals to receive ongoing supervision throughout their careers to ensure best practice. Dupre et al. (2014) suggest that research employing a variety of methodological approaches exploring "the essential aspects of crisis supervision and the qualities of the effective crisis supervisor are needed to increase knowledge in these areas" and provide a better understanding of crisis supervision (p. 95).

"Crisis counseling places helping professionals in demanding situations that require encyclopedic knowledge of mental health disorders, extensive clinical experience, knowledge of family systems theory, understanding of the laws pertaining to civil commitment, and familiarity with community resources" (Dupre et al., 2014, p. 92). Suicide of a client, disaster mental health, and crises in general challenge the counseling rules. Supervisors and agency managers who were flexible and recognized the need to accommodate a new work structure for employees/supervisees were appreciated. Clinical supervision was found to either improve or complicate symptoms of STS (Pulido, 2012) and compassion fatigue, validating the need for supervisor proficiency in critical incidents and crisis response. Continuing professional development in crisis counseling should be a requirement for the resident in counseling and for licensed supervisors.

As supervisors we must ask our supervisees and ourselves:

> What, then, do we do when despite our best efforts, we fail to save our clients from harm? How do we come to terms with the limitations of our power? And finally, how do we accept that we have done all we know to do, and that sometimes what we do will not be enough? Coming to terms with our limitations for effecting change outside our control leads us one step closer toward healing the shattered dream that comes with client loss by suicide. (Juhnke & Granello, 2005, p. 220)

These questions are better pondered preincident and make for crucial supervision discussions. Despite a counselor' s experience level, as part of counselor self-care and wellness, regular supervision, even peer supervision, is considered essential when working with crisis and trauma (Cinamon & Hellman, 2006).

Counselor educators and clinical supervisors have the responsibility to prepare, mentor, and supervise counselors-in-training while they navigate critical incidents of all types. In-the-moment supervision is the most beneficial, and arrangements should be made to provide supervision when a counselor-in-training is managing an incident. Dupre et al. (2006) identify the dearth of literature devoted to supervision and critical incidents. This situation persists despite the prevalence of clients who experience crisis reactions of one type or another. Counselors working with trauma, suicide, and disaster are at much greater risk of developing secondary traumatic stress, vicarious traumatization, compassion fatigue, and burnout, yet this is not covered in supervision literature. Agency support and supervision are invaluable to counselor's ability to process and release this trauma footprint (Cinamon & Hellman, 2006). As supervisors, managers, and consumers of supervision, we must insist on supervisor competence in critical incidents and crisis responses. As supervisors, it is our responsibility to stay current and informed on critical incidents in counseling and crisis-intervention protocols.

REFLECTION QUESTIONS

1. Reflect on and describe the role of crisis response as a process as it relates to your professional practice (current or future).
2. Reflect on and describe the importance of the role a counseling organization or agency plays in critical incidents.
3. What are your expectations about the process of crisis response?

4. What ethical codes and principles are involved in the process of crisis response?
5. What, in your opinion, is the most challenging part of responding to critical incidents?

SUGGESTED RESOURCES

SAMHSA

This site contains free publications and resources on disaster, trauma, and suicide: store.samhsa.gov/home

A suicide screening resource is available at: store.samhsa.gov/ and www.integration.samhsa.gov/images/res/SAFE_T.pdf

PTSD: National Center for PTSD

This site has resources for the public and professionals. Professional information includes screening tools, assessments, articles, training, and more: www.ptsd.va.gov/

ACA Disaster Mental Health Knowledge Center

This site has resources in the form of fact sheets: www.counseling.org/knowledge-center/trauma-disaster

REFERENCES

Afifi, T. O., Enns, M. W., Cox, B. J., Asmundson, G. J. G., Stein, M. B., & Sareen, J. (2008). Population attributable fractions of psychiatric disorders and suicide ideation and attempts associated with adverse childhood experiences. *American Journal of Public Health, 98*, 946–952. doi:10.2105/AJPH.2007.120253

American Counseling Association. (2014). *ACA code of ethics.* Alexandria, VA: Author.

American Psychiatric Association. (2013). *Diagnostic and statistical manual of mental disorders* (5th ed.). Arlington, VA: American Psychiatric Press.

Amir, M., Kaplan, Z., Efroni, R., & Kotler, M. (1999). Suicide risk and coping styles in posttraumatic stress disorder patients. *Psychotherapy and Psychosomatics, 68*, 76–81. doi:10.1159/000012316

Bemak, F., & Chi-Ying Chung, R. (2011). Post-disaster social justice group work and group supervision. *Journal for Specialists in Group Work, 36*(1), 3–21.

Bernard, J. M., & Goodyear, R. K. (2014). *Fundamentals of clinical supervision* (5th ed.). Upper Saddle River, NJ: Pearson Education.

Birnbaumer, D. M. (2013, August 2). *A sad performance by the SADPERSONS scale*. Retrieved from http://www.jwatch.org/na31829/2013/08/02/sad-performance-sadpersons-scale

Boscarino, J., Adams, R., & Figley, C. (2005). A prospective cohort study of the effectiveness of employer-sponsored crisis interventions after a major disaster. *International Journal of Emergency Mental Health, 7*(1), 9–22.

Campbell, J. (2006). *Essentials of clinical supervision*. Hoboken, NJ: John Wiley & Sons.

Center for Personal Protection and Safety. (2014). *Workplace violence*. Retrieved from http://www.fha.org/showDocument.aspx?f=EMP-WPV...pdf

Cinamon, R. G., & Hellman, S. M. (2006). Career development stages of Israeli school counselors. *British Journal of Guidance and Counseling, 34*(2), 209–229.

Clark, D., Thompson, D., & Welzant, V. (2007). *Suicide: Prevention, intervention, postvention* (2nd ed.). Ellicott City, MD: International Critical Incident Stress Foundation.

Council for Accreditation of Counseling and Related Educational Programs. (2009). *CACREP accreditation manual: 2009 standards*. Alexandria, VA: Author.

Curran, L. (2010). *Trauma competency: A clinician's guide*. Eau Claire, WI: PESI.

Deaver, S. P. (2009). Reflective visual journaling during art therapy and counseling internships. Dissertation Abstracts International, Section A: Humanities and Social Sciences. *70*(4-A), 1175. (AA13356758).

Dupre, M., Echterling, L., Meixner, C., Anderson, R., & Kielty, M. (2014). Supervision experiences of professional counselors providing crisis counseling. *Counselor Education & Supervision*, *6*(53), 82–96.

Everly, G. (2006). *Assisting individuals in crisis* (4th ed.). Ellicott City, MD: International Critical Incident Stress Foundation.

Everstine, D. S., & Everstine, L. (2006). *Strategic interventions for people in crisis, trauma, and disaster*. New York, NY: Routledge.

Falvey, J. E. (2002). *Managing clinical supervision: Ethical practice and legal risk management.* Pacific Grove, CA: Brooks/Cole.

Ferrada-Noli, M., Asberg, M., Ormstad, K., Lundin, T., & Sundbom, E. (1998). Suicidal behavior after severe trauma. Part 1: PTSD diagnoses, psychiatric comorbidity, and assessments of suicidal behavior. *Journal of Traumatic Stress*, *11*, 103–112.

Flannery, R., Jr. (1995). *Violence in the workplace*. New York, NY: Crossroad Publishing.

Hipple, J., & Beamish, P. (2007). Supervision of counselor trainees with clients in crisis. *Journal of Professional Counseling: Practice, Theory, and Research*, *35*(2), 1–16.

Howard, E., Inman, A., & Altman, A. (2006). Critical incidents among novice counselor trainees. *Counselor Education & Supervision*, *46*, 88–102.

Jackson-Cherry, L., & Erford, B. (2014). *Crisis assessment, intervention, and prevention* (2nd ed.). Upper Saddle River, NJ: Pearson.

James, R. (2008). *Crisis intervention strategies* (6th ed.). Pacific Grove, CA: Brooks/Cole.

Juhnke, G. A., & Granello, P. F. (2005). Shattered dreams of professional competence: The impact of client suicides on mental health practitioners and how to prepare for it. *Journal of Creativity in Mental Health*, *1*(3/4), 205–223.

Kimerling, R., Gima, K., Smith, M. W., Street, A., & Frayne, S. (2007). The Veterans Health Administration and military sexual trauma. *American Journal of Public Health*, *97*, 2160–2166. doi:10.2105/AJPH.2006.092999

McAdams, C. R., III, & Foster, V. A. (2002). An assessment of resources for counselor coping and recovery in the aftermath of client suicide. *Journal of Humanistic Counseling, Education and Development*, *41*, 232–241.

McGlothlin, J., Rainey, S., & Kindsvatter, A. (2005). Suicidal clients and supervisees: A model for considering supervisor roles. *Counselor Education & Supervision*, *45*(2), 135–146.

McGuire, C. (2013). Workplace violence: Assessing and responding to risks. *Safety Compliance Letter*. Retrieved from https://www.osha.gov/Publications/osha3148.pdf

Mitchell, J. (2006). *Critical incident stress management: Group crisis intervention* (3rd ed.). Ellicott City, MD: International Critical Incident Stress Foundation.

Mitchell, L., & Resnick, H. (1981). *Emergency response to crisis*. New York, NY: Prentice Hall.

Morris, C., & Minton, C. (2012). Crisis in the curriculum? New counselors' crisis preparation, experiences, and self-efficacy. *Counselor Education & Supervision*, *51*(4), 256–269.

Myers, D., & Wee, D. (2005). *Disaster mental health services*. New York, NY: Brunner-Routledge.

Parker, L., Chang, C., Corthell, K., Walsh, M., Brack, G., & Grubbs, N. (2014). A grounded theory of counseling students who report problematic peers. *Counselor Education & Supervision*, *6*(53), 111–125.

Paterson, B., Leadbetter, D., & Bowie, V. (2001). Zero in on violence. *Nursing Management*, *8*(1), 16–22.

Patterson, W. M., Dohn, H. H., Patterson, J., & Patterson, G. A. (1983). Evaluation of suicidal patients: The SAD PERSONS scale. *Psychosomatics*, *24*(4), 343–349. doi:10.1016/S0033-3182(83)73213-5. PMID 6867245.

Peake, T., Nussbaum, B., & Tindell, S. (2002). Clinical and counseling supervision references: trends and needs. *Psychotherapy: Theory, Research, Practice, Training*, *39*(1), 114–125.

Pfeifer, D. (2011). Transforming staff through clinical supervision. *Reclaiming Children & Youth*, *20*(2), 29–33.

Pulido, M. (2012). The ripple effect: Lessons learned about secondary traumatic stress among clinicians responding to the September 11th terrorist attacks. *Clinical Social Work Journal, 40*, 307–315.

Reeves, A., Wheeler, S., & Bowl, R. (2014). Assessing risk: Confrontation or avoidance—What is taught on counsellor training courses. *British Journal of Guidance & Counselling, 32*(2), 235–247.

Robbins, S., & Cenzo, D. (2001). *Supervision today!* (3rd ed). Upper Saddle River, NJ: Prentice Hall.

Roberts, A. R. (2005). *Crisis intervention handbook: Assessment, treatment, and research* (3rd ed.). New York, NY: Oxford University Press.

Saunders, K., Brand, F., Lascelles, K., & Hawton, K. (2013). The sad truth about the SAD-PERSONS Scale: An evaluation of its clinical utility in self-harm patients. *Emergency Medicine Journal*. doi:10.1136/emermed-2013-202781. PMID 23896589.

Skovholt, T. M., & McCarthy, P. R. (1988). Critical incidents: Catalysts for counselor development. *Journal of Counseling and Development, 67*, 69–72.

Thompson, M. E., Kaslow, N. J., Kingree, J. B., Puett, R., Thompson, N. J., & Meadows, L. (1999). Partner abuse and posttraumatic stress disorder as risk factors for suicide attempts in a sample of low-income, inner-city women. *Journal of Traumatic Stress, 12*, 59–72. doi:10.1023/A:1024742215337

Ting, L., Sanders, S. Jacobson, J., & Power, J. (2006). Dealing with the aftermath: A qualitative analysis of mental health social workers' reactions after a client suicide. *Social Work, 51*(4), 329–341.

Tracey, T. J., Ellickson, J. L., & Sherry, P. (1989). Reactance in relation to different supervisory environments and counselor development. *Journal of Counseling Psychology, 36*, 336–344.

Trepal, H., Bailie, J., & Leeth, C. (2010). Critical incidents in practicum supervision: Supervisees' perspective. *Journal of professional counseling: Practice, Theory, and Research, 38*(1), 28–38.

Tyson, L., Culbreth, J., & Harrington, J. (2008). *Critical incidents in clinical supervision: Addictions, community, and school counseling*. Washington, DC: American Counseling Association.

Vincent, C., Stanhope, N., & Taylor-Adams, S. (2000). Developing a systematic method of analyzing serious incidents in mental health. *Journal of Mental Health, 9*(1), 89–103.

Wilkerson, K. (2006). Impaired students: Applying the therapeutic process model to graduate training program. *Counselor Education & Supervision, 45*(3), 207–217.

Ystgaard, M., Hestetun, I., Loeb, M., & Mehlum, L. (2004). Is there a specific relationship between childhood sexual and physical abuse and repeated suicidal behavior? *Child Abuse and Neglect, 28*, 863–875.

Index